Hearts Away, Bombs Away

The Story of Lt. & Mrs. Vincent dePaul Gisriel, Sr.

VINCENT DEPAUL GISRIEL, JR.   7/17/11

MARVIN PRESS, LLC

Printed in the United States of America

First printing

Published by
Marvin Press, LLC
14008 Sailing Road
Ocean City, MD 21842
Phone: 410-251-1360

ISBN: 978-0-615-29424-7

Library of Congress Control Number: 2009904323

Cover design by Denise McDonald, mcnmac@bellsouth.net

Interior design by Sue Knopf, graffolio@charter.net

*This book is dedicated to
Martha and Vince Gisriel Sr.,
for all they endured during World War II.
It is also dedicated to all who serve our nation
in the military; past, present and future.
It is especially dedicated to all those who have given
their lives in defense of our country,
to those who have been wounded,
to those who have been prisoners of war
and to all who are still missing in action.*

Contents

Acknowledgments vii

Introduction ix

Chapter 1   The Early Years 1

Chapter 2   A Kiss from Afar 9

Chapter 3   The Eighth Air Force Arrives in England 29

Chapter 4   The Maturing of a Man 33

Chapter 5   Learning to Fly 43

Chapter 6   Martha Goes West 53

Chapter 7   A Military Detour 59

Chapter 8   The Eighth's First Full Year in England 67

Chapter 9   Vince Arrives in England 71

Chapter 10   The Real Action Begins 77

Chapter 11   And the Real Action Continues 83

Chapter 12   Waiting, and Some More Waiting 93

Chapter 13   30 Seconds Over Hamburg 105

Chapter 14   R & R Doesn't Last Long 119

Chapter 15   Is the End in Sight? 133

Chapter 16   The Telegram 143

Chapter 17   The Best Bombardier in the Whole Wide World 153

Chapter 18   The Best and "Merryest" Christmas 173

Chapter 19   So Close, and Yet So Far 181

Chapter 20   Hampton, Virginia 195

Chapter 21   Patience or Endurance? (Or Both?) 199

Chapter 22   In Conclusion 219

Acknowledgments

I wish to acknowledge my sons and daughters: Vince III, Greg, Kevin, Jeff, Beth and Emily. I want to thank them for all their assistance, input, suggestions and encouragement in my efforts to write this story. Most of all, I want to thank them for their never-ending love.

I also wish to thank my wife, Bonnie, for her love and support throughout this project. She has traveled with me to Alabama, Florida, Georgia and New Mexico in my search for information to complete this book. She has helped me and stood by me throughout the duration. I thank her for the many hours that she sacrificed and endured for me while I read, thought, typed and edited.

I further want to acknowledge and thank three other people who played a vital role in the completion of this book. I list them in the order in which I became acquainted with them. First, there is Whitey Schmidt, author of *The Official Crab Eater's Guide* and *The Chesapeake Bay Crabbiest Cookbook*, among many other books. As my consultant, he has been a mentor, a teacher, a coach, and most important, a friend. Next there is Sue Knopf of Graffolio Book Design & Editing, who is the consummate professional. She works tirelessly to get it right, and I appreciate her diligence, patience and perseverance. Finally, there is Denise McDonald, who designed the cover of this book. She is also a pro at what she does. Just admire the cover and you can see what I mean. I want everyone to know how much I appreciate the effort that Whitey, Sue and Denise put into the completion of my first book. I cannot thank them enough.

Vincent dePaul Gisriel, Jr.

Introduction

It was only after my father passed away in 2003 that I began to realize what a true aviator hero he was during World War II. Upon his death, some of the men who flew with him shared stories about their service with my dad. They served in the 8th Air Force based in England during the war. It prompted me to want to learn more about my father and this time in his life.

I knew that my parents had saved hundreds of letters between them, written while my dad was in the military. My intent was to read them to obtain a better understanding of what was happening back then, particularly when my dad was overseas. As I began to read the letters, I realized that he could not write about war matters or strategy, nor his missions over enemy territory. That would have been a breach of security.

In one of my father's letters to my mother, dated March 15, 1944, he wrote: "I saw something today that sort of shocked me. In the April '43 edition of *Collier's* they had a write-up of a certain base. It was supposed to be so secret and here it was plastered all over the magazine. When we were there they wouldn't even let us mention anything about it. That's what I can't understand about this censorship—we can't say a thing, but magazines can say anything. We could write interesting letters if they'd only let us." In spite of the restrictions imposed on my father, I found his letters to be very interesting.

When I began to think about writing this story, I was somewhat troubled by the thought that I would be focusing primarily on my father, Vince. I felt concerned that I had never even thought about writing about my mother, Martha. However, when I started researching my dad's life, particularly about his service in the Army Air Corps, I realized how interwoven my dad's life was with my mom's life during the war years. It became obvious that I was researching and writing about my dad's war career, but equally about a beautiful love story. It is a story about a young couple who were deeply in love. It also highlights how important it was for a young serviceman to have someone to whom to return.

My parents wrote over 1,150 letters between them over the 34 months my Dad was in the service. Reading them became a real joy for me, something that came totally unexpected at the age of 62. I began to know and understand two people whom in some ways I never knew; how they thought and felt, and how they worried and dealt with life's circumstances at a dangerous time in our nation's history. I read how they had hope and optimism about their lives in a very uncertain future, and how their faith in God the Father, His Son Jesus, the Holy Spirit and the Blessed Mother played a significant role in their young lives. I began to know two people whom I did not know until later in their lives. The letters revealed to me in part how they became the great parents whom I grew to know for the many years that I was a part of their lives.

I was fascinated by the sheer volume of written correspondence between them during the many months they were apart. One of my wise uncles, Jack Holmes, also a veteran aviator of World War II, cautioned me in advance about stumbling upon things in my parents' letters that were not particularly meant for my eyes. In spite of his caution, I have not been embarrassed, for they were a loving couple who not only respected God's laws but they respected each other.

One day I was reading excerpts from some of my parents' letters out loud. My sisters, Rita and Mary, were present along with other family members. Rita's mother-in-law, Grandma Cole, who was present, and as usual very quiet, listened intently to the readings. Later, she commented that it appeared to her as though our parents saved these letters all those years for us to read so that we would know them better. I think she is correct, for my mom and dad could never discard them. At some point the letters were moved to my sister Mary's attic for safekeeping. I retrieved them in 2006 to research this story. I didn't realize the treasure that existed within them until I began the task of reading every single one of them. Apparently, while all of my siblings knew of the vast collection of letters, no one ever had the time or opportunity to sit and read them all.

My son Greg, upon hearing of the existence of the letters and their general content, commented that in the early 1940s there were no cell phones nor e-mail; that letter writing was the way people communicated. Indeed, they did communicate with pages and pages of even the smallest of details, such as my mom borrowing $10 from her father so she could go Christmas shopping in 1942 or my dad going out on a cold day for physical training as a cadet without proper clothing. More significantly, they literally poured their hearts out on paper, longing to be together again.

There are millions of stories of brave young men and women who served during World War II. This is just one of them. Many of the veterans of the war did not talk very much about their combat experiences. Frankly, it was not until after my father died that I began to comprehend what he had accomplished as a young man.

My father enlisted in the Army Air Corps at the age of 19. He was called to active duty for basic aviation cadet training at the age of 20. At 21, he was a second lieutenant dropping bombs over Hitler's Germany. By 22, he was a first lieutenant. My father was a bombardier on a Boeing B-17 Flying Fortress. When a B-17 approached a target, the bombardier took control of the aircraft until the bombs were released. It was an awesome responsibility. Like so many other young aviators, he quickly had to mature, but he lived up to that challenge.

Yes, this is a love story as revealed through my parents' letters, but it is also the story of a real American hero and the woman who stood beside him. I am so proud of both of them and I love them deeply.

1

The Early Years

My parents were both born in Baltimore, Maryland, in 1922. My mom, Martha Owens, was the oldest girl in a large Irish Catholic family. Her father, Daniel Anthony Owens, Sr., or "Willie," as he was called, was born in Baltimore in 1894 to Irish immigrant parents from County Cork, Ireland. Her mother, Isabel Wilhelm Owens, or "Suz," as she was affectionately known, was of German descent. Martha had four brothers and three sisters. One of her younger brothers, Pete, died at a very young age.

My dad, Vincent dePaul Gisriel, was the only boy in his immediate family. He had one sister, Angela, who was two years older. When Vince was about two years old, their mother, Theresa Miller Gisriel, took very ill with tuberculosis and died, leaving her husband, John Jacob Gisriel, with the two young children. From what I have been able to determine, my grandfather John, perhaps because of his tragic loss, became depressed and essentially abandoned the children, leaving them with family members to provide for their care.

Angela was adopted by John's sister Aunt Mary Gisriel. Apparently, the extended Gisriel family had planned to put my dad up for adoption until his mother's sister, Helen Miller BonSeigneur, intervened and insisted that she take care of Vince. Aunt Helen, who became the only mother my dad ever really knew, already had two little girls of her own, Tess and Theona. In spite of her modest means, Aunt Helen was able to provide my dad with all that he needed in the way of love, discipline and

1

Martha—The younger years

*Vince—The
younger years*

nurturing, in fact as much as any natural mother could. Vince's youngest cousin, Theona or "Nonie," as he called her from the age of two, told me recently that Aunt Helen never legally adopted Vince because he was the last boy with the Gisriel name in the immediate family. She wanted to preserve the family name. Otherwise, his name would have been changed to BonSeigneur. Nonie, who was the same age as Vince, and essentially like a sister to him as well as a classmate, recalls that their youthful lives were rather uneventful, that they never got into trouble. They were good kids. Her own father, Earl, who was seldom around, never questioned his wife, Aunt Helen, about taking in another mouth to feed. They apparently accepted it as the right thing to do. As I reflect, what a blessing Aunt Helen was in Vince's life. She was a wonderful woman who obviously did a good job raising her own daughters, but also raised a fine young man, Vince, whom everyone loved and admired.

Vince had minimal contact with his father, John. However, Nonie recalled one event in his life involving his father. Apparently, John wanted to see his son, Vince, so John invited him over to Washington, D.C., where he was living. While there, Vince broke his arm, and the family must have had a good laugh, because John had to pay Vince's medical expenses. As near as we can tell, the Gisriels were from Alsace-Lorraine, an area between France and Germany. In 1850, the first Gisriel appeared in the Baltimore *Polk Directory*. He was Jacob Gisriel, who operated a fruit and produce stall in the old Richmond Market in Baltimore. Vince's father may have acquired his name in part from him.

The Gisriels were a deeply religious Catholic family. Three of John's sisters became nuns with the Daughters of Charity. Two of them were missionaries in South America. Vince also had a cousin who joined the same order of sisters. The Daughters of Charity was founded by St. Elizabeth Ann Seton, who had modeled her religious order after the Daughters of Charity founded in France by St. Vincent dePaul; thus Vince's name.

Vince grew up in east Baltimore, playing a lot of sandlot baseball and soccer. He was a scrappy catcher, who didn't mind breaking a knuckle in guarding home plate or catching a blistering fastball. As an adult, he proudly showed off that crooked knuckle as if it were a well-earned trophy. One of Vince's most memorable boyhood sporting events, besides earning a letter in baseball from Baltimore's Polytechnic High School, was the time he was kicked in the testicles in Patterson Park while playing soccer. He was kicked so hard that he just knew that they had fallen off, so he had his teammates encircle him so that he could drop his drawers and have his teammates verify that they were still intact. He told that story to my sons, who also played soccer, and they got the biggest kick out of it.

Apparently, things were a little tight at Aunt Helen's little row house in east Baltimore. Legend has it that Vince's bed was in the dining room. One day while his older cousin, Tess, was entertaining Ray MisKimon, her future husband, Ray, proceeded to tie Vince's roller skates together while he was sleeping. It is unclear whether Vince went to bed with the roller skates on or whether they were put on his feet as he slept. After Ray tied them tightly together, he yelled for Vince to awaken, at which time Vince jumped up and out of bed only to fall flat on his face. I suspect that Ray was the only one to have a big laugh over this incident.

After graduating from Poly in 1941, Vince went to work for the Chesapeake and Potomac Telephone Company of Baltimore City as a frame hop, maintaining and repairing equipment in downtown Baltimore. It was there that he met Martha, reportedly in an elevator, which sounds almost scripted. Martha worked as an operator and receptionist. Martha and Vince had their first date on March 24, 1942. My Uncle Jack Holmes tells the story of how Martha announced that she was going to bring a young man by the name of Vince Gisriel home to meet the family.

Jack, even as a teenager, was always around the Owens house. He was in love with Rita Owens, one of Martha's younger sisters. Jack recalls how Martha, at this point in her life, hung out with a rather "wild" group. Her crowd liked to dance a lot and went to the "wild" jitterbug dances. The fellows wore the then very popular zoot suits and the women wore those swaying dresses and skirts that went every which way and up as they were thrown in every direction by their partners. Of course, the night out would not be complete without Lucky Strikes, Camels, Pall Malls and probably Coca-Cola. Jack recalls Martha as a beautiful girl who was a great dancer and who fit right in with the hip set. Cass Owens, another younger sister, said that Martha won a lot of the dance contests. So, as the Owens clan anxiously awaited the arrival of Martha's latest beau, yet another one in a long line of guys who were infatuated with the beautiful young Irish lass, they could only envision another wild, zoot-suit Casanova.

When Vince walked in, the family members could not believe their eyes. Here came this conservative young man dressed in a traditional suit and tie. He was fit and trim, and as Cass remembers when she was only twelve years old, he was "so handsome." Jack further described Vince as wearing "a million-dollar smile." Vince was warm and polite and obviously charismatic. Not only did he sweep Martha off her feet, but the whole family liked Vince from the start. They knew that this fellow was different from all the other guys who dated Martha. Time proved them right, for Martha and Vince fell deeply in love.

It was obvious that Martha had swept Vince off his feet as well. From all accounts, Martha was a real knockout and left many a broken heart. Martha attended Seton High School, an all-girls Catholic school operated by none other than the Daughters of Charity. What a coincidence! In digging through the family treasure chest that held my parents' letters, I found an article in the *Seton High News* dated March 23, 1939, entitled "Cheer Leaders Sing Swan Song At Seton S-V Tilt." It reads as follows:

> *For two years the crowning feature of Seton's incomparable team has been its attractive cheer leaders: Martha Owens, Mary Smith, and Laura Marcus. They have made their indelible mark in Seton's Hall of Fame. They really like their job, and in every game they have gained the enthusiasm and interest of the crowd.*
>
> *…on March 17, when St. Vincent's played its return game, Mary, Laura, and Martha made their last public appearance…*
>
> *…who having once heard or seen them could possibly forget Martha's pep, Mary's smile, and Laura's "Hep, hep, Are you ready?"*

Vince and Martha

Cass also remembers one of the times when Vince came to the house to pick Martha up for a date. While Vince was waiting for her to finish dressing, another knock came to the door, and it was a guy named Pete, who had been a rather recent boyfriend of Martha's. Pete was obviously perceived by some to be somewhat of a tough guy. Willie apparently ushered the younger children out of the living room and introduced Vince to Pete. Cass remembers wondering if there was going to be trouble that evening. Apparently nothing serious happened, for I can find no evidence of a fistfight. Pete, however, must have been a persistent fellow, because Cass remembers sitting on the front porch on another occasion when Pete showed up with two other guys and asked Cass if Martha was home. Cass replied, "No," but Pete wanted to know where she was. Cass replied that she did not know, at which point Pete offered to buy Cass an ice cream cone. Cass accepted the offer and Pete bought the ice cream treat. However, he then continued his questioning by asking, "Are you sure you don't know where Martha is?" Cass again said no. The inference here was that Cass, being a good little sister, just may have been covering for Martha, who just may have been out with Vince. Eventually, Pete got the message.

As Martha and Vince fell more deeply in love, they began to talk about their future together. They spoke of marriage and raising a large family. However, our nation was at war. They spoke of Vince's pending enlistment in the Army Air Corps. Vince was like so many young brave men of that era. They willingly enlisted in the service because they knew it was the right thing to do, and frankly, it was either enlist or be drafted.

Vince proposed to Martha on April 27, 1942. She of course said yes. Vince, however, was only 19 at the time, and being under 21 years of age, he needed his Aunt Helen's permission to marry. She withheld that permission. Otherwise, I think that Martha and Vince would have been married that spring.

On June 6, 1942, Vince did enlist in the Army Air Corps, the forerunner of our present-day United States Air Force. However, due to a backlog of aviation cadets already in training, he was not called to duty until much later in the year. Throughout the summer of 1942, he and Martha worked and dated. They spent a lot of their free time together. It must have been a grueling schedule, because John "Butch" Owens, one of Martha's younger brothers, tells a cute story. Apparently, Vince would be so tired after having worked all day and visiting Martha at her home in the evenings that he would fall asleep on the streetcar on the way home, late at night, and miss his stop.

On November 11, 1942, Vince boarded a train at Camden Station in Baltimore and headed to the Nashville Army Air Center in Nashville, Tennessee, where he spent the next several weeks in basic aviation cadet training.

Prior to his departure, Martha and Vince talked about the uncertain amount of time they would be away from each other. They knew they would have to put their personal plans on hold for a while. They promised each other to write often—even about trying to write every day they were separated. Martha promised to pray for Vince, and go to Mass, Communion, Confession and novenas as often as possible to seek God's protection for Vince and for his safe return. Vince made a concerted effort to do the same as time in the military permitted.

2

A Kiss from Afar

In what appears to be Vince's first letter to Martha, dated November 12, 1942, while still on the train to basic training, he wrote: "Today I missed you very much, but it's going to get worse as the days go on. Honey, I wish you knew the feeling I have toward you. It is something that just can't be expressed....This war can't last forever, and when it is over I'll have you all to myself. But before that, there is a job that has to be done, and I think, I have to help do it." On the next day, he wrote: "Right now I am homesick for a letter from home, but more so for you in person. As soon as I think about you being so far away I get all filled up. What I need is a good cry, but I'd feel too much like a sissy if I did."

Vince traveled to Nashville via Cincinnati and Louisville and arrived 28 hours after leaving Baltimore. He and the other recruits missed some meals on the train and on their first day in camp. Several guys had fevers and headaches. Three of them passed out from lack of food. These new recruits were cold on their first night in camp, and they had to sleep in their civilian clothes. On their second day, they were issued their military clothing and gear, and walked two miles to their barracks while "dead tired," only to have "Sarge" run them double-time back and forth to chow. Shortly afterwards, their barracks were quarantined for two weeks, probably due to an outbreak of measles. Vince wrote that he hadn't been able to get a haircut and his hair was growing over his ears. He tried to give himself a haircut and mailed a lock of hair to Martha. That lock of his hair is still in a letter in the family treasure chest.

During his first week of basic training, Vince was optimistic about the war, writing to Martha: "The way things look it won't be long before this war will be over, and we'll have that happy home we always talked about." Later, he wrote: "I want to get home and get that large family of ours started." Within a week, Martha's first letter arrived, which prompted Vince to write: "Just when my morale was very low, you push it back to normal with your sweet letter. I'll treasure it until I die. I received it just before chow and have read it four times already. I am the happiest man in camp. The other fellows are kidding the hell out of me. They can't figure who would spend twenty-two cents on me, and they are tired of hearing me bragging about it." Vince informed Martha that air mail arrives the same time that regular mail does, so she doesn't have to spend air-mail rates.

Vince was not even in camp a week before he and Martha started a little game of writing and agreeing to meet at Charles and Lexington Streets in Baltimore at 1:00 PM, knowing full well that Vince was hundreds of miles from home, and yet chiding each other for not showing up.

As any new recruit likes to complain and yet brag at the same time about military life, Vince wrote to Martha about cleaning the barracks for a general inspection: "All the boys are saying that even if they don't become pilots, they'll know how to house clean. So honey, you're going to marry a man that knows the ropes around the house." Later, after two 2-hour drills, he continued that he "…washed all my dirty clothes. You see! If the army don't make a man out of you, it will sure make you a housewoman."

Vince was feeling sorry for a fellow aviation cadet and former coworker at the phone company who was with him in Nashville. As of November 21, 1942, he had not received any mail from home and was feeling down. Vince asked Martha to telephone the fellow's family back in Baltimore to encourage them to write. Coincidentally, the guy received a letter from home the very next day.

Initially, Martha thought writing every day might become boring, but she wrote to Vince and informed him that she really enjoys it, almost as much as she enjoys receiving his letters. Martha's commitment to prayer, Mass, Communion and Confession was helping her to get through their being apart, and it was changing her for the better by her own acknowledgment.

One of Vince's letters to Martha, dated November 22, 1942, was particularly significant in that it captured what was going on in his mind in the second week of training. Having telephoned her, he wrote: "Gee! It was swell to talk to you today, it helped my morale plenty. When I was talking to you, I made believe I was home and wouldn't be over to your house for a few days. It even brought tears to my eyes to hear your voice. Hon, I miss you very much. More than I could ever put into words.... When I was home, you were very much a part of my life. And now, since I haven't seen you, my life feels real empty. But someday it will be filled again, and when it is will you promise me it will never be emptied again. I promise you that once I am home for good, I'll never leave you, that is, if you would like it that way."

Vince continued in that letter on a different subject: "We were given a talk by the commander of the post, Colonel Wuett, and a cadet who had been washed out at Maxwell Field. The cadet stressed mainly on the fact that in primary training you were on the honor system. He said it was very dishonorable for anyone to cheat on any of their exams, because so many lives depended on each man. So hon, say a prayer that never in my training I be tempted to cheat. I hope I never stoop that low." What an honor to be the son of a man of this integrity. Vince continued: "Colonel Wuett talked on the subject of our training. He said we were getting an education equivalent to West Point, costing the U.S. government close to $50,000 including everything. He said never to forget that we were training to be officers, that we should always conduct ourselves as such."

Vince was in this war for the right reasons. It is obvious that the colonel's good, solid advice and wisdom fell on his fertile ears. This was the way he conducted himself—with dignity and honor and honesty, not only in the military, but throughout his entire life. Knowing my father in person and by his written words, I can clearly see the maturing of my dad in his young life, how important the colonel's words were for him and how seriously he took them to heart. Shortly after, Martha wrote that she knows he would never cheat, that he is a good man. She ended by writing: "I love you, Vince, more than I could ever say."

In that same letter, dated November 25, 1942, Martha wrote: "Tomorrow is Thanksgiving and you are away. I hope to 'hell' this war is over soon. If it isn't I'll go crazy." She continued: "…I thought I had nothing to be thankful for, but when I went to the novena Tuesday night, the priest gave a short sermon. He said that we should be thankful that what has happened on the other side has not happened to us. He also said that we should give thanks that we have been so successful so far, and that we should pray that we keep up the good work. Honest, hon, that is what I'm praying for. It must be a very wonderful feeling to know that a 'war' is over. I do hope that it won't be too long."

Vince wrote a letter to Martha on Thanksgiving Day, November 26, 1942, a letter that Martha wouldn't have seen for a number of days after she wrote her Thanksgiving message a day earlier, and vice versa. Vince wrote: "You probably don't think we have much to be thankful for today, because we are separated. But think about it again—there is plenty. At least we know that someday we'll be together again. If we weren't living in this great country of America, Lord knows what would happen to us. Then there is the thought that we are living and have the great privilege of serving God to the best of our ability. Just that should be enough to be thankful for. Yes! Honey, there is plenty." He continued: "And about us being separated, don't worry about it too much, because I have a feeling it won't be long before we'll be together for our lifetime. This war is going to end mighty quick, and soon." It is refreshing to read the words of a youthful optimist.

Vince spoke with Martha by phone on Thanksgiving Day as well, after trying for "exactly five hours" to reach her. Life in basic cadet training in 1942 left a lot to be desired. Can you imagine just trying to get to a pay phone to call home, competing with hundreds of other guys, each with the same goal? Even when it was your turn, you had to hope the number you were trying to call was not busy. Then, if you reached home, would your loved one be there at that time? Remember, this was an era when you couldn't leave a voice message recording. It was either hit or miss.

Vince was in basic training when the weather tended to be wet and cold. One day he had to clean his shoes five times due to the six inches of mud in camp. On another day he was shivering cold. He finally got warm when the whistle blew for a close formation march. He wrote to Martha that he "...went right to the commanding officer and asked him if I couldn't be released. He liked to jump down my throat. I believe he's trying to make a man out of me. If he keeps that kind of stuff up he will."

He wrote in another letter, dated November 24, 1942: "They are working the hell out of us. From today on we started army regulations instead of girl's boarding school rules, as the commanding officer put it. Whenever a whistle blows we are to form, on the double and in the right uniform. From now on there is to be no excuse for anything. We just take the penalty." On this particular day, Vince wrote: "We've changed uniforms exactly six times today. I am getting to be like 'Queenie of the Burlesque Show.'" He further wrote: "This army life is doing great things to me physically, but heartily it is ruining me. Yes, it is a good life for one who has no one waiting at home for them. But for a fellow like me, it is no good. I'd love it tho if you could be with me always." Finally, he acknowledged receiving a recent "note" from Martha. He teased that her notes were like books, but that he loved them and: "Please don't stop writing them."

Martha wrote to Vince that she was sending him a photo and that when he received it she hoped "...that it doesn't affect you the way yours does me. Honest, honey, when I look at it, I could just sit there and cry. I also kiss it goodnight every single night." Earlier, in one of Vince's letters he drew a heart conveying his "true love." Martha acknowledged it by writing: "...the heart that you sent me was beautiful. I love it. If you should ever change your mind about me, I will take that 'heart' to court and sue you for breach of promise. Do you hear me, honey? No kidding hon, I've never received anything in my life as sweet as that." She ended that letter by drawing little stick figures depicting Vince and Martha with three little boys and two little girls.

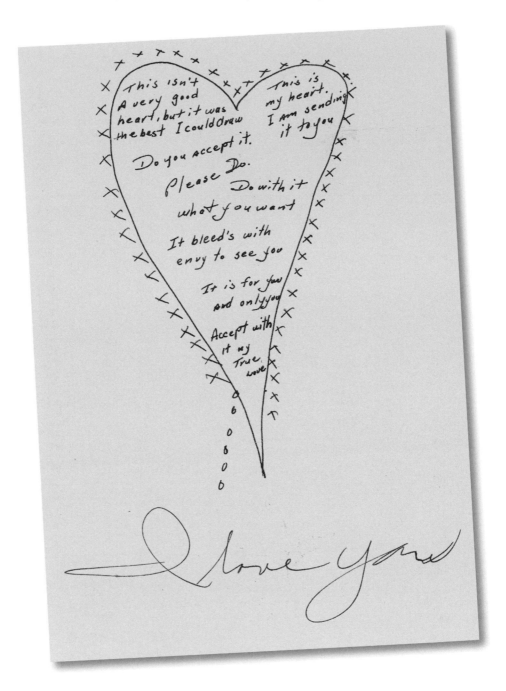

The heart sent to Martha by Vince denoting "True Love"

honey, I feel much worse as the days go on.

"Well goodnight sweetheart"

I love you now, always hour, always will

"Your Martha"

You
me (our boys) (our girls) and who knows what next.

"see ya tomorrow darling"

I love you. I love you, and I love you. (mushy, aint it?)

X X X X X X X X X X X X X X X X X X X X X X X
X X X X X X X X X X X X X X X X X X X X X X X X X
X X X X X X X X X X X X X X X X X X X X X X X X X X
X X X X X X X X X X X X X X X X X X
X X X X X X X X X X X X X X X X X X X X X
X X X X X X X X X X X X X X X X X X X X
♡ ♡ ♡ ♡ ♡ ♡ ♡ ♡ ♡ ♡ ♡ ♡ ♡ ♡ ♡ ♡ ♡ ♡ ♡

Martha's stick people depicting their future family

15

Vince promptly responded by writing: "P.S. You won't ever have to use that heart in court for breach of promise. I'll see to that, because I'm going to marry you when the time permits."

In yet another letter, Martha wrote: "The whole family is making fun of me for writing so much. Willie said that I should use carbon paper and make a copy of each letter to put in a book." How prophetic of Willie, for Martha did save these letters but in a different way.

In Vince's Thanksgiving letter he wrote: "Sweetheart, I want to thank you very much for all the praying you are doing for me. I am also praying for you. With both of us praying, we can't lose." He ended this letter by requesting a lipstick kiss from Martha, to which she happily obliged shortly thereafter.

Also on Thanksgiving Day, Vince wrote a letter to Butch Owens, who was ten years old at the time. Below are excerpts from that touching letter:

> *Hi Butch:*
>
> *I received your letter, and was awfully glad to hear from you. I've been wanting to write sooner, but "this man's army" just keeps us busy all the time.*
>
> *I am glad to hear you're doing fine in school. Just keep "on the ball," as we say down here; and before you know it, you might be a soldier boy yourself.*
>
> *...*
>
> *John, don't think because you are young, you can't help win this war. You can do as much as anyone else. Study hard in school, don't be wasteful with your time or money, help collect scrap metal, and help out with the home defense. Just be a typical American Boy; that is all anyone expects of you.*
>
> *...*
>
> *Love, Vince*

Vince wrote to Martha: "Your heart feels lonesome! That's funny because mine does too. The love bug has got us. And we being separated is one of the 'Horrors of War.' But it won't be long before we're together

Vince had requested a lipstick kiss from Martha, which she gladly obliged.

again. I'm psychic." In this letter, Vince mentioned that out of 208 men scheduled to advance in training, approximately 15 percent "...won't be leaving with the rest of us." Some apparently washed out for physical reasons. Others were hospitalized. Vince also informed Martha that he has been classified as a "Pilot" trainee. He was excited but knew that Martha might be concerned, for he wrote: "You'll probably be disappointed to hear that, but please don't. I'll take care of myself. If this old war would only end....One of the guys was telling us the other day that his wife was a nurse at St. Elizabeth's, and they brought some of the injured men there. She said they were horrible looking. I wish someone would figure a way to stop this old war. By the looks of things, I don't think it will last long." My father was an eternal optimist. I guess that is where I get it.

Later, Martha wrote that while she thought she would hate the prospect of Vince being a pilot, she found herself bragging about it to all the other women. She also found herself saying, "There goes Vince," each time she heard a plane go over. She also said a Hail Mary that the plane would land safely. She followed Butch's example, because he would say a similar prayer.

Reflecting on his marriage proposal to Martha, Vince added to his letter to her on November 27, 1942, an exact verbatim duplication of his words and her responses:

> *Vince – Ah, a honey ah, I don't know how to put it, but, but there is something I want to ask you.*
>
> *Martha – Yes, what is it.*
>
> *Vince – Well you see, it's like this. pause. Oh heck never mind.*
>
> *Martha – Now what is it you wanted to ask me?*
>
> *Vince – Well............Oh nothing.*
>
> *Martha – Come on.*
>
> *Vince – OK You asked for it. Would you marry me if I asked you. I don't mean right now but later.*
>
> *Martha – Yes.*
>
> *Vince – Well then will you marry me.*
>
> *Martha – Yes.*
>
> *Vince – I thought I'd never get that out. I love you. You darling.*
>
> *Martha – I love you too.*
>
> *Then they kissed.*

What a romantic my father was.

Martha wrote to Vince about the promises she made about going to frequent Mass and Communion for him: "It's very amazing, Vince, but I find that I love it. I mean going to Communion each Sunday for you. Also for lighting the candle. I don't know why, but I feel that you will be much safer if you place yourself under the Blessed Mother's care.

I've never felt quite like this before, but I'm awfully glad I do." Martha mentioned that she attended one of her many novenas at St. Alphonsus Church and that the general intention of the novena was for "… 'peace and victory,' and for sending our boys back home, well and very soon."

Vince wrote to Martha: "This afternoon I wanted to go to Mass and Communion. I went to the chapel at 4:45 and sat there until 5:30 until I found out the Mass was down at the other chapel. You see, they have two chapels. On Tuesday they have Mass in Chapel No.1 and on Thursday they have Mass in Chapel No. 2. On our schedule we showed the Mass in Chapel No. 2, but there was some mix-up somewhere. During my 45 minutes in the chapel I did a lot of praying, tho. Honey, you wouldn't know me anymore. I've changed very much! For the best I hope. I hope you still love me after you lay those beautiful blue eyes on me. Before I left, I thought the army would change me very much for the worst. I thought all I'd do was curse and listen to filthy jokes and stuff like that. That is one of the main reasons I went to Manresa [a Jesuit retreat center] and bought so many religious books. I didn't really want to go to Manresa, but I thought it was best, so I went. I'm not sorry now. It's different tho, I don't curse much, never tell dirty jokes, and very seldom listen to them. When I hear some of the fellows curse it really gripes me. I've never felt better in my life. That is, spiritually. I couldn't feel any worse mentally…" for he missed Martha.

Vince finally had the opportunity to go to Mass on November 29, 1942, for the first time since arriving in camp some 18 days earlier. He felt like a stranger in church. Vince wrote to Martha of his plans for frequent attendance at Mass and Communion several times per week: "My intentions are going to be for 'Peace on Earth.' I'm going to start a Novena to the Blessed Mother beginning Dec 1st thru Dec 8th with the same intentions. I am also going to place myself under the protection of the Blessed Mother like you suggested." He ended the letter by drawing a picture of his arm for her to kiss, since he had a sore arm from a typhoid shot. Martha just might have returned that letter, because it has a lipstick kiss on it.

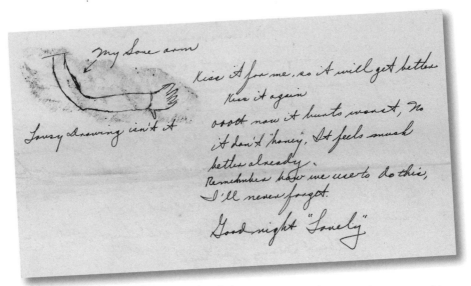

Vince had a sore arm from a typhoid shot. It appears that Martha returned it to him with the kiss that he requested.

The days apart began to affect both of them. Martha wrote: "Vince, gee I miss you, honey. Please try to come home soon, won't you? If I don't see you pretty soon, I don't know what I'm going to do. There are a lot of times when I think I'll go crazy, but then I get your letters out and start to read them all over again." In writing to Vince, in late November, 1942, she hoped that he would be home for Christmas. She further wrote: "Sometimes I wish that you and I could go far away and never have to see or hear anything about the old war. I know that isn't right and I guess, I mean I know, I wouldn't want to do it, either. I guess what I really wish is that the war would end." One day she heard the song entitled "When You're a Long, Long Way from Home" on the radio. "It almost had me in tears," she wrote. That same day she heard the Air Corps song twice. She wrote: "It made me feel very sad and very proud too."

One day Martha was feeling quite depressed, but then she received two letters from Vince and wrote: "Your letters were all I needed. Honey, I wouldn't have taken a million dollars in preference to getting those letters from you."

Martha wrote to Vince about a young woman at the phone company who was pregnant and had not heard from the baby's father for a while. Apparently, he was in the service too. Martha wrote that the young woman said "…that she wouldn't care if she dropped dead tomorrow, she was so disgusted." Martha then added: "But there are so many people who are disgusted in this world today. I wouldn't be if the war was over."

Vince received a letter from his "grand dad." Actually, it was from Pierre BonSeigneur, who was born in France and who was Aunt Helen's father-in-law. Since Aunt Helen raised Vince, this may have been the only "grand dad" he ever really knew. Pierre wrote the following after reading four letters Vince had sent to Aunt Helen: "It made our hearts glad that you are doing your duty and we are proud of you.…If all of us would realize the Seriousness of this Crucial moment there would be no need of a draft—but just a Clear Call to arms and forty million voices would answer, present—for this is the greatest and most wonderful Country on earth…"

It was early December, 1942. Vince wrote to Martha that it had snowed four inches and that it froze when it hit the ground. He further wrote: "You should have seen us trying to march on the icy streets. One guy would fall and about six other guys would come down on top of him. It was really funny."

Earlier Martha had written to Vince asking him how he would feel if she joined the Air WAC (Woman Army Corps). He wrote back: "…don't do anything until after Christmas, as I might get a furlough. If you join now I might never see you until the war is over. I'd love you to join tho. Wherever I get stationed next, you could apply for that city. That would be swell, wouldn't it." Again, his eternal optimism is refreshing.

The Detective Nick Charles radio show was a very popular broadcast in the early 1940s. Martha wrote of one recent episode about a soldier and his girlfriend who had just married. Martha wrote that the minister on the show "…said some very beautiful words. He said, we are fighting this war for ourselves, so that we can have homes and children of our own. He said that some people say this is no time to be married, but he didn't think that way. He thinks that that fellow will fight twice as hard."

Martha continued: "Maybe all the men in the armed forces should come home real quick and get 'hitched,' huh, honey? That man said they would fight twice as hard, so it would be the same as twins or something."

Vince informed Martha that he went to Confession and that his was the last confession to be heard, so he chatted with the priest for a while. The conversation turned to Martha. The priest wanted to know if Vince was in love, to which he responded, "Very much so." The priest asked Vince why he had not gotten married prior to entering the service. Vince wrote to Martha: "I just skipped that question because I didn't really know the answer. That is the main thing on my mind. I keep asking myself, should I send for Martha and marry her, or shouldn't I? I know if I sent for you, you would come, wouldn't you? By your letters you sound like you would." Martha made it very clear to Vince in many of her letters that she was very excited about getting married and could hardly wait for the day to come. Shortly thereafter, their letters started speaking of marriage more and more.

On one occasion, Vince had just come off 15 hours of K.P. (kitchen duty). He wrote on December 4, 1942: "I'm so sick and tired of washing dishes it isn't funny. You finish breakfast and wash dishes, you finish dinner, you wash dishes, you finish supper, you wash dishes. Dishes, dishes, I'll probably dream I'm flying one." In that same letter, he wrote: "It is really lonesome. I can hear my heart saying 'Martha, Martha, where art thou.' Then I say to it, 'She's in Baltimore.' And then it says to me, 'Why is she in Balto. when I'm in Tenn.?' I'm lonesome for her. That's the way my heart keeps going all the time. So as you can see it misses you very, very much."

In a letter dated the very next day, December 5, 1942, before ever reading Vince's letter of December 4, Martha wrote: "Do you know that I love you very, very much? I love you much more than God even intended any one human being to love another one. I miss you very much, and am earnestly praying for the day when you'll return to me, for keeps." They each found hundreds of ways to express their love for each other in their writing. At times, they seemed to anticipate what the other wanted to hear; and as evidenced by the above, each had the ability to answer the other before receiving the next letter.

After writing to Martha that he went to Mass with about 500 other guys in the post theatre, Vince further wrote: "None of the soldiers lose their religion after they're in the service; in fact, I believe most of them get theirs back."

On the eve of the first anniversary of the bombing of Pearl Harbor, Vince wrote: "You asked for my honest opinion of the war situation; well, honey, here it is: This war will be over in six months—in fact, exactly the day I get my wings. That's a prediction, and I hope it comes true." Again, that eternal optimism!

On the one-year anniversary of the attack on Pearl Harbor, December 7, 1942, Martha wrote about how on this day, Baltimore had several things scheduled in recognition of that tragic event. She was on the No.16 streetcar going to work, when at Sun Square, traffic apparently came to gridlock. She wrote: "I'm telling you, chills went up and down my spine. There must have been a million people on that corner. They had tanks, machine guns and big army trucks in the street. Then the army band played all different war songs. It was really thrilling, yet very sad." She further wrote: "Well, sweetie, just one year ago today Pearl Harbor was bombed. I realized then that we were at war, but not 1/1000 as much as I do tonight. I thought then that my life would be changed a little, but never dreamt that it would hit home the way it has." Martha ended this letter with: "I love you very much. Even more than the devil hates holy water. That is the comparison, hon. My love for you is ten times greater than the devil's hatred of holy water. You know I must love you an awful lot. In case you don't, well I do. Please hurry home, honey!"

Vince informed Martha of a visit to the army dentist, a captain. He had to have some teeth pulled. The captain applied Novocain to the wrong side of his mouth before Vince realized what was happening. In fact, the dentist started to pull out his good teeth. Vince had to figure out a way to let him know. When the captain realized the mistake, he apologized, but he could not apply Novocain to the other side, so Vince had to return the next day.

For several days, Martha and Vince wrote back and forth regarding the possibility of a furlough in mid-December 1942, or at least Vince going home for the Christmas holidays. Part of this was fueled by rumors going around camp that Vince referred to as latrine rumors, or more specifically as "latrinagrams." However, in a letter from Martha to Vince dated December 10, 1942, she confirmed receiving a telegram informing her that Vince was coming home in a few days. She was so excited upon hearing the news. Apparently, she woke up that morning and "...had a funny feeling that something was going to happen." That funny feeling stayed with her all day. That evening she told Vince's sister, Angela, that she had a funny feeling about something. Martha wrote that she said to Angela: "Maybe the war is going to end tonight"; and continued: "Then, not an hour later, I got the most wonderful news on earth." It was that Vince was coming home on leave. In this same letter, Martha wrote: "Hon, don't you think we could be married when you come home this time? We wouldn't have to tell anybody. What they don't know won't hurt them. Just my knowing that we were married would make me feel like 'living' again."

The letters between them stopped between December 11 and December 26, for Vince was back in Baltimore for the holidays. In her first letter to Vince back in Nashville, she wrote that her brother, Buster, said: "You know why they sent Vince home?" She continued with Buster's response when asked "Why?": "...because the mail was so heavy and they wanted it to slacken a little for Christmas." Martha continued: "They sent you home, I stopped writing, and it was a complete success. Boy what a ragging I take around here because of you. I love it though, honey."

Martha informed Vince that she fasted for almost twelve hours after he left so that she could go to Mass and Communion. After Mass, she was quite hungry, for she "almost died" before she got home. She wrote: "It was for you, though, and I don't care what it is, I'd go through it for you." She continued to be faithful to her promise to go to frequent Mass and Communion for his safe return.

While Vince was on leave over the holidays, Martha and Vince were formally engaged, and Vince gave Martha her engagement ring. She wrote to him upon his return to camp to say: "I showed some of the girls my ring and they all think it is darling. Even after I got home, a few of the girls called me to congratulate me. Every time I think that I am engaged and you are so far away, I could die. If only this darn old war was over."

Apparently, Vince was called back from his holiday leave sooner than he had expected. In a letter to Martha dated December 28, 1942, he explained: "The reason they called us back is because the 600 boys that got the measles were supposed to ship but couldn't, so someone had to take their place. We were the someones." Vince also mentioned that in addition to the 600 cadets with the measles, there were 500 guys with pneumonia. He arrived back in camp about 10:30 PM and had trouble finding a bed. He and his buddies roamed the camp and found some cots to sleep on. He wrote: "It is really a mess down here. Nobody knows their ass from a hole in the ground."

In a number of Vince's letters, he mentioned the conditions at the Nashville cadet basic training camp. He complained about the mud. He frequently commented on the weather, often wet, cold and misty. He apologized to Martha for "bitching," for he really didn't want to upset her; but at the same time, I believe he wanted to keep her informed and he needed something to write about. Upon his return from leave, it must have really hit him, for he wrote: "You know how much I hated this camp because of the living conditions, well now I hate it 10 times that much. The food has gotten worse and the latrines haven't been cleaned for a week. Last night I walked into the latrine and I swear there was $\frac{1}{2}$ inch of mud on the floor. The other fellows haven't done a damn thing since we left." Upon his return it was raining. He noted that it rained for three weeks prior to his leave, and now it was raining upon his return. He hadn't seen the sun in Nashville for his last 22 days in camp. In fact, on December 31, 1942, when the sun did shine, it was the first time he had seen sunshine since his first week in camp in mid-November. The next day, he informed Martha that conditions at the camp had become so bad, and that apparently "some big shot from Washington" came down, examined the camp and "…he condemned it."

Vince had been looking forward to the day that they would ship out. He knew he was going soon because he had just signed payroll for a partial month, which meant he was to receive about $30. It couldn't arrive fast enough because, he wrote: "Your honey is back with a flash and no cash."

Vince was anxiously awaiting news that he would be shipped to preflight school soon. He wrote: "We were given a lecture by our tactical officer on preflight school. The way he talked, it is very tough but he said you have to be tough to stay in this outfit." With his days in Nashville dwindling down to a few, Vince informed Martha that he planned to sleep in and not make formations. He wrote that he didn't "…intend to meet any formations for the rest of my stay here. I'm going to keep one step ahead of them and lead a life of Raleigh."

He slept in for two straight days, but his plan didn't last long, because the very next day he wrote: "Last night I told you I didn't intend to meet any formations, especially reveille. Well the brutes dragged us out of bed at exactly 6 o'clock this morning. Can you imagine that. And I thought we were going to have it easy. Our squadron commander came back last night and he gave the CQ (charge of quarters) strict orders to drag us out, and drag us out he did. The bully!"

Vince commented on the cadets being sent out for calisthenics only to have it called off once there. They were sent out without proper clothing. He wrote: "Today it has been real cold and a fine misty rain. You know, the kind of weather I hate. Well at 9 o'clock we donned our athletic equipment and marched to the field. We like to froze our ba__s off. After getting us all the way over there, our calisthenics had been called off for the day. Oh boy, did we bitch. That's the kind of stuff they do to us that makes us so damn disgusted with this place. Instead of calling up and finding out whether there was going to be any calisthenics, they let us go out with practically no clothes on at all and let us try to catch pneumonia. Well, we have made up our mind not to get sick. Now we're hoping that we don't."

Continuing, Vince wrote: "This afternoon at 4:50 PM we all went to 'Retreat'. That is the lowering of the flag. Each day a different squadron makes a guard of honor around the flag, and today was our day. It was a very nice ceremony and very impressing. We stood at strict attention while six enlisted men lowered the flag. While the flag was coming down three other soldiers were blowing 'Retreat' on bugles. It really did something to you inside and on the outside it chilled you up and down. You know what I mean, don't you, honey?" Vince continued to mature. He was proud to be what he was, even though he missed Martha something terrible.

On New Year's eve, December 31, 1942, Vince wrote: "The old year is about to go out and the new year is about to come in. Where am I? I am writing to the sweetest, prettiest and most precious girl in this whole wide world. Am I sad? You're damn tootin I am. And why? Because I'm not with that gal. Yes, honey, I miss you awfully, more so tonight than ever before. …Where I would like to be is just impossible and you know where that is, but there will be other years and will we raise hell then. You bet we will." He also informed Martha that at "9:00 AM tomorrow," which would be New Year's day, they would be leaving for some camp out west. They actually departed on January 2. He could not tell her where because their departure was considered a troop movement and it had to be kept secret. However, Martha's next letter to Vince, dated December 30, 1942, was forwarded to Santa Ana, California.

Anticipating that it could be California, she wrote: "I do hope you don't go way out there, honey. I'll let you go if you take me with you. Will you, honey?" Continuing: "Remember the night….You said you were sort of sorry that you got home, because if you hadn't I would have come down there, and we would have been married. Did you really mean that, hon? If you ever want me to come down honey, just let me know."

In Martha's very next letter, also forwarded from Nashville to Santa Ana, she told Vince that her mom read an article in the paper about a guy who had just got engaged over Christmas and was called back to camp unexpectedly, similar to what happened to Vince. She wrote: "When he got back to camp, he called the girl and asked her not to take the matter about the ring seriously, because he had changed his mind. Honey, have I been taking a ragging, especially since I haven't heard from you. I know you wouldn't do anything like that, tho, because I love you too damn much; I know you love me too." Later she wrote: "Buster just got home from work with half a jag on. He is down the basement singing and yelling 'old dumb Vince.' God, hon, it's really a panic. I do wish you were here. So help me, honey, if this damn war isn't over soon, I don't know what I'll do." This letter was dated December 31, 1942. Vince's mail was still going to Nashville while he was traveling across country. Eventually, it was forwarded to California, but he did not receive it for several days.

The year ended with Martha writing to Vince that she loved him more than life itself. Vince reported to Martha that back in Nashville, he and the other cadets rang in the New Year by staging a huge pillow fight that carried over into other barracks. From all accounts, it was Vince's group that started the whole thing.

Between November 11, 1942, when Vince left Baltimore, and January 2, 1943, when he left for Santa Ana, I have counted one telegram, three postcards and 69 letters between them. I would say they did a very good job of living up to their commitment to write often.

3

The Eighth Air Force Arrives in England

While not everyone in the military agreed that strategic precision bombing was the way to win the war in Europe, aviation experts and leaders persevered, eventually overcame opposition and convinced those in command of the need and the potential of such a campaign. British and American officials became convinced that the way to break Hitler's back was to launch an all-out effort against Germany and Nazi-occupied Europe. It was not to be an air attack on cities or mass concentrations of civilian populations as Hitler had done for seventy nights over London. It was to be a progressive, well-planned bombing assault of Hitler's factories and plants that produced aircraft, tanks, vehicles, machine guns, tires, fuel and equipment. It was to be an attack on his airfields and his railroads and transportation network that moved men and military equipment to the front lines.

Hitler's communication system was to be knocked out, along with his submarine bases that were heavily protected by tons of concrete under which subs hid in port. In short, it was to be a long and steady campaign against his industrial might, which had produced one of the fiercest war machines in the history of the world. The British had the experience, the stamina and the courage to do it. They just needed the help of the industrial strength of America's mighty work force consisting of hard working men and women on the assembly and production lines. They also needed the brave and well-trained men of the American armed forces.

By the summer of 1942, American bombers and crews of the Eighth Air Force had begun to arrive in England to help the Royal Air Force (RAF) defeat Germany. August 17, 1942, was the first time an all-American group of twelve B-17s took off on a mission over Rouen, France, to attack German marshalling yards. All twelve safely returned to England, and the mission was considered a success. The 92nd Bombardment Group, to which Vince Gisriel would eventually be assigned, was there from the beginning, arriving in England within just a few days after August 17. Over the next few days, these early B-17 missions met with success, and no planes were lost. Morale was lifted for the British and Americans because the prospects seemed high in these early missions. No one ever really underestimated the enemy, however. On September 6, 1942, thirty B-17s took off on a mission to bomb a repair depot used by the Luftwaffe, Germany's air power. It was the Eighth Air Force's first loss of B-17s. Two planes went down in air combat, and one of them belonged to the 92nd Bombardment Group. It was the first mission of the 92nd Group.

In the early days of the air war against Germany, the American aviators learned some valuable lessons. For example, if a squadron of B-17s stayed in tight formation, they would have a better chance of surviving against German fighter planes. The crisscrossing of B-17 machine guns from their gunner positions on the aircraft provided a strong defense against enemy attack fighters. On the other hand, the Germans would learn to go after a plane that for any reason fell out of formation. They would single out the weaker or lone aircraft to try to take it out. Later, they focused on attacking the last bomber to head for the target on a bombing run. When British fighters escorted our bombers, the Americans were more successful. However, the Allied fighter planes could not penetrate deep into enemy territory because of limited fuel capacity, at least in the early days of the war. By the fall of 1942 things were heating up, and the American crews were seeing heavy defensive action by the German fighter planes. When the winter of 1942–1943 came, there was limited American action because bombers and crews were being diverted to other hot spots such as North Africa and the Mediterranean.

Throughout the early days of the combined British and American air effort against Germany, it was agreed that the RAF would continue their night missions against the Germans, while the United States air forces would concentrate on daylight strategic precision bombing of pre-selected targets. Part of the American strategy called for alternate targets when weather conditions were not right for the primary target, thus conserving valuable fuel and bombs.

By the spring of 1943, air action over occupied Europe began to increase. The Eighth Air Force slowly went forward, learning things from their initial mistakes that would prove invaluable in the months to come. Throughout the war, particularly in the early days, the loss of crews and bombers was staggering.

In preparing to write about my father, I traveled with my wife, Bonnie, to Maxwell Air Force Base in Montgomery, Alabama, to visit the Air Force Historical Research Agency. We also visited the Mighty Eighth Air Force Museum in Pooler, Georgia, just outside of Savannah. It was there that I learned that the Eighth Air Force was never turned back by the enemy. While weather, mechanical or technical problems could turn back a mission or an individual aircraft, the Germans never did. Once the mission started and the bombers left English soil for Germany or occupied Europe, the mission went forward in spite of the sometimes fierce opposition sent up against the Americans. We could have been losing half our planes on a specific mission, but it would continue onward. The bravery of these bombing crews continues to amaze me. Their bravery and determination to defeat Hitler turned the tide in Europe, and in my opinion this was one of the main reasons we won the war against Germany.

It is estimated that more than 350,000 men served in the Eighth Air Force. By D-Day, an estimated 200,000 aviators were based in England. Approximately 26,000 men of the Eighth were killed in action. Roughly 28,000 were held as prisoners of war (POW), and well over 19,000 were reported as missing in action (MIA). What a price to pay for our freedom!

4

The Maturing of a Man

After leaving Nashville on January 2, 1943, Vince was on a train bound for Santa Ana for four days. In a series of letters, he described to Martha what he saw as the troop train traveled west. He had hoped to see cotton fields in Alabama, but the crop had already been picked. He only saw one cowboy rounding up some cattle in all of Texas. He described the state of Arizona as "…about the prettiest I've ever seen." He continued: "You see nothing but prairie for hundreds and hundreds of miles and in the distance you see mountains that look like they're only a mile or two away, but when you start heading for them they are miles and miles away. Just looking at them makes one realize how small he is in this great vast country." Vince arrived at Santa Ana Army Air Base on January 6, 1943, and he wrote to Martha: "I love you with every inch of the 3,000 miles that separates us."

Compared to the cold and damp weather of Tennessee, Vince loved the sunny, hot, dry weather of southern California. His second day in camp found him digging around the barracks in an attempt to get grass growing on this new air base. He wrote: "Besides trying to make pilots out of us I think they are trying to make us farmers."

Work details made way soon, however, for classrooms and study. Within a few days, he began to tackle the following subjects: Math, Physics, Airplane Recognition, Military Hygiene, Naval Forces, Maps & Charts, Morse Code and Ground Forces. Some of the work came easily from his high school days, but like anything else, some of it was tough. Vince buckled down and studied and worked hard. In the early days, he struggled with completing two words per minute of Morse code, knowing that he would have to master eight words per minute by the end of the course. His hard work paid off, because his final grade in Morse code was a 98. The course schedule was designed to be a nine-week program, but toward the end they were told that they would finish in seven weeks, an early indication that the military was beginning to need replacements along the battlefronts. Vince completed the preflight training with an overall average of 93.1 percent.

One of the more interesting parts of Vince's preflight training involved the altitude chamber test. It was a big iron chamber into which the men entered, and then the pressure was reduced to simulate any height or altitude. Vince explained to Martha: "As you probably know, that also reduces the oxygen. Without oxygen you pass out. Under normal conditions a person can't fly above 12,000 feet to 18,000 feet more than 8 minutes without an oxygen mask. Above 18,000 feet it's just a matter of seconds before one passes out." The cadets were intially taken up to 5,000 feet and then brought right back down again to see if they could take it. Then they were taken up to 38,000 feet with oxygen masks on.

Vince continued: "On the way up four fellows passed out completely. When anyone passes out they level the chamber off and take them out in what they call a locker, which is attached to the chamber and at the same pressure as the chamber. They then lower the chamber at about 2,000 feet to 3,000 feet per minute until it reaches sea level. See, hon, they can't bring you down fast because that would bust your eardrums, etc. After getting up to 38,000 feet we had to stay there for three hours. Boy, that was really tiresome just sitting there doing nothing. During the three hours all but 15 of us passed out or got the bends. There were 35 boys to start. When we were brought down everyone had trouble trying to get their ears to clear. Couple times our ears wouldn't clear, so they had to take us back up again. It took 40 minutes to get down from 38,000 feet."

Continuing, Vince wrote: "We then went back up to 18,000 feet without any mask at all. That was the funny part about it. At 18,000 feet you stay for eight minutes without oxygen. Towards the end you get real anoxic. They ask you all sorts of questions and stuff. The instructor told me to subtract two from four, and I just laughed at him—I wouldn't even do it for him. That's how you get, real silly. I just laughed and laughed and laughed. When I finally decided to do the question I couldn't figure it out. I knew the answer was two but I wasn't sure, and I couldn't write it. At eight minutes we were all about to pass out, so we had to put our mask on. After we got our sense, we went to 24,000 feet and then to 28,000 feet and then we came down to sea level again. All in all we were in the chamber five hours. It's the first time they tried anything like that. All the other times the boys were just in the chamber about an hour. Hon, it's getting to be that our squadron are human guinea pigs. It seems that we are always the first to do something."

Part of Vince's training at Santa Ana involved his initial experience of going to the range for gunnery practice. The range was located right on the beach of the Pacific Ocean about 15 miles from camp. He fired a .45 caliber tommy gun and a .30 caliber machine gun. Apparently, the cadets went to the range only once while at Santa Ana. After gunnery practice, they went swimming in the ocean. Then, to their surprise, they were served dinner on the beach by the enlisted men of the post. After eating, they had a mock beach invasion. Vince wrote: "That's when the fun started. I was assigned to the invasion squad. We didn't do so good either. All of us were thrown right back into the ocean. Clothes and all. …All in all I had a helluva good time."

When Vince arrived at Santa Ana, he was assigned to an upper-classman by the name of Bill, who immediately took Vince under his wing and was a great help to him. They became good friends. Vince informed Martha that Bill was a national jitterbug contest winner. That prompted Martha to ask where Bill came from. She jokingly suggested that the best jitterbug dancers were from Baltimore.

On one of Vince's first passes off post, he went into Santa Ana. He wrote to Martha that he enjoyed his visit but noted that while it was a busy little town by day, at night they took up their sidewalks. Martha apparently had never heard that expression and wanted to know where they put the sidewalks at night. Vince enjoyed writing back to explain and called her a "square."

At camp, the boys had a mascot named "Blackout." He was an all-black spitz who at the first sound of a whistle or bugle was the first to fall into formation. He would sit on his hind legs until the formation was dismissed. They wanted to take him to their next assignment, but his home was at Santa Ana Army Air Base.

Vince wrote that one of the guys and his wife had just had a baby born three months premature, so they got together and gave the new dad a fifty-dollar war bond for the baby. Vince wrote: "It was really funny how we did it. All of us got around in a big circle and put him in the middle. He didn't know what was coming off. He made a little speech for us; this is what he said, quote, 'Half of us are Yankees and half are Rebels, so junior's going to be a half-and-half baby.' You see, honey, he's always fighting the Civil War with the southern boys here and I guess he felt a little bad about it. Anyway he sure was tickled with the bond."

Upon hearing that his Aunt Helen was breaking up her home in East Baltimore, Vince was a little saddened. He wrote: "I know it is the best and only thing she could do, but I liked that house so much. I feel like a soldier without a home now, but I shouldn't, I know." Aunt Helen's oldest daughter, Tess, was living in Omaha, Nebraska, and expecting a baby. Aunt Helen planned to move out to Omaha to stay with Tess's young family. Her other daughter, Nonie, was going into the Air WAC soon. Vince continued: "This damn war is the cause of everything that is wrong in this world. I'd like personally to choke everyone that has anything to do with it."

There was a fun side to Vince's stay in Santa Ana. On a couple of occasions, he went to Hollywood, where he heard Tommy Dorsey's band play at the Palladium. He even met the actor Mickey Rooney there and spoke with him for fifteen minutes at the bar. Vince wrote: "Our conversation ended when his wife came over and dragged him back to their table." On another occasion, Vince saw the Andrews Sisters at the

Municipal Auditorium in Long Beach, California. In one of his letters, he told Martha about some of the stars who were in camp with them. There were the actors Robert Sterling and Tim Holt. John Kimbrough, an all-American fullback from Texas A&M, was there as well as Joe DiMaggio, the New York Yankees great, who had just been appointed athletic director at their post.

One of the things that was unexpected in his letters is the fact that for recreation, Vince participated in some boxing bouts while at Santa Ana. Apparently nothing formal or staged—he just went a few rounds on a couple of occasions. I knew my father was a tough young man, but it was a surprise to learn that he was that tough. He wrote that he hoped the Army would develop a more organized boxing program.

While Santa Ana overall may have been a good experience for Vince, there were certainly some gloomy days. In his second week of camp, his barracks was quarantined again for measles. A weekend pass was cancelled. Vince wrote: "For a bunch of guys that are quarantined for two weeks, we are really slap-happy. I guess it's because we're so disgusted we don't give a damn about anything. You should hear them, honey, singing like they don't have a worry in the world. That's what I like about the boys—they don't let anything get them down, and in case we do we won't show it until the lights go out. You see, honey, when I feel low or anybody else feels low we try to hide it until lights out, and then you can cry your eyes out if you want to, and I have done it already. Please don't think I'm a sissy tho. As the saying goes, 'it takes a man to cry about something that has him down,' or something to that effect."

Martha wrote back: "…I don't think you're a sissy because you cry. No matter what you do, I think you're wonderful. As soon as I get a 'definite word' from you, I'll be out there, and there will be no need for us to cry." Actually, Martha pressed the issue even further when she indicated that she would quit her job and "…come out there to stay if we could get married. Hon, I'm sure we would both feel better if we were married. If it wasn't happening every day, I wouldn't even suggest it, but everyone is taking a chance. You never can tell what tomorrow will bring; we ought to get what little happiness we can out of life. I wish you'd think about it, honey." At the phone company, she was getting pressure to put in her vacation request, and she was trying to decide between a vacation and a furlough.

While Vince was stationed in Santa Ana, he and Martha wrote extensively about her coming west to join him and about their upcoming marriage. Vince appeared slightly hesitant until they knew more about where he would go next for primary flight training. Martha became frustrated because things were so much up in the air. She found herself feuding at times with her immediate family. She discussed it with Angela, who shared a similar experience, since her husband was away in the army. They conclude that it was the war and the separation they were both enduring that had them so anxious, distraught and short-tempered. After all, being alone at home without their fiancé or their husband and not knowing for how long could be nerve-racking. The uncertainty of their loved one's future and safety could take a heavy toll.

Two songs of the day that often played on the radio while Vince was at Santa Ana and that made him particularly homesick for Martha were "Tangerine" and "That Old Black Magic."

Vince and Martha went to great lengths to plan a telephone call in the latter part of February, 1943. While they had spoken by phone once since Christmas, the connection was so poor that they had hardly understood each other. Vince gave Martha the phone number of a pay phone that was located in camp. He informed her that he would be next to the phone every night over an extended period from 9:00 PM until 9:55 PM, West Coast time. Vince had to be in bed by 10:00 PM. Martha, being an operator at the phone company, was to try to reach him every night until they spoke. While she was on the night shift, she tried between 12:00 midnight and 12:55 AM, East Coast time. Despite several attempts, they never could connect, and both were very disappointed.

When Martha heard of another quarantine and an apparent small outbreak of spinal meningitis, it prompted her to write: "I think it's a crime before the Lord to take perfectly good and healthy fellows and then stick them in some old army camp to pick up all sorts of disease."

In one of Martha's more reflective moments, she wrote: "I often sit and think about the fun we used to have. Sometimes we wouldn't go a single place and yet we were so happy. If I only had you here right now. Gee, Vince, I love you. It makes me mad, too. I try to think that you are only away from me because it's your duty, but I still wish you were home, duty or no duty. That isn't being very patriotic, is it, honey? I guess when you love someone the way I love you, you don't bother about being patriotic and stuff. Anyway, honey, I'm very proud of you, and when the war is over and that long-awaited-for 'peace' comes, we can say that you helped to make it so 'peaceful.'" While Martha wrote this on the East Coast, that very same day, Vince wrote on the West Coast regarding a drawing sent by Martha: "I received your dented heart and am very sorry it is that way. You know it isn't my fault, it's this damn war's fault, and if it isn't over soon me and about 4,000,000 other boys are going to have to do something about it."

While at Santa Ana, it was evident that Vince was beginning to settle into military life. While he still longed for Martha and a return to civilian life, he wrote: "...Oh, for the life of a civilian. It isn't that I don't like the army, because I like it very much, but I miss you so doggone much it hurts. I'd be willing to stay in the army all my life if I knew you could be with me. Let's get the president to pass a law permitting soldiers to live with their wives on the post. That would be swell, wouldn't it?"

From time to time, Martha continued to ask Vince in her letters how long he thought the war would last. Up until this point, Vince had been optimistic that the war would end soon. Perhaps he wanted to comfort Martha. He may have been somewhat naïve. That all changed for Vince in early March 1943. Toward the end of his preflight training, he answered her in the most candid and sobering way since his departure.

Vince wrote to Martha on March 4, 1943: "We were just given a talk by a captain...who has just come back from active service, and he has seen plenty. I want to pass on some of the things he told us. Thru him my outlook on this war has really changed. Hon, after listening to him, we are far from winning this war. I hate to say that but facts are facts. The American people don't realize what our soldiers are up against and what our boys are going thru. From now on I refuse to do anymore bitching. If you could have only heard some of the stories he told. One boy asked him how the boys on the other side felt toward the people at home who were striking and laying down on the job. All he said was they'll handle them their own way when and if they get back. Another boy asked him how they felt toward us soldiers." Apparently, the captain was speaking on behalf of ground forces. Vince continued: "He said they don't envy us, that is, if we make good use of our time. They all realize that when the war is won, it will be won thru the air. But if we are wasting our time, they would like personally to kick our ass up between our shoulder blades. So you can see how the boys over there now are holding the burden waiting for the ones training now. As I said before, the American people don't realize what's going on; that also includes us soldiers. We have all been letting them down. They aren't getting half the equipment they need. Like I was reading in this mornings paper. If they could get 7% of a month's airplane production, they could blast the Japs to kingdom come, but they aren't getting it. That was from a General who knows."

Vince continued: "He also gave us a few pointers in the technique of the Japs. Hon, they are really sneaky….I can now see why we go thru so much training. They want no one who can't think faster than the Japs. It's no getting around it, the Japs are tough and smart and shrewd, but we have to be one point higher than them."

Continuing, Vince wrote: "This captain was in command of an army gun crew on a transport. He said he's hauled many men back and forth from the war zone. Most of them back have been in boxes. He's seen men—strong, big men—cry like ladies when they've seen the golden gates. I don't know whether I should be telling you all this, but I believe that's the trouble with most of the people—they don't get enough of the true facts and horrible facts of war. Too much is kept back from the people. Hon, from here on in we're going to be taught to be killers, and that's the only way to win this war. We are learning the tricks of the Japs and some of our own also. They're teaching us to be tough, so tough we'll have to be. Sounds funny to me when I write about it. I just can't picture myself killing anyone, but I guess I'll soon change. The talk today was the first of a series of seven we're to be given." Vince continued to mature, perhaps sooner than he had hoped, and was well on his way to becoming an officer.

There was some evidence from back home that the war was at a critical point. Martha informed Vince over a series of letters that in mid-January 1943, pleasure driving had been banned in Baltimore; and shortly thereafter, one could not take a taxicab for pleasure purposes. As a result, even Baltimore Society was traveling on the streetcars to the Lyric Opera House in their formal wear. By early February 1943, shoes had been rationed—only three pairs per person per year. When Martha bought Valentine candy for Vince, she was limited to half a pound of one kind of chocolates—such as butter creams—per customer, and only one two-pound box of mixed chocolates per customer.

Vince received word from Martha that Jack, her future brother-in-law, had been called to duty on February 19, 1943. His first placement was in Miami, Florida, where he was assigned to ground crew training before being moved into a cadet program in the air corps. Martha reported that her sister Rita cried that night, understandably, and that Martha cried right along with her. Martha knew full well what her younger sister would have to endure.

Martha continued to be faithful to her pledge of frequent Mass and Communion and her other devotions to Our Father, Jesus, the Holy Spirit and the Blessed Virgin. At times she made at least two different novenas over the same period. Vince remained faithful when his military schedule allowed. He wrote about one sermon he heard at Mass, which he called one of the best he had ever heard. The priest's theme was "Soldiers of Christ—either change your conduct or change your name." That theme was repeated throughout the sermon. Vince wrote: "Then he told about the language that went on in the barracks and the conduct of the boys in town with the girls. He really put it across nicely and I know everyone that was there will benefit by it."

Two isolated quotations in the letters between Martha and Vince while he was at Santa Ana sum up their feelings at the time. Martha wrote: "I have my whole life planned on you, and just the thought of us being together keeps me going." Vince wrote in reference to a question from Martha: "Honey, you can call me anything except late for my wedding date, which I hope is soon."

Vince left Santa Ana on March 10, 1943, bound for Phoenix. Keeping up with their previous commitment, between January 2, 1943, when Vince departed from Nashville en route to Santa Ana, and his departure from there on March 10, 1943, I have counted two telegrams, five cards and 145 letters between them.

5

Learning to Fly

Vince arrived at his new assignment at Thunderbird Field, near Phoenix, Arizona, on March 11, 1943, where he took his primary flight training. He wrote to Martha his second day there: "Honey, this place is the closest thing to a Country Club that I ever saw....Our living quarters are Spanish-style connected bungalows which form a circle with a patio in the center....In the center and around the outside is the greenest grass you'd want to look at. There is also a swimming pool in the center." Vince went on to describe flowers growing that throw off an elegant scent. Unlike in barracks, there are ten cadets to a bungalow, with beds that have innerspring mattresses. There is a private latrine for each bungalow. He wrote: "Our beds and study hall are separated by these tall, roomy lockers. It's going to be a pleasure not to live out of barrack bags and footlockers." They even had individual desks for study and homework. Obviously, he had come a long way from Nashville in his brief military career.

Some things did not appear to change, however, because Vince was not there a week when they were quarantined yet again. That was the fourth week in a row, and that was only the beginning. By March 28, 1943, they had been quarantined for seven straight weeks including the weeks at the previous post. At one point Vince reported to Martha that he had been quarantined 10 out of the 18 weeks he'd been in the service. Eventually, their group was confined to post without leave for nine straight weekends. By early April, a small outbreak of scarlet fever was added to the list of diseases that confined them. Vince was concerned that some of the guys would be washed out for breaking quarantine and going AWOL. Two men with wives in the Phoenix area did go one night, but they got back without being discovered. On one occasion, a quarantine was announced fifteen minutes before the fellows were to go on a weekend pass. Six went over the hill anyway but were not caught. Vince was tempted, but he did not go. Later he felt bad for even thinking about going. He did not want to wash out for any reason. He did write to Martha reflecting the frustration of the group: "Four cadets have just upped and quit because of all the 'chicken shit' we have to take. Sometimes, hon, we are treated like boy scouts. I sure will be glad when we're upperclassmen." That had to wait until April 12, 1943, when they did become upperclassmen.

Thunderbird was more disciplined than previous bases. As underclassmen, they had to eat with only one hand while the other was placed in their lap. Vince explained that his hair was much shorter—only three-eighths of an inch long—a post requirement. He wrote: "In the towns nearby, that is the way a Thunderbird cadet can be distinguished. Out here a Thunderbird man is hot stuff. So they say, anyway." When they walked, they had to square their corners. He wrote: "The post is strictly military tho. Everything has to be perfect. From here on in is where you are really noticed. We're potential officers and we have to act and look as such."

When the cadets moved to new bases, their mail was delayed. After four days Martha had not heard that Vince arrived safely at Thunderbird, so she was ready to telephone the president to see where her fiancé was. Already down in the dumps, she heard the following three songs on the radio within a short time period: "Tangerine," "That Old Black Magic" and "Don't Cry." She almost cried.

At Thunderbird, Vince's subjects were Engines, Theory of Flight, Weather, Navigation, Maintenance and Airplane Recognition again. He acknowledged that some of these are tougher courses. While he got a final grade average of 84 percent in his ground school, he did not enumerate to Martha all of his final grades at Thunderbird. He did mention that the general average for the whole course at Thunderbird since it started was 78 percent, so he was feeling pretty good about his grades. Apparently, most cadets acknowledged that the courses were getting harder as they advanced. Vince commented in a letter to Martha: "Now I know what they mean when they say this training is one that can't be bought and is worth a million dollars. Hon, we learn about everything, and I wouldn't trade it for any other in the world." Vince continued: "In navigation we were given a problem for homework and it goes something like this. We start off from an aircraft carrier somewhere in the Pacific and fly to San Diego, then to San Pedro and then back to the carrier, but of course the carrier is in a different spot. Well, to get to the point, I started off on the trip correcting for wind and variation and all that stuff, but hon, I've wound up in Michigan someplace, and I can't seem to get out. Sometime before tomorrow afternoon, when we have class, I just have to get back on that carrier. I've been over it 20 times and I can't find my mistake. I'm as bad as the ensign that finds his battleship somewhere in Texas."

Vince had been looking forward to flying for some time now. He wrote: "I just can't wait to get in a plane. I'm excited as hell about it. I'm a little scared, tho, not of flying but washing out. I have my heart and soul set on getting my wings, but I have that fear of washing out." Apparently, his fears were well founded, for he informed Martha at the end of April, 1943, that 94 of their starting class of 207 cadets at Thunderbird had washed out. Some of the cadets just gave up. Flying was the program at Thunderbird that Vince obviously enjoyed the most.

On March 15, 1943, Vince flew for the first time—with an instructor, of course. This was known as dual flying. He wrote: "Honey, flying is wonderful. When you're up there above the ground you feel so free and at ease, you wouldn't think there was a war going on. It's just perfect." Later, he wrote: "The air was so smooth and nice." Before long, he was learning banking turns, climbing turns, gliding turns, glides, climbs, engine stalls, field patterns and the fundamentals of taking off and landing. He was flying a Stearman aircraft. On March 30, 1943, just two weeks following his first dual flight, he went up solo. It was a tradition at Thunderbird that after a guy went up solo, he got dumped in the swimming pool fully dressed. However, Vince experienced things the hard way throughout his early training. For some reason, the guys that went solo this particular day were dragged by their feet through six inches of water and mud fully dressed. He wrote to Martha: "…I had mud from head to foot; my clothes look like hell. This is one experience I'll never forget—it was really funny. After the other boys got done with us, we just had a mud battle among ourselves, more fun."

Vince needed at least 60 hours of flying, dual and solo combined, before he could advance to the next level of training. Some days it went well. Other days he had trouble with spins. While soloing he would wonder if he was high enough at 4,000 feet to attempt a spin, so he'd go up to 5,000 feet. He'd be "scared silly," but he'd do one and be all right, and then do three more. On his third solo he had trouble with his landings. As he gained experience, though, he learned chandelles, loops, snap rolls, slow rolls, split-S's and lazy 8's. While he was on his own, he was scared to do a snap roll, but he did one and got over the scare. After every 20 hours or so of flying, he had to go up with an instructor for a check flight. He sweated each one of them. Sometimes the instructor made them sweat it out just waiting to be called for the flight. The first was at 20+ hours, the next at 43 hours and the final one at 60+ hours. Each time Vince passed.

One evening back in Baltimore, a plane had been flying around the neighborhood all evening and it sounded very low. Martha first heard it at Angela's house. Before leaving Angela's for home, Martha convinced everyone there that it might be Vince. When she arrived at her house, the plane flew over again and her Mom said: "That darn old plane," at which Martha spoke up and said, "That's Vince." Martha wrote: "Mom told me to tell you to cut out all that 'racket'. Was it you, hon? Let me know."

Vince wrote to Martha that a group of Chinese aviator cadets was training with the Americans at Thunderbird Field. He wrote: "After chow a whole bunch of us went over to the Chinese quarters. Hon, are those boys clever—I never saw anything like it. Most all of them can speak English, but they say they can't understand us because we talk too fast and use too much slang. We had a nice lengthy conversation tho. It's really interesting the way they put things across, and they love to be corrected. They're really eager to learn. And what a sense of humor. If they're not talking they're laughing like hell. I can see where we're all going to get along nicely. They're in the same class with us, but most of them have about 50 hours in the air, so they are much more advanced than us." Later, Vince wrote: "Today we had a basketball game with the Chinese cadets and they beat the heck out of us. They've only been playing about two months, but you should see them go. I never saw one race have so much coordination. It's remarkable. They're so eager to learn our language that they come over to our rooms and just listen to us talk."

Calisthenics, drilling, marching, parading and athletics were still a major part of life at Thunderbird. In athletics one day, Vince ran the 75-yard dash in 7.8 seconds. "It was unofficial, but the instructor couldn't believe it. I broke the post record by .2 seconds. You know it's funny, hon—I didn't know I could run until I got in the army. I found out in Santa Ana when I ran the '75' in 8 seconds and tied the record. The instructor was so damned surprised he's going to run me again in a couple days to make sure it wasn't a mistake."

In early April, 1943, there was a major inspection at the post. Vince wrote: "Boy, hon, did our post put on a show today. We had some visitors and we really strutted. Under-Secretary of War Patterson, three senators, one general, three colonels and a lot of other officials were the visitors. Thunderbird was picked out of all the primary fields to be inspected by them. They wanted to see just what kind of training we got in primary. They inspected our rooms, the mess hall, and the flight line, etc. They were only here for an hour, but it made us all feel kind of big to be inspected by the Under-Secretary of War. You know, he even outranks General Marshall."

While Vince stayed focused on his flying and his schooling, he and Martha wrote frequently about their marriage. They continued to want so much to be married. They began to write about Martha coming west, and she was anxious to see Vince. As time went on, their correspondence centered on the possibility that when she came westward, they might get married. Martha inquired where the wives of the married cadets lived while their husbands continued training. They wrote about Martha getting a job to support herself living off base but near the training facility. Vince became anxious about washing out of pilot training. It was not just because he really wanted to succeed in his efforts to become a pilot, but also because he realized that washing out could alter their marriage plans significantly because it would mean uncertainty as to where he would be assigned. Martha became increasingly frustrated as the weeks dragged on. Not knowing for certain whether they would get married when she came out to see Vince was difficult for her. Her frustration was reflected when she wrote to Vince in early April, 1943: "If I don't see you very soon, then I am going to give up, and I don't care what happens to me. If this old war would only stop." Letters from Vince could turn her mood around very quickly, though. She cherished receiving them very much. Most of Martha's letters were uplifting and chock-full of news from back home. Vince enjoyed hers equally as well.

During World War II, it was quite common for a couple to get married on a weekend, while the guy was home on leave, only to have him back on base the following Monday. Apparently it was the uncertainty of the times that prompted many a couple to marry abruptly, since they were not sure when they might have the next opportunity. Martha wrote to Vince about a young woman at the telephone company who went to West Virginia on her vacation to visit her fiancé, who was stationed there in the air corps. Martha wrote: "Down work we have a 'hook-your-man club.' You see, we put money in, and then we place a bet on whether or not the girl leaving will get married. Now, if she comes back a 'Mrs.,' we will buy her a present. If she comes back 'Miss,' then the ones who bet she wouldn't get married will get the money. I hope nobody gets their money back when I leave." She continued: "Hon, do you think we will get married? If anything happens to make you change your mind, I think I will die."

Martha was so eager to see Vince and to get married. She wrote: "I miss you very, very much, and hope we can get this business of my coming out there settled. Hon, when I do come out, you're going to have one awful time getting rid of me." She told Vince's sister, Angela, that very day: "…when I get out there, I am going to get you real drunk and then make a mad dash for the church. Then, darling, we'll be married. I wish I had done that last September…" Martha wrote to Vince that she was kidding, and that she only wanted to be married if he really wanted it. It is most evident from Vince's letters that he wanted her to be with him out west and getting married was only a matter of time and timing. There had been some talk of Martha losing her vacation if she didn't request it soon. Vince wrote that if that happened: "…I think I'd die." He suggested: "See if you can't get your vacation right away or as soon as possible, before I leave here if you can."

Within a few days, Martha had all the train routes and fares mapped out, but things continued to remain up in the air. However, plans were resolved, at least for the moment, when on April 10, 1943, Martha and Vince spoke by telephone for the first time since February. During the telephone conversation, they both decided that Martha would come out to be with Vince in May. Two days later, Martha informed Vince that her vacation had been approved from May 30 to June 19. Initially, she was to get two weeks' vacation. However, she asked her supervisor for three weeks. Her supervisor said: "Miss Owens, may I ask why you are making such a ridiculous request in these times?" Martha wrote: "I got scared then, so real bold-like, I said, well, I'm going to see my boyfriend, and it is going to take me 3 or 4 days to get where I'm going. She laughed and said, 'The extra week is yours'. Boy, I was so glad when she said that, I could have kissed her." Martha was going to request a furlough, but another supervisor had advised that she wait until she reached her destination and then let the company know.

While it was resolved that Martha would be going west at the end of May 1943, the question of marriage still remained a lingering question as the days unfolded. Martha asked Vince to let her know if he thought they would be married when she arrived. She wrote to him: "You always write things that make me think we will, but it's always so indirect. You have never once come right out and said that we were." In response to many inquiries, she told family members and friends that she did not know whether they would be married or not during her upcoming visit. Apparently, most suspected they would, but Martha was reluctant to say for certain until Vince made a definitive statement. Vince continued to be concerned about washing out. He wrote: "I just can't wash out now. It would just about ruin me and all the plans we've been making. Say a couple extra prayers that I don't, huh, hon." And further: "Gee, hon, I'm looking forward to you coming out here so much that if anything happens to our plan I don't know what I'll do. I love you so much, it hurts."

Martha wrote to Vince and asked if she should bring pajamas or nightgowns. She wrote: "Hon, I've got another plan. I have to get either some new pajamas or nightgowns. I don't know which to get, if you know what I mean. Now, if you think we won't get married, you write and tell me that you saw a darling pair of pajamas, but if you think we are going to get married, then you write and tell me to get the blue nightgown. Is that OK, hon? Listen, hon, please do that, will you?" Martha tried every trick in the book to obtain the answer she was looking for. Eventually, Vince answered this particular question by suggesting the nightgown, but not until he was ready to commit. In the meantime, he wrote: "I don't want to get your and my hopes all up and then something happen."

As Easter approached, Martha tried to find Vince some candy or an Easter egg. She tried for three weeks, but the stores were empty. She was told that they had been that way for the past month. She wrote: "Hon, this damn war—you can't even buy a little jelly bean."

On April 29, 1943, Vince wrote to Martha: "You're saying those prayers that I don't get shipped to Pecos, Texas, aren't you? If I go there, our plans are practically wrecked unless it isn't as bad as everybody says." However On May 11, 1943, Vince informed Martha that his next assignment *is* in Pecos, Texas. He had heard that the field and the post were swell, "...but it's out in the middle of nowhere." Continuing, he wrote: "What I'm afraid of is that I won't be able to find a place for you to stay. I've been talking to some of the married men, and they don't know what to do with their wives. They don't know just what kind of a town it is or whether they'll (the wives) be able to get jobs there. Boy, this sure has put us all in a helluva mess." Jokingly, he asked Martha if she would live in a tent if he had to pitch one, and she responded yes. She went on to write: "I'm coming no matter what. There must be someplace for me to stay. I'm little, hon—I could squeeze in someplace." She told Vince that she would stay in "somebody's old barn" if she had to, or perhaps the next closest town. Martha was determined to come regardless of the circumstances.

In preparation and in the event they were to be married during her stay, Martha obtained proof of her baptism at St. Edward's Church and proof of Vince's baptism at Corpus Christi Church, both parishes in Baltimore. Further, she received the necessary dispensation from the diocese that was required by the Catholic Church to be married in another parish, out-of-state and within a brief time period. Not knowing whether Vince would need it, Martha even secured a note from his older sister, Angela, giving him permission to marry, since he was two months shy of being 21. The dispensation form had a time limit of 60 days, and if it wasn't used by that date, it was to be returned to the chancellor of the diocese. Vince wrote: "If I can help it, that dispensation won't be turned in because of not being used—how about you? I'm looking forward so much to you coming out here." Father Manns, the priest who helped Martha with her dispensation and who had known her for years, offered to write a letter of introduction to the priest in Pecos. Now, Vince was getting excited about Martha's upcoming trip.

Vince's cadet class would be leaving Thunderbird Field, and it was a tradition to have a graduation dance prior to departure. Vince wrote: "Our dance is coming up tomorrow night, and myself and the other boys are set for a rousing time. Four of us are going stag. A couple of the boys have been asking me to let them get me a date, but I keep saying no soap to it. That is unless they fly back to a little house on Ellicott Drive and get the sweetest gal on this earth." From her home at 2842 Ellicott Drive, Martha had been feeling down and wrote in response about the dance: "I think that's why I felt so bad last night, thinking about what a wonderful time I could have been having."

As in the past, they found more ways to say they loved each other. Martha wrote the following within a short period of time: "I love you with every ounce of life in me, plus plenty"; and "I love you 6 million times more than I ever did, plus another day's worth"; and finally: "I know there has never been a love so great as my love for you."

Between March 11, 1943 and May 20, 1943, while Vince was stationed at Thunderbird, I have counted one card and 129 letters between them.

6

Martha Goes West

The next assignment for Vince was the Army Air Forces Basic Flying School in Pecos, Texas. He arrived there on May 21, 1943, by train. Almost immediately, he became concerned for Martha traveling to Pecos. She was set to leave Baltimore on May 28, 1943. He wrote a week before her scheduled departure: "Darling, I'm about to ask you a question that's hurting me more to ask than it will when you read it. Do you think you could have your vacation delayed for 9 weeks—that is, until I finish here at Basic and move on to Advance? Honey, please don't think I want it that way. You know damn right well I don't, but they say it's almost impossible to get a place to stay. Let me know how you feel about the matter, as if I didn't already know. Darling, we'll figure out a way; both of us haven't been praying for nothing." What do you think Martha's reaction was? There was no way she was delaying her trip to Pecos.

While things appeared again to be somewhat up in the air, everything was definitely resolved during a telephone call between Martha and Vince on May 25, 1943. It was deadline time, and Martha had to know, for she was scheduled to leave in three days. She reached Vince by telephone and it was finally settled. Everything was a go! Vince wrote by special delivery: "Oh, sweetie, am I happy, knowing that in a week or so we'll be together again as we should have been all along. While walking over to the phone, all different kinds of thoughts were running thru my mind. I thought maybe you had decided not to come, and then I felt real funny, but now I feel better than anybody on this earth. Well, I guess next to you I do." He continued: "I had so many things I had planned to tell you, but it seems I lost my tongue when I was talking to you. Or maybe it was because you were doing all the talking, huh, hon? It was so good to hear your voice again, Oh, sweetie, if you only knew how much I love you and how happy I am right now, but I guess you know." Vince was finally feeling a lot more at ease, for he wrote: "Now all we have to worry about is that we can see each other. By the way you talked, it won't be hard finding a place to stay—that is, if that priest wrote to the priest in Pecos."

Martha had been concerned when Vince raised the possibility of a nine-week delay, but once they spoke and she knew that Vince wanted her there, she wrote: "I'm so happy....Hon, I feel better tonight than I have felt in months....Oh, hon, won't it be heaven? The prayers we said have not been said in vain, darling. Now, I'm going to pray twice as hard."

Prior to her trip, Martha's older brother, Buster, gave her a pocket-size cookbook. He had written a note inside that read: "If this doesn't help Vince's stomach, send me a wire, and I will send you some iron & hammer," apparently referring to Arm & Hammer bicarbonate of soda. Buster further wrote: "The lettuce is for new can openers. They do get dull." Martha looked for a lettuce recipe, thinking it was some sort of a fresh salad. It was two $5 bills. She was obviously very touched by his thoughtfulness. Buster had contracted polio as a young boy, and it had left him crippled. He walked with crutches all of his life, but he never let his handicap get him down. He had a full and active life, and he had a heart as big as Texas.

The long-awaited day arrived. Martha was scheduled to leave Baltimore at 5:16 PM on May 28, 1943, and arrive in Pecos at approximately 4:00 AM on May 31. The next thing we know is that Martha and Vince were married in a Catholic church in Pecos, Texas, on June 5, 1943, by Father Yannes. Since they were now together, there was no written correspondence between them, so the record is silent regarding a lot of the details surrounding their wedding. It appears, however, that Martha was married in an outfit and hat that were made in Baltimore for the special

The newlyweds.

occasion. Her sister Cass, who was 13 years old at the time, recently re-called putting rice in that outfit before it was packed. Cass wrote a letter to the newlyweds on June 6, 1943, pointing out to Martha: "Remember, you were the girl who wasn't going to get married, and my God, you've only been there 4 days & you're married." Cass wrote that when she heard the news of their marriage she nearly fainted and couldn't talk. She wished them good luck, but had one word in the letter for Vince: *Sucker*. Mary Jane, another sister, who was 15 years old at the time, re-cently reflected on how it was sad when you think back and consider that Martha and Vince were married all alone. They were strangers in the Texas community. They had a small, quiet wedding in the church. However, there is no doubt in my mind that Martha and Vince were the happiest people on earth at that moment in time!

Numerous telegrams, cards and letters of congratulations were sent to room 230 of the Hotel Brandon in Pecos, where they undoubtedly stayed for their honeymoon. Martha apparently resided there for a brief period following their wedding. For some reason, Vince was sent back to the Santa Ana Army Air Base by the third week of June 1943. On or about June 20, 1943, Martha's mail from her family and friends started being forwarded to what appears to be a rooming house in South Gate, California, approximately 33 miles from the Santa Ana Army Air Base. It is unclear exactly what brought Vince back to Santa Ana, but Martha was able to continue to be near him. While in South Gate, she found a job in a defense plant, Rheem Manufacturing Co. It appears that she worked in an office and occasionally worked on the telephone switchboard.

Martha's first letter to Vince following their marriage was dated July 18, 1943. She wrote to him at Santa Ana from South Gate. She wrote: "Here I am, back again. It's been quite a while since I wrote to you, hasn't it? But I'm a married woman now, and I'm really busy. You see, I'm working now (to support my husband) and I don't have much time for writing." Vince wrote his first letter after their marriage on that same date. Since there are no letters between them from the end of May until July 18, they apparently spent a fair amount of time with each other. They probably spent a lot of weekends together during this time, and they likely spoke frequently by telephone, perhaps daily. Legend even has it that Martha walked guard duty with Vince, she on the outside of the base fence and he on the inside perimeter.

Perhaps for at least a brief period, there may have been a strike going on that involved the streetcars and buses in Southern California, because transportation between Santa Ana and South Gate presented challenges for them for a while.

Suz wrote to Martha in the middle of July 1943. She obviously missed her oldest daughter when she wrote: "It's pretty funny when one is so far away. You know, you could have 30 kids and one away, and that's the one you miss. That's life, I suppose." This letter, written on or about July 18, 1943, included one of the first indications that Vince would become a bombardier. Suz writes: "I'm sorry he is a bombardier, though. But God will take care of him; he is a good kid." Cass wrote to Martha in July as well. Cass asked her older sister to "...tell my brother-in-law to write to me. Since he doesn't have to write you a book, he can write me a little letter. Do you know that I'm the only one whom he hasn't written to?" It is apparent that the Owens girls had no trouble being assertive. God bless them for it.

Again, due to the lack of correspondence between the end of May and Martha's first letter in mid-July, a lot of details regarding Vince's training and status are unknown. At some point Vince washed out of pilot training, but when and where is not known. It probably occurred in Pecos at the Army Air Forces Basic Flying School, but that has not been confirmed. It was always my understanding that the Army Air Force selected more pilot candidates than they actually needed. Perhaps their plan was that as cadets washed out they would be assigned to other specialties as the need arose.

I read a book by John Steinbeck, author of *The Grapes of Wrath*. Mr. Steinbeck was asked by the United States Army Air Forces to help in the effort to recruit young airmen candidates during World War II. He wrote a book entitled *Bombs Away: The Story of a Bomber Team*, published in 1942 by Viking Press, New York, New York. His goal was to inform young men and their parents about what was involved in the selection, testing and training of the members of a bomb crew.

I found a paperback reprint in a locked cabinet in an antique mall and purchased it during a trip to Ohio. It was reprinted in 1990 by Paragon House of New York, New York. I found the book fascinating, partly because I wasn't looking for it and didn't even know it existed. I simply stumbled upon it. Most interesting to me was its account of what went into the selection of the various members of a bomb crew. The author went to great lengths to explain how the Army Air Force put together a team of some of the best psychologists in the nation to come up with aptitude tests to find the right talent for building a proficient and successful bomb crew. Mr. Steinbeck discussed the kind of background, schooling and athleticism a young man might have experienced in his growing years that would make him the ideal candidate as a member of a bomb crew. As I read his explanation, I could not help but feel that he had my father down pat. He left the reader with the impression that only those who were above average mentally and physically were selected for the Army Air Force. The kind of training a bombardier had to undergo and master was presented in such a way that you knew the author had thoroughly researched the matter and lived through the process. Mr. Steinbeck left no doubt that a bomb crew and the bomber in which they flew and worked was only as good as the whole team, each member being a vital part of that team—from the pilot to the tail gunner, from the radio engineer to the navigator. Each member had an important role to play, and the mission was successful only if the team as a whole functioned as one. After reading Mr. Steinbeck's *Bombs Away*, I believe I know why my father was selected as a bombardier. He was meant to be there at that point in history.

Between May 20 and July 29, 1943, while Vince was stationed at Pecos and then subsequently moved back to Santa Ana, I have counted one telegram and 28 letters between him and Martha. While letter production had decreased significantly, at least they were together or close to each other during most of this time.

7

A Military Detour

Vince was moved to Victorville Army Flying School, in California. He arrived there on or about his 21st birthday, July 30, 1943. It was there that he took his advanced bombardier training. Within two days, he was writing to Martha encouraging her to move to Victorville and seek a job there. On August 5, 1943, Martha learned that she had to vacate her room at the rooming house in South Gate to make way for a mother and her baby who were friends of her landlady, so moving to Victorville appeared to be the timely thing to do. On her first weekend visit to Victorville in early August, Martha gave Vince his birthday present—his wedding band. Perhaps it is worth mentioning here that Martha and Vince did not have a lot of money. Vince was receiving a very modest amount of pay as an aviation cadet, probably in the range of $50 to $75 per month when they were married. He was able to save a little. Martha probably traveled to Pecos with a couple of hundred dollars. As mentioned, she worked when she could find a job. While they didn't have much, they were rich in all the important ways. They were practical, and to a degree frugal, but they relied heavily on the love between them and their faith in Almighty God.

Vince had a close call returning from one of his weekend trips to South Gate. He wrote to Martha: "Boy, I really had a scare last night. I thought for sure I wasn't getting back on time. When I left you I went to get the bus, which wasn't a bus, but a P.E. train. The doggone thing didn't pull out until 5 o'clock, and everybody was saying it took four hours to get to San Bernardino. Well, I just sweated the whole trip. I was in San Bernardino at 7:20, and that sure did relieve me. The next bus to Victorville was at 9 o'clock, and then it started all over again. My only chance was bumming a ride, and that's just what I did. I walked down to the avenue that leads out of San Bernardino and into Victorville and started the old thumb a-moving. Well, the road turned out to be the wrong one, so I got a ride over about a mile to the right one and started over again. By this time it was 8 o'clock, and Victorville 42 miles away. There weren't many cars going to Victorville, and each minute made me more nervous. Finally the bus that the boys hired came along and picked me up. It's a good thing I knew all the fellows. The bus was about 15 minutes late, and the driver really had to step on it. We got into the post just about 9:20, and I called you immediately. Do you love me for that? I love you. Hon, from now on I'm gonna allow myself enough time, so I don't have to sweat another ride like that." Apparently, a P.E. train was a passenger train, the coaches of which resembled trolleys.

By August 28, 1943, Martha was staying in room 15 at the Stewart Hotel in Victorville, where she probably resided until late October 1943. There was no written correspondence between Martha and Vince in September 1943. They were obviously living close to each other and seeing each other frequently. Even though they might have known about it earlier, one of Martha's October letters contained the first reference to her being pregnant. In her letter dated October 10, 1943, Martha first mentioned "Junior." The next day she wrote asking Vince to let her stay with him "…to have our baby." The baby was due in May 1944. Vince's training and future assignments would eventually dictate what was to come. In mid-October, in a letter to Martha, her mom wrote: "My heart breaks when I think of the innocent who are going thru hell because somebody is mad with somebody else."

Some of the subjects Vince took at Victorville were Calibration, Navigation and Combat Record. Part of his program involved a bivouac type of training in the desert, where the men lived out of tents and engaged in flying and exercises, pistol range and bombing practice. His bombardier training appeared to be going quite well. He wrote to Martha on October 13,

Lieutenant Vince Gisriel, bombardier

1943, c/o pickup at the post exchange, that he had "15 hits with 20 bombs to go." He added that he only needed 13 hits to successfully complete the course. Vince wouldn't be satisfied with that, though. Vince's aunt, Sister Dorothy of the Daughters of Charity, wrote to Martha on September 19, 1943, asking about Vince: "Has he hit the target yet? In his last letter he said he got closer to it at each mission. Tell him to pray to the Holy Spirit for his success—and I shall join with him." It never hurts to have an aunt who is a nun working on your behalf! Vince did succeed—he passed bombardier training. On October 23, 1943, he graduated and he was commissioned a second lieutenant. He was discharged as an enlisted cadet on October 22, 1943.

Martha worked at the Victorville Army Air Field from September 4, 1943, until October 14, 1943, probably in some sort of office position. Between July 30, 1943, and the end of October 1943, while Vince was stationed at Victorville, I have counted another 27 letters between them.

It appears that upon Vince's graduation and appointment as a second lieutenant, he and Martha went back to Baltimore on leave. After a week or so, Vince had to return to a new assignment at the Salt Lake City Army Air Base in Utah. After a brief visit with his Aunt Helen and his cousins in Omaha, Nebraska, Vince arrived at the Salt Lake Air Base on November 3, 1943. He returned west alone, leaving Martha back home, a move he later regretted. However, she joined him shortly thereafter in Salt Lake City. When Vince first arrived at the air base, there were no beds for him and some of the other fellows, so they had to go back to Salt Lake City and spend the night at the Hotel Temple Square at a cost of $3.00 per man. By November 19, 1943, Martha had arrived; she stayed at the Milner Hotel in Salt Lake City. Vince did not remain in Salt Lake City for long. By November 30, 1943, he received a letter that was forwarded to Dalhart, Texas. During the month of November 1943, I have counted two telegrams and seven letters between Martha and Vince. These were their last letters of 1943, which indicates that they stayed close to each other for the balance of that year.

By late November 1943, Vince moved on to an unknown air base in Dalhart, Texas. It was at Dalhart that Vince met his fellow crew members, the guys with whom he would be flying over the next several months. The crew members were Lt. Charles "Grubby" Hodges, pilot; Lt. Paul Robertson, copilot; Lt. Vince Gisriel, bombardier; Lt. George Ray, navigator; T/Sgt. William Talbot, engineer/top turret; T/Sgt. Robert Heare, radio operator; S/Sgt. Robert Noble, ball turret; S/Sgt. James Meeks, right waist gunner; S/Sgt. Earl Dahlgren, left waist gunner; and S/Sgt. William Moggs, tail gunner. It was at Dalhart that they got to know one another very well. They worked and practiced together as an efficient bombing crew. They learned to function and operate as one entity. It was here that they received their air combat training.

Martha stayed in room 6 of the Bray Hotel in Dalhart. Her mother, Suz, wrote encouraging Martha to plan to return home to have the baby delivered in Baltimore. Suz strongly suggested in her letters that Martha limit her travel, and to rest and keep regular hours, and stop spending so much of their money traveling around the country by train. Suz acknowledged that she was beginning to sound like a mother-in-law, but she was genuinely concerned for Martha, Vince and the baby's well-being. By December 27, 1943, Martha was residing in cabin 19 of Casa Mia Courts in Dalhart.

While at Dalhart, Vince was engaged in night flying. Suz wrote to Martha on December 26, 1943: "What will Vince have to do now that he has finished night flying? I think of him so often at nite when I hear those darn planes go over. I hope and pray this darn mess will be over soon. I think I will be in the bug house before long." Suz was concerned about the safety of her other loved ones in the military as well.

Suz indicated to Martha that she would turn the upstairs front bedroom into a nursery and Martha's room for when Martha returned. Due to space limitations, a younger sister might have to share the bed. Suz

The crew at Dalhart, Texas, in 1943: Back row: Noble (ball turret), Dahlgren (left waist gunner), Moggs (tail gunner), Heare (radio operator), Meeks (right waist gunner), Talbot (engineer/top turret). Front row: Hodges (pilot), Robertson (copilot), Ray (navigator), Gisriel (bombardier).

understood Martha's reluctance to return home and knew that she wanted to remain with Vince for all the obvious reasons, but felt that Martha had to think of her own health and safety and that of the baby. Suz was not shy in expressing her concerns, but yet she was sympathetic to her daughter's plight. Knowing that Vince could be shipped overseas reasonably soon, Suz wrote in January 1944: "…The nights I lie awake and wonder what in the world the future holds for any of us." She wrote earlier: "If only this dam war was over and people who love each other could be together."

Willie and Suz reserved a room at Maryland General Hospital for Martha for her upcoming labor and delivery. Apparently, rooms at hospitals in Baltimore were hard to come by, and to secure one, it had to be reserved in advance.

Lieutenant Vince Gisriel

By the end of January 1944, Martha had moved from the Casa Mia Courts. It is not known where she stayed for her remaining days in Dalhart, but it was probably a rooming house. By early February, Vince knew that he would be going overseas soon. By mid-February 1944, Martha and Vince were in Kearney, Nebraska. Here they said good-bye, not knowing when they would see each other again. It was in Nebraska that the crew members went as a crew together and picked up a new B-17 that they would fly overseas to deliver to the campaign.

Martha and Vince were fortunate that they were able to be together or be relatively close to each other between late May 1943 and mid-February 1944. However, now they would be separated again while Vince was shipped over to England to accomplish what he had been trained to do. Sixteen months of training had brought him to this point. On her way back to Baltimore, Martha stopped in Omaha, Nebraska, to visit with Vince's Aunt Helen and his cousins. In Omaha, Martha returned to her frequent letter writing to Vince. On February 23, 1944, she wrote in her first letter to her husband since his departure: "There is no need for me to tell you how much I miss you, Vince. I am practically lost already. You can be sure that you will be in my heart and my prayers constantly. Even though we are far apart, you will always be with me spiritually. I am going to make the novena, as I used to, and also go to Communion every Sunday for your safety and speedy return. I know that Our Blessed Mother will watch over you and keep you safe."

The crew left Kearney on or about February 23, 1944, and headed for Manchester, New Hampshire, where they were snowed in for a week. Vince wrote in a letter to Martha on February 24, 1944: "Already I miss you something awful. My heart yearns for you. I'll be back to you soon and then nothing will ever separate us." In this letter, he could not tell Martha where he was, but he assured her that he was safe and that he felt fine. While traveling by train back home to Baltimore,

Lieutenant and Mrs. Gisriel back home

Martha wrote: "You know, it's 10 times worse being away from you now than before we were married. I tell myself that the months will fly by, and you'll be home soon, but I'm not very convincing. I guess that I'll have to be brave, just like millions of wives are, and keep praying." She continued: "I say a rosary every night for your safety...Please be very careful, and don't forget to say a prayer before every mission you go on."

Aunt Helen sent a letter to Vince just prior to his going overseas. She wrote: "Nonie said her prayers will follow you and, my dear, mine will too, and I know Martha's will. She felt real good and you need not worry about her—she is a brave darling. I love her dearly. I must say she loves you very, very much. Always be good to her. I have no doubt that you will. God bless you, my boy, and be with you always." As Vince prepared to leave the United States, bound for England to do his part to stop Hitler, he went with hundreds of prayers from family and friends. While he was growing up in East Baltimore, he developed a close-knit group of friends—about thirteen guys in all. Many of them wrote or inquired about Vince and wished him well in his assignment abroad. They were very proud of what he had accomplished to date. They sent their prayers as well.

Martha arrived home in Baltimore on February 27, 1944. It seems that everybody came to see her upon her return. She was delighted with her freshly painted, light blue bedroom and nursery. She was overwhelmed by all the gifts for the new baby.

Vince wrote on February 26, 1944: "Well, I'm writing from the same place as my last letter. I'm sorry I can't say where it is. I will say it's in the good old U.S.A., but that's all." On March 1, 1944, the day before he was to leave for England, he wrote: "Are you beginning to get scared yet? Please don't. I'm with you always, maybe not physically, but spiritually. Whenever you feel bad or depressed, just think of the future years when we'll have a home of our own and five or six little ones growing up in front of us. It'll be a struggle, but we'll be the happiest people in the world." Martha responded: "I miss you so much and already am dreaming of the day when you will be home and we have our family. Gosh, that will really be wonderful, and I know that rich or poor, we will be the happiest people in the world."

Martha's sister, Reet, wrote to her on March 2, 1944, from Arkansas, where Jack was stationed and where they had been married in January. Reet wrote: "…my heart aches for you. But don't forget you are still lucky. In just a short while you will have the baby; that will be a great comfort to you. You can take pictures so often and send them to Vince—he will be so proud of you. I know it seems hard now, but think of all the time you've been with him. Think of how lucky you have been—then you won't feel quite so bad. I prayed so hard that Vince could stay here until things were more settled for you. But the war may be over soon, and you'll have him back before you know it. Vince is a swell guy, and a good guy too. God will take real good care of him, I'm sure, so don't you worry. Just keep writing to him, and tell him you are so happy. Everything will be fine."

In the short period between February 23 and 29, 1944, when correspondence between Martha and Vince started up again, I have counted nine letters between them.

8

The Eighth's First Full Year in England

As the American bombing campaign progressed through its first full year, our aviators began to perfect their strategic precision bombing techniques, but no one was resting just yet. By the time of the Eighth Air Force's first anniversary in England on August 17, 1943, there had been some success, but the war was far from over. However, if there were any skeptics still around, they were becoming believers in what the U.S. Army Air Force was capable of doing. As a steady stream of well-trained replacements arrived and new aircraft were produced in record numbers and delivered to England, the future looked optimistic for the Allies.

The strategy of going after the German factories and infrastructure was paying off, and Germany knew it. With the growing success of our bombing campaign, Germany began to shift its production from offensive bombers to defensive fighters in an attempt to stop the Americans. Our aviators simply responded by focusing their attacks against the factories that produced the German fighter planes.

On that one-year anniversary of the arrival of the Eighth Air Force in England, a massive aerial assault was initiated on the Nazis' second largest Messerschmitt fighter factory, at Regensburg, Germany. Bombing was extremely accurate and it all but put this manufacturing facility out of business. On that same day, an attack on a plant in Schweinfurt, Germany, was very successful in knocking out approximately 50 percent of the Nazi production of ball bearings. Some estimates have the

Luftwaffe losing over 285 fighter planes on this day, and the Americans may have lost as many as 60 B-17s on that same day. The price of success was very high.

As the war progressed, and our bombers went deeper into enemy territory, we equipped our escort fighter planes with extra fuel tanks. Our bomber crews were able to concentrate more on their targets while our escort fighters fought off the Luftwaffe, which resulted in improved bombing accuracy and a reduction in our losses. More American fighters with greater fuel capacity were rushed overseas.

The plan to go after Hitler's production capability was accomplishing its goal. Keep in mind that when a factory in Germany was successfully damaged, the impact on the front lines was not necessarily seen immediately. Unlike a direct hit on a naval destroyer, which could result in it sinking within minutes of its fatal blow, the results of significant damage to a factory might not be seen right away. While there may have been many explosions and billowing smoke going up thousands of feet in the air, the impact was not necessarily immediate. However, when that factory could not produce the 500 tanks that were needed as replacements six months later, then the real impact was felt by the enemy. The American strategy was brilliant. It was slow, deliberate and methodical. It was patient, well planned and well executed. It was decisive, and it was the beginning of the end for Hitler.

Great thought went into the strategy and design of bomber formations. Equal thought went into the creation of the 10-man crew, the role of each member and how they fit and functioned in the B-17. How these crew assignments were created, how these men were trained and how the crew members carried out their jobs so well was amazing.

The war record is filled with the heroic actions of our aviators. It speaks of men who, in spite of being severely injured, continued to fight the enemy with everything they had. Gunners who were wounded still manned their gun turrets to protect their crew and the plane. Pilots who were wounded still kept the plane in formation because they knew that was the safest place to be up there. As crews watched other B-17s go down in flames, they still pressed on. They would watch and count, hoping to see 10 open parachutes drifting gently downward from the damaged fortresses. Sometimes men jumped but their chutes did not open. Often only part of the crew made it out of a plane going down. Sometimes the pilot remained, regained control of the plane and landed it somewhere. At times, pilots had to land in enemy territory, where they might be taken as a prisoner of war; or they might walk for days and escape. Occasionally, they might have to ditch the plane in the English Channel, where rescue boats patrolled and were quick to respond. At other times, they died trying. And yet those remaining in the formation went forward. The bravery of these men has not ceased to amaze me.

B-17s were not called "flying fortresses" by accident. Their design and durability were technical marvels. Two of their four engines could be knocked out by the enemy, and they could still fly. Some even made it back to safety on one engine. Their windows could be shattered and all their flying instruments could be damaged, and yet they continued to fly. Some planes had gaping holes and damaged and dangling stabilizer cables, and they would still fly. In spite of the damage to their planes, at times the brave men who flew them somehow found a way to continue to complete their missions; at other times they simply attempted to return to friendly soil.

It is a testament to our engineers and designers and the men and women who labored to build these marvelous planes. It is a testament to the men who flew them and who navigated them. It is a testament to the crew chiefs and the ground crews who serviced and maintained them and kept them in tiptop condition. As an American, I am extremely proud of all of these men and women and what they accomplished.

9

Vince Arrives in England

On March 2, 1944, Vince and his crew arrived in Goose Bay, Labrador. They landed on a snow-packed runway in the middle of the night with the temperature at minus 25 degrees. They left Goose Bay in the middle of the night on March 11. By March 12, the crew was in Ireland. En route to Ireland, their B-17 ran low on fuel and they had to land at the first available location in Ireland, which was in Ballyhalbert. Later, they moved to their original destination, Nutts Corner. It was there that they turned in the B-17 they were assigned to bring overseas. From Ireland, they traveled to a temporary location in Bovingdon, England. They arrived there on March 13, 1944.

Over the several days between their departure from Nebraska and their arrival in Ireland, the crew had a fair amount of down time. When not traveling, Vince wrote Martha, they were able to catch up on sleep and engage in a lot of recreational activity. Upon reading this, Martha wrote: "I'm so glad you have so much time off. Naturally, when the wives can't go along, you have quite a lot of free time, but boy, didn't they keep you busy when we were together? I suppose that's life, isn't it?"

Vince wrote to Martha about the different adjustments he has had to make such as getting used to the British currency. He wrote: "It's gonna take me a long time to get used to the way they speak. It's English they speak all right, but it doesn't sound a bit like ours. They say six or seven words before I even begin to catch on to what they're talking about. I'll learn in due time tho." Vince commented on the English drinks. He wrote: "Now about the spirits (as the English call it), I can't go for them much….I've had…Scotch, Irish whiskey, and English beer. You know how I hate Scotch, and the English beer affects my kidneys about 16 times during the middle of the night, so I've decided to give up drinking until I get back to the States." He also told Martha that the only kind of milk they get is powdered milk and he hasn't seen an egg yet, but in spite of the rationing they had been served very good meals, especially in the U.S. mess halls. He did, however, ask Martha to send him some "cat-hup" (catsup/ketchup) for his meat. Vince acknowledged that he was not sure how to spell it. However, he was in good company, because apparently the correct spelling has been debated for the last three centuries.

For months, Martha and Vince had been referring to their unborn baby as "Junior." Vince addressed one letter to his Darling Martha and son. He caught himself somewhat, for he wrote: "Honey don't get me wrong when I say 'son.' Please don't think that I'd rather it be a boy than a girl, because I wouldn't. It's halfway with me. What ever the dear Lord pleases to send us will be just perfect with me. He knows best, and one can't go wrong by His judgment. So boy or girl, I'll be the happiest man in the world when the little one arrives. I can hardly wait—how about you? Never before has anyone been as thrilled over a newborn baby as I am now. I mean that too, honey. Words cannot express my thanks to God for letting us be so fortunate. To think that soon we'll have a child of our own makes me the happiest man in the world. Believe me, I am so grateful."

Can you just imagine how this makes me feel, to be so wanted in life? Please God, that all babies will be so wanted! My mother shared in my father's joy. She made it very clear that she would be equally happy whether it was a boy or a girl.

Vince recounted to Martha a sermon on marriage he had heard during a "religious mission" service. He thought Martha would get a kick out of reading about it. The priest told the story of a soldier in England who wanted to marry an English girl. They were being married in an Anglican church and everything was going along fine until the minister got to part that said, "Do you, so-and-so, take _____ to be your wife in sickness and in health, etc., until death do you part?" Then the soldier raised his hand and said, "Whoa there, not 'til death, only for the duration." The minister responded, "Only for the duration? I can't marry you under those circumstances." The soldier responded, "Well, that's the way I want it to be....Why only a couple months ago you married a couple and they separated and divorced, and if you can marry them that way, why can't you marry us?" Meanwhile the minister was getting very embarrassed, so he took the couple into the sanctuary. After a lot of back and forth, the soldier still insisted that they be married only for the duration. He said to the minister, "Why after the war, I'll be going back to my wife at home. Right now I can't see her and I want to marry her (the English girl) until the war is over." Needless to say, the minister refused to marry them and sent them on their way. The priest who gave the sermon on marriage said this actually did happen—it was a true story. Vince explained that the priest used this account to point out how some people don't take marriage seriously.

Vince was very impressed with the attendance at the religious mission, which was held over several evenings, and explained that 175 men would line up for Communion and the chapel was filled every night. What really impressed him was the way these aviators would come back from a seven- or eight-hour mission over enemy territory, attend a briefing or interrogation, and then rush to attend the religious mission, skipping dinner just to get there. Vince really looked up to each and every one of these men—keep in mind, they faced death every time they took off on a mission. They had their priorities in order.

Vince wondered to Martha whether the censors who read his mail would understand the difference between a "religious mission" or retreat and a bombing mission. He was careful in his letters to make that distinction.

By March 26, 1944, Vince and his crew were located at their permanent station in Podington, England, where he enjoyed delicious food. On March 26, Vince wrote to Martha: "Hon, what do you think of the war situation these days? The Russians are running the Germans' little tails off, and we aren't doing so bad on this side of the continent. Won't be long now and the second front will get under way, I hope. I guess all of us over here will play a big part in it." Earlier in the month Vince had asked Martha in a letter to "...pray for me."

Vince received his first letter in England on March 31, 1944. It was his first mail in five and a half weeks. Once mail started to arrive, it was often two to four weeks late.

On a lighter note, Vince wrote Martha about their copilot, Paul: "Boy is Paul taking a razzing nowadays. You know we've all been wearing long johns over here. Well, they've rubbed Paul's butt raw. So now his nickname is 'the Red A__', if you know what I mean. You should see him walk—he looks like a baby with a load in his pants."

On April 5, 1944, Martha wrote to Vince that the baby had been kicking quite a bit, and when he arrived she intended to tell him that "... it isn't polite to kick ladies, especially your mother." She went on: "Well, hon, if the doctors are right, one month from today we'll be very proud people. I sure wish you were here. That's the only thing I mind—your not being somewhere within reach."

On April 9, 1944, Vince wrote to Martha: "Hon, I've been wanting to tell you this for quite some time now. I don't know why I've put it off this long. When the time does come and in your hours of labor, it's going to be a little hard for you. Well, I want you to remember, even tho I'm so far away I'll be right with you in spirit. Remember that, will you, darling. I'm praying for you every day, and I'm sure the Dear Lord will be with you in your hours of labor. If I could only be there, everything would almost be all right. Please honey, don't be afraid."

On April 11, 1944, Martha wrote to Vince about another couple, who would be together for the birth of their coming baby. She wrote: "Gosh, Vince, I'd give anything if you could be here when ours is born. That's all I think about, but I know that just as I am with you spiritually at all times, so are you with me."

Given the length of time it took for mail to arrive overseas, there is no way that Martha or Vince could have known about the contents of each other's letters within this short time span, yet they continue to anticipate each other's moods and thoughts. Love is amazing. I think I now know the meaning of the term "soul mates."

In early April, Vince wrote to Martha: "Hon, how do you like the way the Russians are going to town? Sure does look good for us right now, don't you think?" Martha tended to be optimistic when Vince was. She ended virtually every letter now with: "May God and His Blessed Mother bless you and protect you always."

On April 15, 1944, Vince went to the post office to see if he had any mail. When he inquired, the postal clerk said, "…not if your name isn't 'Gisrielio.'" Right away, Vince knew it was his. People have always had trouble with spelling or pronouncing "Gisriel," which rhymes with "Israel." The clerk told Vince, as he handed him the pile of mail, "… there's 46 for you, and get away from here before somebody murders you." Thirty-five of the letters were from Martha. He wrote: "Boy, honey, I can't get over it, I'm so happy." Paul had received 18 letters one day and he thought he was doing well. Now Vince would capture bragging rights. Two days later, Vince received 12 more letters, nine of which were from Martha. Six days after that, he received two cards from Martha and another six letters. By April 27, 1944, when Vince received another seven letters and two cards from Martha, he figured that all the back mail from March had finally arrived. He was a happy camper.

10

The Real Action Begins

From March 31, 1944, until April 9, 1944, the crew had a few aborted missions. Some were scrubbed before the group took off; others were called off while they were in the air. Weather often was a factor when missions were aborted. However, on April 10, 1944, Vince's crew had their first completed mission since arriving in England almost a month earlier. Their first mission was to bomb the Evere airdrome at the Melsbroek Airfield, north of Brussels, Belgium. They carried forty-two 64-pound incendiary bombs. The crew was initially briefed to expect as many as 200 German fighters, but none showed up. Their B-17 did sustain seven holes, probably from flak, otherwise known as "ack-ack," or bursting shells fired from anti-aircraft artillery. There were no injuries to the crew. Their flight time was 4 hours and 15 minutes. The mission was deemed successful. Vince described the mission as an easy one—a "milk run," as they called it. Incidentally, all of Vince's comments were remarks that he wrote following the missions. He never wrote regarding mission details in any of his letters; that would have been a security breach. These one-word or short-phrase notes were written on foreign currency found with his personal papers following his death in 2003, almost sixty years later.

On April 13, 1944, Vince wrote to Martha: "Hon, I want to tell you how much I appreciate your going to church for me so much, especially when you should be home. Please don't go wandering around by yourself, in your condition, when the weather is bad. I don't want anything to happen to you. Again, I love you to death for praying so hard. I'm sure with God with us we can get thru this thing OK." A few days later, Vince wrote to Martha that he found out that the chaplain is down in Operations before every mission. Vince learned that he could receive Communion before taking off and without even fasting. He wrote: "From now on I'll go to Communion before each mission. Won't that be swell?" Martha later wrote: "Hon, I'm so glad you're able to go to Mass and Communion so often. I know that sometimes it must be a sacrifice for you, but please keep on going, as often as you can." Martha's faith convinced her that God would keep her husband safe. Vince wrote: "Darling, you don't know how much I appreciate the novenas you are making for me. Believe me, it does my heart good to know you are with me constantly, by prayer. Thanks a million, hon." Martha went out of her way to be faithful to her novenas and her frequent receipt of the sacraments. Later, she wrote: "Honey, I think you're a darling for going to Mass and Communion for the baby and me so often."

The time was getting close for Martha to have the baby. Vince was anxious to hear the news and he wanted to be notified upon the baby's birth. The doctor had for some time indicated that the due date was May 5. After hearing that a crew member was not notified right away about the birth of his baby, Martha wrote to Vince on April 24, 1944: "Honey, you can be sure that you will be notified immediately. Everyone has their orders around here regarding the cable that will be sent to you." In one of her letters, Martha explained how difficult it was getting dressed, particularly when trying to put on stockings and shoes. Vince wrote back: "I got quite a kick out of you trying to dress with your big stomach. I was just telling Ray about it and we've been laughing for five minutes. You're a killer, hon, and a 'square,' and I love you for it." In spite of the distance between them, both Martha and Vince kept their sense of humor alive and well.

As the days drew closer to Martha's delivery date, she acknowledged to Vince that she did tire easily and often took naps to deal with it. Vince wrote: "Honey, I can plainly see why you have been so tired lately. After all, you are just on the verge of performing one of your most beautiful duties as a woman and a wife. You've been carrying a lot around with you lately. And I love you for it. You haven't complained a bit…"

The crew's second mission came on April 18, 1944. This time they flew to Oranienburg, not far from Berlin, and they encountered no flak. One of the crew reported a German Me-109 fighter coming in at 10 o'clock high, but it blew up within seconds of being seen. Allied fighter support was excellent that day. Apparently, while other planes attacked marshalling yards, their payload on this mission was pamphlets. They dropped thousands written in German with President Franklin Roosevelt's face on them. Vince characterized this mission as "rough," probably because it lasted 8 hours and 15 minutes.

The third mission came the very next day, April 19. This trip was to Kassel, Germany. They encountered no enemy fighters, but they met with heavy flak, and a piece of shrapnel hit their windshield. They were apparently bombing German training aircraft at a Luftwaffe aerodrome and carried thirty-six 64-pound bombs. The bombing was characterized as "good." The mission lasted 6 hours and 34 minutes. Vince described this mission as "very rougher."

On April 20, 1944, their fourth mission was over Linghem, France, where they bombed high-priority construction sites, possibly rocket manufacturing plants. The bombing was very successful. Thirty-six planes took off that day for two different construction sites, and all returned safely. That day marked the 92nd Bombardment Group's one hundredth mission. They carried a "V-1" bomb load consisting of twelve 500-pound bombs. The duration of this attack was 4 hours.

The crew's fifth mission was to Hamm, Germany, on April 22, 1944. They encountered no Nazi fighters and no flak. They carried thirty-six 100-pound bombs and hit marshalling yards with very good results. This mission lasted 7 hours and 15 minutes. The crew received the Air Medal for completing five missions.

On April 25, 1944, Vince's aunt, Sister Dorothy, wrote to him: "What a delightful surprise was mine upon receiving your very interesting letter. I thought you would be too busy to think of writing to me, but, as you say, one's thoughts naturally turn to the dear ones. According to the accounts in the papers, there has been quite a bit of action in the European theatre, and I can almost picture you in the midst of it. And just as often I whisper a prayer for your safety." Sister Dorothy realized that Vince would not be home for the arrival of his new baby. She wrote: "What a grand source of merit you can make of this sacrifice, if you will but cheerfully offer it to the good God. May He give you all the strength you need. Yes, I'm sure He will."

When Vince's crew members had their first 48-hour pass on or about April 24, 1944, they went to London. He described London as being a lot like New York City, where everyone seemed to be in a hurry. He said that there was no relaxation there. He thought that on his next pass he would spend his time somewhere peaceful. Vince had apparently written to Martha's parents and had made a request of her father. Martha wrote: "Listen honey, what do you mean by asking Willie for the addresses of some of those French babes he knew? Boy, have I been taking a ribbing. I'm just kidding you, darling. No fooling, Mom and Dad were very glad to hear from you." Later she wrote "...Willie asked Mom to get out his discharge papers and his little black book (from the last war) so he could send you those addresses. Of course, he's just kidding, the same as you, but we had a lot of fun over it."

Martha wrote that she was glad that Vince had the opportunity to go to London. She wrote: "Boy, we're going to have a lot to tell our grand-children, aren't we?"

As new aviators arrived in England day by day, Vince met guys with whom he had trained in the States early on. He enjoyed seeing the fellows he had met previously.

The crew's sixth mission occurred on April 27, 1944, over Pas de Calais, France. They were to bomb rocket buzz-bomb launchers. They carried sixteen 500-pound bombs, but they returned to England with no bombs dropped, because they could not identify the target. The Americans would not bomb indiscriminately; they would only bomb targets that were positively identified. They encountered no enemy fighters but went through some very heavy flak. Their plane sustained three holes: one in the nose, one in the waist and one in the tail. The mission lasted 4 hours.

The seventh mission was over Avord, France on April 28, 1944. The target was a Nazi airplane repair depot. The crew again encountered no enemy fighters. They did go through some bitter flak, but their plane sustained no hits on this trip. They carried 36 clusters of "6 frag" bombs. The length of the mission was 5 hours and 45 minutes. Vince described it as "long but a snap."

The crew's eighth mission, and the last of April 1944, occurred on the 29th, when they flew to Berlin. Vince wrote, "The name scares me." Apparently, the target was the industrial center. The formation encountered very aggressive enemy fighters, and there was heavy flak over the target area. Vince's B-17 sustained seven holes. They carried five 1,000-pound bombs on this mission, which lasted eight hours. While returning to England, Jim Meeks, their right waist gunner, was injured by shrapnel in the back of the arm. He was treated and bandaged in the radio room. He was awarded the Purple Heart for his injury and was grounded for several months. Later, he was assigned to a B-26 crew. Before returning home, he was credited with 60 missions.

While over Berlin, three B-17s were seen going down. One went down in flames about three minutes before "bombs away." Only five parachutes were observed floating down. Another plane was observed going down in flames with only one wing intact. A third went down spiraling, with an engine on fire. Sadly, no chutes were seen following the latter two aircraft. As many as 350 enemy fighters engaged our American bombers in defense of Berlin that day. Later, two more B-17s were seen going down. One went down in the English Channel, and the other was seen burning in an English field. At least two of the planes lost were from the 92nd.

After returning from their mission to Berlin, the officers went to a party at the Officers' Club. Vince indicated that they were having quite a party over there. He felt worn out and tired and went back to their quarters in the Quonset hut to retire for the evening. After all, they had just flown three missions in three days. Apparently, some of the other officers in the squadron stayed later. They had the next morning off, so Vince slept in until 11:00 AM. He wrote to Martha: "I never slept so sound in my life; no one could have gotten me up with a sledgehammer." The officers who had stayed at the club later apparently were still sacked out when Vince awoke. He heard moaning and groaning out of one of them, and at least two of them were not exactly sure how they got back to quarters. In retrospect, these fellows probably needed to unwind a little.

Martha ended one of her last letters of April by writing: "I love you 10 million thousand times more than I did a minute ago. I couldn't possibly love anything so dearly as I love you. I miss you so much, I can hardly stand it." Vince ended one of his last letters of April by writing to Martha and his unborn child: "If you two only knew how much I loved you. My love has gone beyond infinite and is heading for something that's never been heard of before."

Between March 1, 1944 and April 30, 1944, which is essentially Vince's time overseas to date, I have counted two cards and 175 letters between them. Martha was now writing two letters per day at a minimum. Vince wrote when he could and was doing pretty well himself. On some days Vince was on an eight-hour mission, which made it impossible for him to write to Martha. From time to time, he apologized to her for missing a day or so. She wrote back that she fully understood and that she appreciated the effort he made to write so often. She was very much aware that some wives rarely received mail from their husbands who were overseas, partly because they did not make the effort. Again, the letters between them were so important for their morale. Hearing from each other so frequently also assured them that they were both safe and well. In addition to writing to Martha, Vince wrote many, many letters to other relatives and friends over an extended period. Martha indicated that she enjoyed corresponding with the wives and girlfriends of the aviators, many of whom she met while traveling with Vince after their marriage.

11

And the Real Action Continues

May 1944 started off as busy as April had ended for Vince's crew. Their ninth mission was to LeGrismont, France, on May 1, 1944, and was the crew's first and only known night mission. Their bomb load was twelve 500-pound bombs, but no bombs were dropped due to cloud cover. They encountered no enemy fighters and no flak. Vince described this trip "like flying over England." The flight lasted 7 hours and 45 minutes.

The tenth mission, on May 4, 1944, resulted in a recall. They had only traveled halfway to the destination when they were ordered to return due to weather conditions. They encountered no Nazi fighters, but they did see some fairly accurate flak. Their bomb load had been 30 incendiary clusters, but none were dropped. The crew members received oak leaf clusters for their Air Medals for having completed ten missions.

On their eleventh mission, they flew to Berlin. It was May 7, 1944. Vince noted, "had my 1st real scare." The target was the center of Berlin's industrial area. They encountered no enemy fighters, but flak was heavy. They dropped 30 incendiary clusters and three 1,000-pound bombs. A total of 326 bombs were dropped by 30 planes from the 92nd Bombardment Group. It was one of the largest air assaults on Berlin. The mission lasted 8 hours and 45 minutes.

On May 7, 1944, Vince wrote to Martha that based on the number of missions he had flown to date, he was one-third through his tour of duty. On May 8, 1944, before Martha read Vince's letter, she wrote:

"Hon, I know that you want to get your missions over and hurry back home, and that is what I want also, but remember what I said about rushing through them. You just go when you're assigned, and please be very careful always, darling, and pray hard." With that said, however, ten days later, Martha sent Vince a preprinted card showing an American G.I. kicking the daylights out of a German soldier and Hitler with a black eye. On the card, she wrote: "You just do your share, hon. I mean your missions and no more!...I don't want you to wait until those two 'rats' are licked, I just want you to complete your missions, and then hurry home to us."

On May 8, 1944, their crew manned the squadron's lead plane over Berlin. The target was again the center of the industrial area. This was their twelfth mission, and they carried the same payload as on the previous mission. During flight, two American planes had a midair collision, and one of them fell on a third plane. This tragic crash narrowly missed Vince's aircraft. He noted later that he was "lucky on this one." This mission lasted 8 hours and 45 minutes, just as the eleventh mission had. One plane from the 92nd Bombardment Group landed along the English coast with fire streaming from one engine, a second engine hardly functioning, and all navigational equipment destroyed. In another B-17, the navigator, the bombardier and the copilot bailed out after the plane took a hit in the nose. The top turret gunner filled in as the copilot and the tail gunner assumed the role of navigator, and they flew on.

Vince's crew flew to bomb the airdrome at Thionville, France, on May 9, 1944. It is uncertain whether Vince was bombardier on this flight, but it is recorded as the crew's thirteenth mission. The bomb load was ten 500-pound bombs. They encountered no enemy fighters and no flak. The length of the mission is not known.

The attack on the Thionville airdrome was the beginning of the Allied strategy to weaken the German air force during the month prior to the invasion of Normandy. The Allies intended to create a situation whereby Hitler would not have time to recover from his losses before the invasion.

On May 12, 1944, the crew was on its fourteenth mission. The destination was Merseburg/Leuna, Germany, and the target was one of Germany's largest synthetic gasoline and oil production facilities. The plane carried a bomb load of fifteen 310-pound bombs. They encountered no German fighters, but the flak was bitter. Vince was lead bombardier on this mission and made a direct hit on this target, for which he was awarded the Distinguished Flying Cross. The other bombardiers in the formation keyed off of Vince's bomb drop and dropped on his command, with excellent results. This was a direct hit from an altitude of 26,000 feet. It was reported that smoke could be seen billowing to near bombing altitude as the planes headed back to England.

The plant they bombed employed more than 25,000 workers on round-the-clock shifts and had produced approximately 600,000 tons of liquid products annually before it was first attacked on May 12, 1944. It was estimated that 40 percent of its liquid production was aviation fuel, 40 percent diesel oil and 20 percent gasoline. It was estimated that the damage caused by the initial attack on May 12 put the plant out of production for approximately two and one-half months. However, later attacks by American bombers caused further damage and even longer periods of production loss, and Merseburg/Leuna never fully recovered. It was attacked another 21 times after Vince's first bomb drop. Wow, did this put a dent in Hitler's war plan!

In addition to synthetic fuel and oil, Merseburg/Leuna also produced fixed nitrogen, methanol, other higher alcohols and synthetic ammonia. It was reputed to be the largest producer in all of Europe of synthetic ammonia, which was needed for the manufacture of explosives. There was also some indication that the Germans had planned to make synthetic rubber at the Merseburg/Leuna facility as well.

I am so proud of what my father did over Merseburg. Not only did he receive the Distinguished Flying Cross for his efforts, but he was also part of the first Eighth Air Force attack on oil production at this location. The combined damage to this facility from the 22 air attacks was massive. In the spring of 1945, one war correspondent described the damage at Merseburg/Leuna as the biggest pile of junk that he had ever seen. It was beyond anything he had seen damaged in Germany. He offered it as proof that strategic bombing worked.

Keep in mind that during World War II, the Americans did not bomb with guided missiles fired from great distances. The bombs had to be delivered literally to the doorsteps of the enemy. As the squadrons approached the target, the lead pilot would make a number of course corrections. This was done primarily to cause confusion so that the enemy did not know precisely where the bomber formation was headed. In the seconds immediately preceding the bomb run, a final course correction was made and the planes headed for the target. At that point, the pilot engaged the autopilot and the bombardier took over control of the aircraft until "bombs away."

It was the bombardier who made adjustments for airspeed, wind, weather conditions and altitude. He adjusted the bombsight with any revised data, which in turn made corrections to the plane's autopilot system so that the plane stayed on target. This is when the real danger occurred, because although it was crucial for the bombardier to keep the plane level and straight, this made it easier for the enemy on the ground to get a better fix on the altitude of the squadron and attempt to knock the American planes out of the sky with flak.

Enemy fighter pilots could also see the bomb bay doors open, and when they did, they knew that the Americans were on their final approach. Fortunately, enemy fighter pilots tended to keep their distance, because they did not want to be shot down by their own flak. Enemy pilots who ventured too close were susceptible to the awesome firepower of the B-17 gunners, who fired from both sides of the bomber as well as from the rear, forward, top and belly of the aircraft.

During all this activity, the bombardier had to maintain a cool head and keep the aircraft steady. Even when the enemy flak was extremely accurate, the bombardier had to keep the aircraft steady and level, for any evasive action at this point could jeopardize the accuracy of the bomb drop. This was extremely dangerous work, and only very brave and courageous aviators could successfully accomplish the goals of a mission.

Much later in life, during his retirement years, Vince wrote a brief article for a community publication that featured stories of veterans' experiences while in the military. He wrote about the strategy of precision bombing and how three squadrons of B-17s would fly in tight formation, with one squadron high, one low and one in the middle. The middle squadron led the group. The lead bombardier sighted the target and dropped his bombs, and the other planes then "toggled" their bombs so that all the bombs fell in a cluster on the target. What he did not write about was the danger that he and his crew and the crewmen in the other planes in his squadron put themselves in as they went into a bomb run that could last as long as 10 minutes.

Many duties were required of bombardiers in preparation for a bombing mission, particularly the lead and deputy lead bombardiers. They had to be thoroughly familiar with the primary target as well as with backup or secondary targets if the primary could not be bombed. They had to check their equipment prior to takeoff. They were responsible for the bombs. At an altitude of 5,000 feet, the bombardier removed the pins from the bombs. If the plane returned to the airfield with any bombs on board, he had to replace the pins prior to landing. The bombardier functioned as the oxygen officer and the gunnery officer during the mission, frequently checking with the respective crew members, sometimes at three- to four-minute intervals. At "bombs away," the bombardier was also responsible for making sure all cameras were turned on.

A bomb crew had one main function, and that was to bomb the designated target. It took a crew of ten to accomplish this: the pilots to reach their destination; the navigator to see that the pilots stayed on course; the radio operator to communicate with other planes and the ground; the engineer, or crew chief, to make sure the aircraft was in proper working order before takeoff and during flight; and the gunners to protect the plane from enemy fighter plane attack. This is not said to diminish the role of any of the crewmen, because the bombardier would be the first to say that the entire crew accomplished a successful mission, but the truth is that it was all for naught if the bombardier missed his target. What an awesome responsibility!

The techniques a bombardier used to accomplish his objectives still boggle my mind. Can you imagine dropping 500-pound bombs, either in unison or in rapid succession, from a moving aircraft, with open bomb bay doors, on a target perhaps 26,000 feet below? The speed and altitude of the aircraft, the speed and direction of the wind and the nature of the weather all had to be taken into account, and a bombardier was trained to do just that. Altogether, Vince was lead bombardier for about 18 of his total of 35 missions. It was a phenomenal feat and, again, I am so proud of my father's efforts and accomplishments.

Prior to the crew's next mission, they got another pass and went to London again. They ran into so many other guys with whom they had gone through different phases of training that it was like old home week. They obviously had a great time seeing many old buddies, and it was good to relax away from their bombing raids and have the opportunity to see more of London. Some of Vince's crew members scribbled notes to Martha on his letter from London—so scribbled, in fact, that they are a mess to try to read.

In a letter from Martha to Vince dated May 6, 1944, Martha asked how the English girls danced. She wanted to know: "Are they jitterbugs?" Martha had read an article that indicated that the English girls liked to dance with the "Yanks." She further understood that the English girls think that "Yanks…kiss much better than the English fellows." Vince responded by writing on May 17, 1944: "Yes, honey, the English girls like to dance with the Yanks, but they can't jitterbug. They think they can, tho. They're too wild with their movements or something. I don't know about the kissing part. I'll have to find out from somebody else."

Martha's due date of May 5, 1944, had come and gone, and she was getting anxious. Vince was extremely anxious awaiting word of the baby's arrival. Martha's friends were apparently anxious too. Two girlfriends from the telephone company called her by phone and teased her. Martha wrote: "They can't imagine what I'm up to. Now they want to know if I'm pregnant or not. They think I'm trying to fool someone, but I told them that if I'm not, someone is sure fooling me." One of the girls said that the women at the telephone company were not surprised that the baby was late. Martha wrote about when she worked there: "You know how I used to be late every day. Well, I'm still hearing about it." Martha also wrote: "I'm going to put on some of my dark red nail polish. I haven't worn any for over a month, because I didn't want to have it on when I went to the hospital. Well, tonight I'm going to put some on and see if I can't start things rolling." In that same letter, she wrote: "I think the little guy is waiting for you to come home. Anyway, hon, the longer he puts things off, the younger he'll be when you get back. Then, you can watch him grow. Oh, boy, that will be a wonderful day, when you come back from over there."

During this period of their separation while Martha was pregnant, she and Vince had an ongoing dialogue in their letters that included their unborn child. They gave each other additional messages, mostly of love and affection, but attributed the words to and through their unborn infant. For example, Martha wrote the following: "Jr. is raising heck right now. He's just dying to make his 'debut,' and so am I. Honest, darling, these last few days have been just awful. This waiting! Anyway, Jr. just kicked me with a 'thud' and said, 'Hey, Maw, you tell my daddy that I love him more than any kid ever loved anybody.' He loves you so much, Vince, and if he takes after his mother, he'll never stop loving you." Vince wrote: "Kiss the baby for me and tell him I love him dearly, and to take good care of his mommy. Also you take good care of him and save some of those kisses for yourself." Later, he wrote: "Will you do me a favor, hon? Tap Jr. a code for me telling him how much I love him, and how much I love you. And it is an awful, awful lot." Martha closed many a letter with words such as the following: "Oh, honey, I love you so much. Jr. loves and misses you very much also."

Within two weeks of his arrival in England, Vince wrote that he was considering the purchase of a used bicycle. The buildings at the air base were dispersed at great distances, obviously by design for defensive reasons, but the aviators had to walk for great lengths on any given day. Eventually, he purchased a secondhand bike and called it "Herman." It must have been a piece of junk when he bought it, because Vince had to work on it extensively to keep it in riding condition. It had missing spokes, and the tires were a mess. On one occasion, he had to patch five holes in the tires, only to find one flat again. He put three holes in one inner tube just putting the tire on. He wrote: "By the time I get done with it, the tire will be nothing but patches. That's life tho!" He thought he had it fixed and then the brakes fell off. It was undoubtedly an English bike with the hand brakes up on the handle bar. Vince considered throwing it away if he could not fix it.

In one of Vince's letters in early May, he wrote to Martha: "I am also enclosing a buttercup. Don't ask me why, tho. It's the only one I've seen over here, and it looked so lonesome by itself. I thought I'd pluck it and send it to you for company. You'll take good care of it, won't you, darling? It might be a little mashed, but give it your tender care." Martha acknowledged the buttercup and put it back in the letter for safekeeping. It still remains "mashed" inside that letter over six decades later.

During the war years, motion pictures were a favorite American pastime. Martha and Vince saw a lot of movies while they were apart. They liked to share films by highly recommending the really good ones to each other. They enjoyed going to the movies even more when they could go together. Writing about them would have to do for when they were apart.

While stationed in England, Vince saw one film that he particularly enjoyed—*Going My Way,* starring Bing Crosby. He described it as a "very, very, very good picture." He encouraged Martha to make sure that she didn't miss it. He wrote: "It was one of those pictures that reaches down into your heart."

Being born and raised in Baltimore and Baltimore County, I am often teased even now for the way I speak like a Baltimorean. For example, I still pronounce Baltimore as "Bawlimer." Well, over my lifetime, I have been equally teased for the way I pronounce "sink," as in the kitchen sink. I actually pronounce it "zink." Now I know that I got that pronunciation honestly. In one of my mother's letters to my father, she was explaining that the kitchen sink was stopped up and that Willie and Buster were trying to fix it because they could not reach a plumber. In the letter, she actually wrote about "our zink in the kitchen." No wonder I say it the way I do! At one time, I thought they might have been made out of zinc.

As May wore on, Martha still had not had the baby. Her family was teasing her more and more. She wrote to Vince: "They make fun of me 22 hours a day. Every time any of them come in from school or work, they say, 'Well, is she still here?' Now, they're going to give me until May 22nd, and if Jr. still isn't here, then they're going to blast."

Sister Dorothy wrote to Vince in mid-May and thanked him for a recent letter. She was delighted to hear that he was safe. Like so many others, she was also anxiously waiting to hear whether he was a father. On another matter, she wrote: "Perhaps by now you have more than half finished your allotted assignments, eh? Won't it be grand when you start your return trip to the good old U.S.A.? Well, I know you want to perform your duty first, so you won't mind waiting, even if the time does seem long. Just think what a grand part you are taking in the Victory which is sure to be ours, please God."

12

Waiting, and Some More Waiting

On May 20, 1944, Vince and his crew took off to bomb Orly Airfield, south of Paris, France. This was the crew's fifteenth mission. Their bomb load was six 1,000-pound bombs. Their crew was the lead squadron. Originally, 36 planes were scheduled to take off. However, a major tragedy occurred during takeoff. The 19th plane to take off crashed off the end of the runway. The pilot of the 20th plane saw the red flares fired by the takeoff controller, heard the radio orders to stop taking off, and slammed on his brakes halfway down the runway. The pilot turned his plane around and was heading back when it collided head-on into the 21st plane, whose pilot apparently had neither seen the flares nor heard the order to stop takeoff. The weather was a contributing factor in that the fog produced poor visibility. While some of the crewmen escaped, a total of 21 aviators lost their lives in these two separate accidents. Four of those who escaped had severe injuries, but they did survive. The remainder of the planes did not take off that day. The first 18 to go airborne went on to bomb the target, and Vince's crew was one of those 18. Because of the fog, they had to execute an instrument takeoff. The mission took 6 hours and 30 minutes. Upon their return they had to land on an auxiliary runway because the collision of the two B-17s had caused four explosions of 1,000-pound bombs, creating a huge crater in the main runway. It took engineers and British workers four days to repair the damage.

The day after this mission, Vince wrote to Martha: "No one could love another person as much as I love you, and my love for you triples as the seconds go by. I also miss you beyond words. I sometimes think I can't go on without you—in fact, I couldn't if you weren't waiting for me. I know that someday we'll be together again, never to be separated, and that's the day I live and long for. So long for now, darling. I love you so much."

The crew's sixteenth mission occurred on May 24, 1944. This raid was to bomb the industrial center of Berlin. Vince was lead bombardier but with another crew. His regular crew was part of the raid but was in another plane. Vince's comment was simply, "Figure it out yourself." They carried 32 incendiary bombs and ten 100-pound bombs, and the bombing results were good. They sustained medium flak but encountered no enemy fighters over Berlin. However, as Vince's bomber left the target area and turned east, they saw some of their B-17s being attacked by Nazi fighters just ahead of them. Three of our planes were shot down. One such B-17 took out two enemy fighters before it went down, including the very fighter that shot it down. Earlier, there had been American fighter support, so someone called for additional support, but apparently our fighters were running out of fuel, ammo or both, for they had left the area. This mission lasted 9 hours.

Their seventeenth mission occurred on May 25, 1944. It was to attack the marshalling yards at Thionville, France. Fifty-six planes in all took off on this mission, but some had to return to England because of mechanical problems. Their bomb load consisted of ten 500-pound bombs. Vince was again lead bombardier. Bombing netted good results, and Allied fighter support was characterized as good. Vince described this flight as a "snap." After the crew dropped their bombs and were heading for home, a formation of American B-24s, on their way to a bombing destination, came through Vince's formation of B-17s. The scene was described as like that of being in the middle of a deck of shuffling cards. Fortunately, no one collided. The duration of this mission was 6 hours and 20 minutes.

On May 25, 1944, Vince wrote to Martha that he was halfway through his missions. A few days earlier he had written: "…boy, how the time does fly over here. The weeks and months go by like lightning, but boy, it seems like years since I've seen you. I hope the coming months go by as fast."

On May 23, 1944, Suz sent Vince a short letter informing him that Martha had been admitted to the hospital with labor pains. Suz wrote again on May 24 that Martha was still in labor. Things were moving very slowly. Suz was convinced that Martha would have a boy "…because they are always slow." Vince didn't receive these letters for more than two weeks. On May 26, Martha finally delivered her baby boy, Vincent dePaul Gisriel, Jr. Martha and Vince were right all along—it was a "Junior." Later, Vince made it clear to Martha that he really didn't want the baby called "Junior"—that was just the name they shared for their unborn baby. Thus, we were called "Big Vince" and "Little Vince" for many years thereafter.

On May 28, 1944, Martha wrote to Vince, her first letter in almost a week. She had a good excuse for not writing for a while. In addition to having a long, lingering labor, she also had complications. The baby's birth was a breech delivery and Martha sustained a serious infection as well. She wrote to Vince: "Before I go into details, hon, we have only God and Dr. Brown to thank that he is alive. But please don't worry, we are both doing fine." Martha began having pains every ten minutes at 1:00 AM on the morning of May 22. She didn't awaken her mom until about 4:00 AM. The pains were much worse but farther apart. She and her mother delayed calling the doctor until about 10:00 AM. Dr. Brown came over to the house at 10:30 AM and advised taking Martha to the hospital. They arrived there at 12:00 noon.

On May 22, at 11:45 PM, the nurses took Martha to the labor room. As she wrote to Vince: "Well, honey, I had an awful lot of trouble, and was in real labor from Tuesday night 11:45 PM until Friday at 1:04 PM., when the baby arrived. I had everyone pretty worried, both at home and at the hospital, and Vince, honey, Dr. Brown was more than a doctor. He spent from 2:00 AM Thurs. until 9:00 AM right with me. Then on Thursday evening and Friday afternoon, he cancelled all of his appointments in case anything happened. He was wonderful to me and really saved both the baby's and my life. That's all the details I'll give you, but I'll tell you all about it when we are together. Believe me when I say that everything I went through was well worth it, because we have our little boy, and he is just like you. We are both fine now, so don't worry about a thing. I am nursing the baby, and Dr. Brown is tickled pink about that."

I never knew about the difficulty that my mother had in my delivery until I turned 60. For whatever reasons, I was never informed about the complications. Knowing my mother, she probably didn't tell me because she never wanted me to think that I was a bother. No one could ever convince me that a mother's love for a child is not the greatest kind of love with which God has blessed humanity. I hope to find the words to thank Him and her one day.

Martha explained to Vince how much her own mother and father helped her during this very difficult time. She wrote: "Vince, they have really been swell to me, and stuck by me thru it all. Mom was so glad that I was home, after all the trouble I had." Maybe mothers-in-law do know what is best, after all. Martha ended this letter by writing her standard closing but adding: "May God and His Blessed Mother bless you and protect you, as They have Jr. and I…"

I was told by my Uncle Jack that the physicians at the hospital did not want to take responsibility for whatever had to be done to facilitate my birth. It was Dr. Paul Brown who then took charge and assumed full responsibility. What a gem of a man he was. He had a tremendous family practice. He visited his patients in their homes at all hours of the day and night. Long before the baby was born, he stopped by the Owens house if he was in the neighborhood just to check on Martha's condition. He held office hours in the evening as well as in the daytime for the convenience of working people. Apparently, Dr. Brown visited Martha and the baby every day in the hospital until her discharge on June 5, 1944. Afterwards, he stopped by the house almost every day until Martha had fully recovered from her difficult delivery.

Shortly after Vince, Jr.'s birth, Rita and Jack, who were then stationed in Denver, Colorado, learned that they were expecting a baby. Rita asked her parents to have Dr. Brown reserve a room at the hospital for December 1944, because reservations were still required in advance. Dr. Brown learned that December was booked, so he simply changed her expected delivery month to January 1945 to secure the room, knowing full well that if Rita "came early," as he expected, she would already have the reservation secured. Dr. Brown went overboard to help the Owens family.

I remember that the last time I saw Dr. Brown was in 1953 or 1954, when my younger brother, Mike, was an infant and was very sick. The good doctor traveled a long distance to make a house call to our home near Parkville, Maryland. It was a different era then, one which is a loss for all Americans.

In late May, Martha wrote to Vince: "Honey, you'll just have to complete those missions and get home quick, to see your little son." The wife of one of Vince's crew members wrote to Martha: "I only pray this old darn crazy war ends soon, so we can all have our husbands home safely with us." This was the thought shared by millions across our great land.

In late May 1944, Vince wrote to Martha that he had been moved. Ever since he was stationed at Podington, England, he had been assigned to the 326th Squadron, 92nd Bombardment Group. Now he was assigned to the 364th Squadron, 305th Bombardment Group stationed at Chelveston, England. He was with a P.F.F. (Pathfinder) Group that flew radar-equipped bombers in overcast conditions. Apparently he saw it as a good opportunity, but he missed his regular crew. He didn't know if the move was permanent or temporary. He wrote: "You see, honey, here's what the whole deal is: Hodges is a damn good pilot, one of the best in the 92nd, and he was really going places, and we were going with him. It so happened on our 12th mission that our squadron was to lead and the crew that usually leads was on pass. Well they took a chance and let our crew lead and we did a damn good job. Boy, did I worry tho. I was shaking from the time I took off until we landed. After that mission, we were one of the group lead. It's a good deal, but lots of responsibility.

So then yesterday the wing called for a group bombardier for P.F.F. and it just happened that I was picked. Now if every thing goes alright I'll be leading a wing instead of a group. It might be a little more responsibility, but it's one of the safest spots in the outfit. That's about the whole thing in a nutshell, but I'd still rather be back with the boys. I guess it's all for the best tho." He continued: "Looks like I'll be pretty busy from now on too. They sure started on me today. I'm kind of glad tho, helps take the loneliness away, and that I've been. I met the crew I'll be flying with, and they seem to be a swell bunch of boys." Vince closed the letter by writing: "Say a little prayer that my mail will hurry up and catch up with me, so I can find out about my little family." He referred to their unborn baby as "slow poke," for he still didn't know about the birth.

Later, Martha responded to Vince: "I gather from your letter that you must be doing alright, even though you are too modest to admit it. Honey, I'm so proud of you, and know that no matter how great the responsibility is, you'll do your job, and do it well."

On June 3, 1944, while Vince was assigned to the 305th Bombardment Group, he was on a mission to Pas de Calais, France. The target was the airdrome. His crew was group lead and he was lead bombardier. He described the mission as a "milk run." On June 4, 1944, Vince's crew went back to Pas de Calais. They were group lead again, and Vince simply commented, "Ditto." While Vince was assigned to the 305th, most of his original crew from the 92nd eventually joined him. One particular exception was Lt. Paul Robertson, their copilot, who now had assumed the duties of a pilot with his own new crew. Vince flew a few extra missions when he was initially at the 305th before his original crew joined him.

Vince did not find out that he had a son until June 8, 1944, when he received a V-mail from his sister, Angela, dated May 26, 1944. He still had no idea of when the baby was born or any other details, although he surmised that his son was born on May 26, 1944, because that was the date of Angela's V-mail.

Incidentally, V-mail, short for Victory Mail, was based on a British idea. People could write a letter to someone overseas in the service on a special sheet of paper that folded into its own envelope. These letters were microfilmed, and the film was sent overseas and printed at reduced size—about 4 x 5 inches. Sending the film instead of the letters themselves saved a great deal of weight—150,000 letters on paper would have weighed 2,575 pounds, but the microfilm containing the letters' images weighed only 45 pounds.

Vince was moved to the 364th Squadron on or about May 28, 1944. Again, it took weeks for his regular mail to catch up with him. The cable that Suz sent to Vince immediately following the birth of his son never reached him, in spite of the fact that Suz called three times to verify its delivery and was told that it had been delivered. Apparently all cables to and from England were put on hold during the days leading up to and following the invasion of Normandy. Vince really began to worry when he eventually received Suz's letter dated May 23, 1944, indicating the beginning of a lengthy labor—but of course, no mention of how long it would last. However, he suspected that Martha experienced a long period of labor if the baby was in fact born on May 26. Angela's V-mail did not indicate the exact date of birth. She was simply sending Vince a congratulations message regarding his new son on that date, and she probably assumed that he had heard the news by then.

Upon learning in Angela's V-mail that he had a son, he wrote to Martha on June 8, 1944. He was obviously excited, writing: "Darling, I am just about the happiest man in the world right now. I just found out that you delivered me a son. Hon I'm so proud of you and love you so much. How I wish I could be there with you, so we could both share in our joys. I'm so happy, darling, I hardly know what to say. I've been gleaming all over myself ever since I found out. If you only knew how happy and relieved I am. When I think of being a father of my own son I could jump with joy. I bet you were really happy when you found out it was a boy. I know I was." Vince continued: "All I could do was let out a yell and fight like heck to get the letter out. I still haven't calmed down from the excitement—in fact, I don't think I ever will." Vince was eager to hear all the details from Martha. He had a lot of questions, including whether the baby looked like her. When her later letters finally arrived, she joyfully informed Vince that everyone thought the baby looked like him. (That torn-open V-mail envelope still sits in the family treasure chest.)

Vince actually started the above letter on June 5, wishing Martha a happy anniversary. He wrote: "Just think, we've been married one whole year today. To me it seems like you have been mine all my life. You really have, but it took me 20 years to find you. It was really worth waiting for." He stopped the letter of the 5th, but continued it on June 8, writing: "You are probably wondering what happened between the 5th and 8th. Well, darling, you will have to forgive me for not writing. Right in the middle of your letter, I was called on to perform my most important feat of this war, and I've been going ever since. I'll have a lot to tell you when I get back, but can't mention anything at the time. You might even be proud of me—Slow Poke, too. You do forgive me for not writing those three days, don't you? I think you realize I had something important to do."

June 6, 1944, or D-Day, as it will forever be known, just happened to have occurred between the day my father started this particular letter and the day he finished it, which was the same day he learned that he had a son.

I think that was a pretty good reason for pausing in the middle of a letter. I think he can be excused for that delay. He certainly did not want to hold up one of the most significant events of the war and perhaps all of history to finish that letter. Beside, the rest of the free world could not wait any longer. Mankind could not wait any longer. I know my mother forgave him for that little delay, and I believe that all good, freedom-loving people throughout the world would forgive him for being pre-occupied during those days. For he was a part of the Allied invasion that would lead to the liberation of France and the ultimate defeat of Hitler and Nazi Germany. Again, I am so very proud of him.

Martha later assured Vince that while she was eager to hear what he did between June 5 and 8, no matter what it was, it couldn't make her or the baby any prouder than they already were at that moment.

The role of the Eighth Air Force on D-Day was to attack German beach batteries to cause maximum destruction and neutralization of the enemy in support of our landing assault forces along the coast of Normandy, France. The planning and coordination that went into D-Day to time the air attacks at precise moments prior to the landing vessels arriving on the beaches were remarkable. Vince's crew was a part of that effort. His crew flew three missions on D-Day in support of the Normandy Invasion. In his personal notes, Vince commented that D-Day was "Easy but touchy."

More than 1,700 heavy bombers from the Eighth Air Force took part in D-day. Combined, they dropped almost 3,600 tons of bombs on the enemy. Because of cloud cover, some bombers on the second mission of the day returned to England with their bomb load. The Eighth flew a total of four missions on D-Day, and they lost three bombers in that effort. The third mission of the day was against the important communication center located in Caen, France. The losses of the German war machine were staggering.

Vince's mail continued to be delayed, partly because of his re-assignment. Also, for some unexplained reason, perhaps because of D-Day, mail to and from England was disrupted. It was not until June 13, 1944, that Vince received some of the particulars surrounding the birth of his son in newly arrived letters from Martha. And it was not until June 20, 1944, that Martha finally learned that Vince even knew about the baby.

Prior to that date, she had no confirmation that he had even received any word about the baby's arrival. While Martha had been through some of the roughest days of her young life in labor and delivery, and Vince had been through some of the most important days of the war, each also had the added anxiety of not knowing for weeks what the other knew about the birth of their baby. The sacrifices this young couple made during the war continue to amaze me, and yet it is but one couple's experiences, multiplied by millions of others all over the globe.

After reading some of the details of Martha's extended labor and delivery, Vince wrote on June 13: "Hon, you must have been in terrible pain those three days, and it has me worried silly. Darling, please tell me if anything is wrong—I can't stop thinking that there is. I am sure thankful to God and Dr. Brown for pulling you both through. I'll never be able to repay them in full, for it. I prayed for you always and will never stop." In closing, he wrote: "My eyes are just about burning up from the lack of sleep. Maybe a little from some crying I did. I couldn't help but [cry] when reading your letters. I hope you don't think I'm a sissy. Do you, darling? If you knew how much I loved you, you would realize. It hurts me mentally when I know you suffer." Martha assured Vince that she and the baby were fine. She also responded: "Vince, I don't think you're a sissy for crying. You're only human. Another thing, the bravest and strongest men that ever lived have been known to cry when their hearts ache them. But hon, when you come home, I assure you, you will never have need to cry except if it's for joy. We're going to make you so happy. Well, darling, if I don't stop, I'll be crying myself. One of these days, everything inside of me is going to explode, and I'm going to cry until there are no more tears. I feel like doing so, so often, but everyone around here goes out of their way to make me happy, and I know I would upset them, so I keep it in my heart."

Martha also wrote: "Vince, I'd give every cent I have if you could only be here. I'd even give an arm or a leg, just anything. I'm just hoping and praying that it won't be too long before you see him." She shared her joy with Vince when she wrote: "Then after I nursed him and he was asleep, I held him halfway up, to make him burp. Well, honey, if you could have seen him, I would have been very happy. Here he was, sound asleep, arms over his head, cheeks as fat as can be, and the little fat belly, just as pretty as any picture you ever saw. He's so precious and just like you, that I almost cry when I lie here and talk to him." She wrote further about the baby: "He looks more like you every day. When you talk to him, he just laughs. He can hold his little head up so well, and looks all around. You should see his little face when I show him your picture. He always gets a half-frown and half-smile on his face. The past few days, he looks like he's all ready to talk to it. I mean he opens and closes his mouth and throws his little hands around, just like he's going to say something. I swear, Vince, I honestly believe that he knows just who you are."

Vince wrote: "I miss you both something dreadful. How I'd like to hold you in my arms again. And let little Vince cuddle up to me as he does you. I dream about him doing it often. I too hope I can hurry home before he gets too big." And he wrote: "In one of your letters you mentioned how Vince would lift his little head from your shoulder and look around and smile. I can just see him now. Yes, honey, they stay babies but such a short time, and I'll probably miss most of his early baby life, 3 or 4 months of it anyway. I say 3 or 4 months hoping it'll be sooner. He's now almost a month old and it shouldn't be more than 2 months before I can hold him close to me and hear him breathe soft and smooth. My eyes get all filled up every time I think of being away from him and you, especially while he is so young." Having had six children of my own, I believe that I understand how my father was feeling.

Later, Vince wrote in regard to the baby's birth weight: "…all the fellows are very proud of the 7 lbs., 1 oz. our baby weighed. They are especially proud of the 1 oz., if you get what I mean. Isn't that awful of them, honey?"

Martha had written to Vince about the tremendous appetite the baby had. Vince wrote jokingly: "…you tell that Doctor Brown to give our baby more to eat or he'll have to answer to me. What's he want to do—starve the little thing?"

I find it somewhat awkward to write about myself, but my arrival was so important to Martha and Vince that this story cannot be told without it. Having children was very important to this young couple. Sharing how they felt and what they wrote really helps to define who they were. Having a wife to return to was extremely important to Vince. Now he had a son to return to as well. It made him a more determined aviator. Having a baby made Martha more determined to bring her husband safely home from the war through prayer and personal sacrifice.

In a letter to Vince shortly after D-Day, Martha wrote: "…I have to tell you this. You should hear Willie. You know, the papers are filled with news about the 29th Division, in France. That's Willie's old division, and he's been singing their theme song and drinking toasts to them ever since the invasion started."

Willie served as a first sergeant with the 29th Infantry Division of the Maryland Army National Guard in France during World War I.

He was very patriotic, and I can just see him beaming from ear to ear as his old unit advanced. Willie reportedly fibbed about his age and initially joined the 29th Division at the age of 16. By 1916, he found himself near the Texas and Mexico border when military action broke out between Pancho Villa from Mexico and the United States. It was the first nationwide call-up of the National Guard in our nation's history. I often asked him if he saw any action down in Texas, and his consistent stock answer was always: "One night a gunshot rang out," but he never saw who fired the weapon. However, I am sure he saw plenty of action in France. If the legend is accurate, Willie would have enlisted with what was probably a Maryland militia unit in about 1910. Interestingly, I enlisted in that same 29th Infantry Division on April 14, 1964.

On June 7, 1944, the mission of Vince's crew was to bomb an airdrome at Kerlin-Bastard, France, some two miles from Lorient. They flew with a bomb load of thirty 100-pound bombs. They encountered no enemy fighters but did see light but accurate flak. The duration of the mission was 5 hours and 40 minutes. Vince's crew may have flown to Cherbourg and/or Le Havre, France, shortly after D-Day. They probably would have been group lead; however, details are very sketchy at best. Also, it appears that Vince's original crew was together again on June 14, 1944, for a mission to Etampes/Mondesir in France, but I have no details of this flight. Because of the additional flights surrounding D-Day, I am not clear about the number of missions flown by the original crew at this point.

Even though there is no record of the crew's involvement, it is interesting to note that on June 15, 1944, bombing raids were initiated all over France and Germany involving 1,361 bombers. On this day, 747 B-17s and 614 B-24s took to the skies. It was only a matter of time for Hitler.

By now, Vince and his crew had received another oak leaf cluster to add to their medals. The crew had had extensive training in evasive action and safety throughout the many months of their service, but nothing would prepare them for what happened next.

13

30 Seconds Over Hamburg

On June 18, 1944, the original crew was together again. Along with the crew was Lieutenant Gaylord "Corky" Corlis, a pilot who was flying in the nose with Vince, just as an observer. Lieutenant Fabec was also with them as a radar navigator. Their target was an oil refinery known as "Eurotank," in Hamburg, Germany. Their plane was to fly as deputy lead with Lieutenant Robert Crutcher as command pilot sitting in the copilot's seat. Lieutenant Charles "Grubby" Hodges was the pilot. Grubby said later that he had a premonition that it wasn't going to be his day. The first problem to occur was that their plane did not receive the signal that takeoff had been delayed for 30 minutes. Then, while circling the perimeter track around the field, Grubby made a 90-degree turn, only to discover their plane had no brakes. As he made the turn, the plane slid, spun around and got stuck deep in mud, with its nose sticking out over the perimeter track. As Grubby cut off the engines, a colonel arrived on the scene. He climbed into the B-17, started the engines and saw for himself that the hydraulic system had failed. The system was leaking brake fluid. The next problem was that they were blocking all the other planes behind them that were fully loaded for takeoff. Those planes now had to taxi out on the grass and go around their disabled plane.

Grubby told the colonel that this was not his day, but the senior officer stomped his feet and informed Grubby that he intended to have him flying in 10 minutes. It took four vehicles, including fuel trucks, to do it, but they pulled the B-17 out of the mud even though it was weighed down with a full bomb load. The brake fluid leak was promptly fixed, and then they took off immediately, since they were already late. As deputy lead, they had some catching up to do, but they caught up and slid into their position in the formation. As they were flying over the island of Helgoland, Germany, the pilot of the lead plane sent an urgent message to Grubby that the lead plane had lost its radar. So, as deputy lead, Grubby's crew assumed the lead position, guiding 35 other planes into the target area. Flying at 150 mph, they dropped their bombs and began to pull away at 170 mph. While Lieutenant Fabec was prepared to bomb with the use of radar in the event of cloud cover, Vince was able to bomb visually as they approached the target. The results were later noted as "good."

As the bomb bay doors began to close, Vince yelled: "Look out for the flak." Within seconds, their plane was hit by an 88 mm shell that entered the lower side of the fuselage forward of the nose escape hatch. It angled up, taking Grubby's foot off and exploding along the left side of Lieutenant Crutcher's head, killing him instantly. The explosion wiped out all of the instruments. The only electrical line still functioning was to the radio room. The dead command pilot in the copilot's seat slumped over and wedged against the controls, and the plane rolled right and went into a dive. It dropped 15,000 feet, but somehow Grubby, already seriously injured, was able to pull out of the dive at 13,000 feet. He leveled it out and flew for 15 more minutes without any rudder controls.

Grubby motioned to Sergeant William Talbot, the engineer. At first they thought Grubby was telling them to bail out, but he was not. The injured pilot was motioning for some help in getting the dead command pilot off the control column where he had slumped. In the meantime, a fire broke out in the electric motor that operated the bomb bay doors, and Sergeant Talbot put it out with a fire extinguisher. Grubby's next problem was to get the tip tanks turned on so that the plane didn't run out of fuel. They had no fuel gauge. Vince was able to turn on the tanks. Next, they had to determine in which direction to fly, because Grubby had obviously lost his bearings after the dive and had no instruments to aid him. Vince and

Lieutenant Fabec were able to determine the right direction and inform the pilot. Grubby later characterized the scene as though it were one from the movies. He described how his bombardier, Vince, rushed backed to the radar operator and came back and said, "Go that-a-way." All this was happening while they were still under enemy attack.

When the crew realized how badly injured Grubby was, they pulled him out of the pilot's seat and placed him in the nose, where Vince, Sergeant Talbot and Ray Alexander, the navigator, tended to his injuries. They administered morphine and sulfonamide, used prior to penicillin. In the meantime, Lieutenant Corlis took over as pilot. Earl Dahlgren, the left waist gunner, had to finish closing the bomb bay doors. He did so by climbing across the catwalk and manually cranking the doors closed as someone held him by his parachute harness and as flak shells exploded below them. Earl also helped get the dead command pilot off the controls by propping him up in his seat.

Vince went on the radio and announced that they were going to try to make it to Sweden, and if there was any doubt about making it, the crew was free to bail out. He went on a second time to inform the crew that if they could make it to Sweden and get Grubby to a hospital, they could probably get back to England; but again, if there was any doubt, they could jump before they reached the North Sea. However, Grubby would not hear of it. He knew they still had all four engines, and he wanted them to head for England. He attempted to pull himself out of the nose to return to the controls, but Vince held him down. At least twice they encountered flak barrages over enemy territory. And although twice the crew was given the opportunity to bail out, they all stayed with the plane. They honored Grubby's wishes and command, and they flew on to England. They never did head for Sweden.

As they flew on for over three hours, they felt totally alone. However, they found out later that fellows in the group above them had their eye on their damaged plane as they too flew back to England. Fortunately, no enemy fighters were encountered on their return trip. While not aware of the B-17s above them, Lieutenant Corlis did see a single B-24 above, which he knew was flying back to England. He followed the B-24 for as long as he could see it, but eventually it disappeared in the clouds, because it was a faster aircraft. He stated many years later that once the crew decided to stay the course and not bail out, he began talking with the "Man upstairs." Lieutenant Corlis was a man of faith who later in life served as a minister for ten years.

Eventually, they pulled the dead officer out of the seat, and Ray Alexander attempted to run the rudder pedals from the copilot's side, but the windshield and the roof window had both blown out during the explosion. Sub-zero temperatures forced Ray out of the seat. His hands were frostbitten when he tried to board up the open windows. Earl Dahlgren used a piece of a flak suit to deflect the wind from Lieutenant Corlis, who had to scrape blood off of his windshield so that he could see. Earl commented that Lieutenant Corlis was flying their plane with what he had left, which wasn't much. He did a remarkable job of flying the crippled plane in extremely cold conditions with air pouring into the cockpit. He held it level and maintained altitude. There were loose cables in the waist, probably rudder cables since the rudder pedals on the pilot's side were gone. One of the throttles was jammed. He flew the plane 650 miles, crossing the North Sea and entering England at the exact location from which they had earlier departed, which was a coincidence.

As the plane approached the English coast, Lieutenant Corlis asked the crew to open Grubby's parachute and drop him from the plane in the hopes that he would be picked up promptly and provided immediate emergency medical treatment for his serious injury. It was then that the young pilot learned that the crewmen had thrown their parachutes out of the plane, along with anything else they could grab, to ensure that they had the lightest load possible in an effort to conserve fuel.

Vince called out their airspeed from his bombardier position and Lieutenant Fabec navigated them straight to an airfield at Langham, near the English coast. Lieutenant Corlis advised the crew that they were going in for a belly landing, and the men positioned themselves as best they could. Some sat on the floor with their backs to the bare bulkhead of the bomb bay. Prior to landing, they unscrewed the cable to the radar to avoid sparks. Since they had no radio contact and were unable to respond to a Royal Air Force request for identity, the British began firing on the plane. The crew fired red flares and the RAF ceased fire. Due to crosswinds and the damaged controls, their plane was actually flying "sideways"—somewhat cockeyed—as they flew into England, and they narrowly missed taking out the control tower.

Lieutenant Corlis was able to straighten the plane out and made a couple of passes over the field. His main problem was how to slow the aircraft. He had no flaps or gear to reduce their speed. He had no airspeed indicator and no instruments. In the meantime, Grubby was still insisting that *he* land the plane, but he couldn't in his condition. Amazingly, Lieutenant Corlis had the presence of mind to fly beyond the airfield, which was on high ground, to a spot approximately a mile away where there were hills and a valley. He flew down into that valley to kill the aircraft's speed as he flew back up the hill, and then he approached the field.

The crew could feel and hear the plane slowing down. On his third attempt at landing, Lieutenant Corlis got the tail on the ground, then the belly, and then the props started hitting the ground. The plane was equipped with a radar dome instead of a ball turret underneath, which resolved the problem that would otherwise have occurred in a belly landing. The plane gently settled and slid across the field and then filled with a vapor, which entered the fuselage through the machine gun openings; it was caused by aluminum scraping against the ground as they slid across the field. The plane slowed, turned to the left and stopped. The crew exited the escape hatch and went around to the nose, where Sergeant Talbot was attempting to break the Plexiglas with his .45 pistol so that he could retrieve Grubby. The ground personnel put Grubby in an ambulance. The crew was taken to a building where they were served hot beverages until their group could send a plane for them. Grubby later characterized Lieutenant Corlis as a novice pilot who made a beautiful landing.

What is both amazing and miraculous is that not only had Lieutenant Corlis never flown in combat previously, but he had never flown a B-17 before. He had trained only on two-engine aircraft such as the AT-9 and the AT-10, having aspired to be a fighter pilot. And yet he flew that severely damaged aircraft all that distance back to England. He obviously was not very familiar with the B-17—he did not even know that the B-17 was equipped with tip tanks with reserve fuel in them.

Grubby was later awarded the Distinguished Service Cross for his accomplishments in pulling the B-17 out of the dive and flying the plane for the next 15 minutes, and for his failure to relinquish command of his plane and directing its course of flight back to England. Vince later said that he had never seen such a brave man as Grubby. He also said that while Grubby was in great pain and had lost a considerable amount of blood, he desperately wanted to help Lieutenant Corlis get the plane back to England. Vince had to actually hold Grubby down to prevent him from going back to the cockpit. It was a miracle that they made it, and it was a miracle that Grubby didn't bleed to death. He later explained that his arteries were somehow sucked back into his leg and became swollen, and that stopped the bleeding.

For his bravery and heroism under the most difficult of circumstances, Lieutenant Gaylord Corlis was awarded the Silver Star.

Below is the entire narrative from the official damage report of the plane dated June 29, 1944, and submitted to the Commanding Officer of the 305th Bombardment Group:

1. *Ship belly-landed with major battle damage. Damage beyond repair.*
2. *All props bent and engines damaged due to sudden stoppage. Flaps and bomb bay door damaged. Bulkheads #4 and #5 damaged. #3 nacelle buckled. Ball radar sheared off and chin turret crushed in.*
3. *Anti-aircraft projectile entered left side of fuselage just below pilot. The shell cut the main lead of electrical lines, ripped out pilot's rudder pedals, cut numerous flight control and engine control cables, blew the instrument panel in two rendering all instruments useless, damaged*

> pilot's control column, bent the throttles and mixture
> controls, rendered the control toggle switches on the
> control stand useless, broke all the bulletproof glass
> enclosing the cockpit, and blew the bulletproof glass in
> front of the co-pilot completely out.
>
> 4. The R.A.F. said the pilot made an excellent 'belly' landing
>   in spite of the condition of the ship."

I do not know how this plane flew for so long back to England. I believe the hand of God held it in the air. I know Corky Corlis would agree, because I had the honor and the privilege of meeting him and discussing these matters with him in April 2008, in his hometown of Albuquerque, New Mexico. After serving in the Army Air Corps during World War II, he later joined the Air Force Reserves and served for many years, attaining the rank of lieutenant colonel. I am very proud of him, as well as the entire crew. In my opinion, the entire crew was a group of brave men.

Corky passed away in August 2008. I am so glad that I had the opportunity to meet him and to personally thank him for saving my father's life as well as the lives of the other crew members.

Lieutenant Colonel Gaylord "Corky" Corlis and the author
(April 2008). Photo by Bonnie Gisriel.

Location where 88mm shell entered the fuselage

The damaged cockpit, controls, and instrument panel

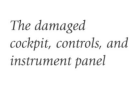

The damaged cockpit, controls, and instrument panel

*Blown-out
windows
caused by the
explosion in
the cockpit*

Two days after this near-tragedy, on June 20, 1944, Vince wrote to Martha: "...finally after three days I am back with you again. I am sorry I went so long without writing, but it just couldn't be helped. A lot has happened since my last letter, but as usual can't say anything about it. I am feeling fine and healthy and will tell you all about it when I get home, which I hope is very, very soon." On June 22, 1944, Vince wrote: "Darling, I'm just about eating my heart out right now. Fred Waring is playing 'That Old Black Magic.' That song just about drives me crazy, especially when he plays it." He continued: "Went to a U.S.O. show here on the field tonight and it was really good. Very different for a change. I could go for them more often."

Vince had been reassigned to the 305th Bombardment Group from approximately May 28, 1944 until June 23, 1944. Afterwards, he returned to the 326th Squadron, 92nd Bombardment Group. Shortly thereafter, his crew rejoined him back in their original location. His reassignment had delayed some of his mail. Waiting for him were nine letters and two cards from Martha. He wrote to Martha that while over at the 305th, he had his bike, "Herman," all fixed up. He was reluctant to say too much on the positive side about his bike, for he wrote: "Oops, you know I'd better not say anything good about Herman, 'cause every time I do, something happens to him." Martha responded: "I'm so glad that 'Old Herman' is working OK. Tell him to 'keep on the ball,' hear, hon!" Later, Martha wrote to Vince that Butch, who was then 12 years old, wanted to have his own bike fixed up so Vince could ride it when he returned home. Martha was very touched by her younger brother's thoughtfulness.

Vince wrote to Martha that he wanted her to start thinking about the kind of house she wanted and where she wanted to live when he returned. He saw a kitchen advertised and he wanted to cut the clipping out and send it to her, but new rules did not allow him to mail clippings. He wrote: "I was going to cut it out and send it to you..." Martha responded: "Hon, I got the biggest kick out of your letter, when you were telling me about the cute kitchen you saw advertised. I thought for a while that you were going to send me the kitchen. I read that part to Mom and thought she would die laughing." Martha continued: "I haven't made any plans about a house yet, honey…I could live in a soap box as long as you were with me, and be more than happy. Little Vince said that he could, too."

Mail continued to be delayed and unpredictable. Martha was still upset about delays. She wrote: "…I get so mad. I know, only too well, that there's a war on, but when they separate people from those they love, I think they could speed up on this damn mail situation."

Vince continued to be concerned about Martha's well-being and recovery following her lengthy labor and delivery. Martha acknowledged that concern and wrote on June 23, 1944: "Honey, please don't worry anymore. I was in pain for an awfully long time, but Little Vince, after his arrival, made me forget every pain I had. I still have to take it pretty easy, but I am as good as new, and Little Vince is perfect. He's just as healthy as could be….So don't you worry about anything at home, hear, darling?" Vince recognized that Martha was getting a lot of hands-on experience in becoming a good mother and made reference to the fact that he would have a lot to learn from her and to make up for lost time. She put that to rest quickly when she wrote: "Hon, I don't think you'll have to practice or study on how to be a good father. You're a wonderful husband and you're bound to be a wonderful father."

It was evident from the correspondence that Vince was enjoying being a father. His crew and buddies were all giving him congratulations as the news of the birth of his son traveled around the airbase. Some of his close friends, who shall remain nameless, even got pretty "stinken drunk" in celebrating Vince becoming a "Daddy," and Vince wasn't even there to celebrate with them due to his reassignment.

Vince informed Martha that two of his close buddies were promoted to first lieutenant in mid-June. While Vince was delighted for them, he wrote to Martha that he thought he should have been promoted too. He wrote: "I was talking to the major about it and he apologized all over himself. It seems like he thought he had put me in. He can't understand how he slipped up. Had me believing him." This prompted Martha to write: "Honey, I don't know what you're doing over there, but it sounds as though it is pretty important. If you can, darling, will you please let me know what it is? But listen, darling, it doesn't matter to me in the least that you haven't been promoted. All I pray for is that you get back real soon and safely. I'm very proud of you, right now, as I have always been and I know that no matter what task you are given, you will do your very best. Of course, hon, I would like it very much if you were to be promoted, but you just be very careful. I've loved you for a very long time now, and although my love for you increases as the seconds go by, your little gold bar didn't make me love you any more. I love you for your own sweet self, and would love you just as much if you were a buck private or anything else. Just don't you worry about those old promotions honey! Roger?"

It must have been an oversight on the part of the major, because on June 27, 1944, Vince was promoted to first lieutenant. Grubby was also promoted to captain. While admittedly I am biased, I think these promotions were well deserved.

Vince and a number of the crew were off to two different rest homes by June 29, 1944, for some well-earned time off following the events of the preceding several weeks, particularly the near-tragedy in the air over Hamburg on the 18th of June. The officers were sent to one rest home, and the enlisted men were sent to another. However, before they could rest and relax, the crew apparently had one more mission on June 28, 1944. They flew back to Merseburg, home of Germany's gigantic fuel and oil production facility. It was the crew's second attack there. They carried a bomb load of ten 500-pound bombs. They encountered heavy flak again, but no enemy fighters. The original crew rejoined Lieutenant Paul Robertson, now a pilot, on this mission. Vince may not have been on this particular mission, which lasted 8 hours and 50 minutes.

On June 29, 1944, Vince wrote to Martha from the rest home, which was, from all accounts, an English estate with vast grounds and many amenities. He was awakened at 9:00 AM by the butler, who served him a glass of tomato juice. He was then given the option to either go back to sleep or enjoy breakfast. Vince opted to go down to breakfast. The morning recreation consisted of snooker (a form of billiards) and ping pong. After lunch, nine of them went horseback riding. At 4:00 PM, they had tea and crumpets. Afterwards, they played bridge, snooker and ping pong. By 6:00 PM it was time for a shave and a bath prior to dinner at 7:00 PM. The evening was topped off with a party. He wrote to Martha: "How's that for a day's work, honey?"

Vince went on to describe the house, but of course, he could not write regarding its location. It was a large white stone building with about 20 rooms. All around the front of the house was an open porch, and each room in the front led to the porch. There were big glass doors. Vince described the landscaping, which consisted of just about every kind of flower imaginable. They had access to a modest-size swimming pool. There was a big lawn with volleyball and badminton courts. The rest home was complete with its own golf course. The only thing lacking was mail delivery, and he was really missing letters from Martha. Vince had time to rest, but he also reflected on his family. He ended this particular letter wishing that he could hold his son in his arms and sing to him or tell him stories. He wrote: "Darlings, I love you two so much it hurts. And I miss you both something awful. Too, too much to suit me. So long for now darlings." Martha later responded to this by writing: "How I do wish you were here, to sing to him and hold him very close to you. He knows you love him very much, though, 'cause I always tell him so. I also kiss him good morning and good night for you."

Martha ended another letter to Vince by writing: "...I love you with my heart and soul, and every breath I take. There has never been a greater love than I have for you, since the beginning of time. I miss you more than words could ever express. Little Vince loves and misses you the same way." Martha was wrong. She *could* find the words to express her heartfelt feelings. Their words to each other simply flowed because they were so pure and so sincere. This is very evident when you read the hundreds and hundreds of letters between them.

Between May 1, 1944, and June 30, 1944, I have counted one telegram, four cards and 143 letters between them. An awful lot occurred in the lives of Martha and Vince on both sides of the Atlantic Ocean during this time, and yet written correspondence between them still flourished.

Vince Jr. and Martha

14

R & R Doesn't Last Long

Vince continued to enjoy the rest and relaxation offered by the rest home. One evening a "gang" of them, as Vince called them, went "pubbing." They had a great time. The only thing available to drink, though, was "Mild and Bitter," a then popular beer or ale in the United Kingdom. Vince said, "…no one got a buzz on." They enjoyed an evening of table pool and darts, which apparently were very popular in the British pubs. Their last full day at the rest home was July 4, 1944, and the fellows decided to celebrate American style. They had a picnic out on the lawn where they cooked hamburgers and roasted sausages. Vince wrote that they went over to a British airfield nearby and borrowed "…a flare gun and loads of all different colors of flares. Really did the sky up, just like back home. Lord knows what the people around the countryside thought." Knowing Vince, this probably took place prior to dark, due to blackout requirements.

On their last evening they played bridge. Vince wrote: "You know it's funny, here at the house rank doesn't mean a thing and there's a colonel here who is commanding officer of one of the groups. Well, anyway, we were playing bridge, and I kept calling him Pete—that's his first name. Finally, he got very indignant about it, but we soon put him in his place and told him one of the rules of the house was to call everyone by their first name or nickname. Ever since then he's been a good Joe, and we struck up quite a friendship." Vince ended the letter by writing: "I can hardly wait to get back and get all your letters that should be waiting there for me. I sure have missed them. It seems as though I've lost contact with you and Vince, but I haven't 'cause I think of you both every second of the day, and love you something terrific. I don't know what I'd do without your love. I know I couldn't go on living without you." Martha did not disappoint Vince, for upon his return to the base, there were 12 letters with six pictures of her and the baby waiting for him. Three days later, another seven letters from her arrived.

In her Fourth of July letter, Martha had the sad task of informing Vince that Oriole Park had burned down early that day. This was a park used by the International League team before Baltimore acquired the Major League Orioles in 1954.

In her letter of July 5, 1944, Martha reflected on the thirteen months since their wedding day. She wrote: "It seems like only yesterday, doesn't it, honey? An awful lot has happened since then, though. Some good and others very unpleasant—meaning when we were separated, of course." Martha wrote that she had started another novena for Vince. It was the Sacred Heart Novena for all the men in the service. Martha's recovery following her difficult delivery took extra time. However, once she was back to her normal self, she continued her frequent attendance at Mass, Communion, Confession and novenas for Vince. Her mother and family often watched the baby so that she could continue her prayerful routine.

Vince and the other guys left the rest home on July 5, 1944. On their way back, they stopped in London to spend the day. That afternoon, they went to a movie and saw Danny Kaye in *Up in Arms*. Vince thought the movie was wonderful. He wrote that he laughed until his sides hurt. It was the first time he had ever seen Danny Kaye in a movie and thought he was really good. He encouraged Martha to see this movie. Vince also ran into a lot of other aviators he knew but had not seen for some time. One such fellow had been a cadet along with Vince when he was in basic training in Nashville. They talked at length about the whereabouts of all of the men who had gone into the service with Vince. The fellow knew where all of them were, and Vince really enjoyed their long conversation.

The men had planned to stay overnight in London but quickly changed their minds and left right after dinner. In his letter, Vince did not say why; however, during this period the Germans had been launching buzz bombs at London. Vince probably could not write about such a thing even if they did encounter it.

During the day they also went to the PX to pick up a few things. While there, they saw Edward G. Robinson, the movie actor. Vince found him to be quite timid and not a bit boastful and was thrilled to have seen him.

Once back at the base, the missions continued. On July 7, 1944, the crew was on a mission to Leipzig, Germany. The target was the Aero Engine Works. Grubby was still recovering from his serious injury, so Lieutenant Paul Robertson was back again as their pilot. They carried a bomb load of ten 500-pound bombs. They weathered heavy flak but encountered no enemy fighters. The duration of the mission was 8 hours and 50 minutes. On that very day, Martha wrote to Vince that she wanted him to see their baby. She wrote: "Hon, won't they let you fly home to see him every other day or so? I guess they won't consent to that, though, will they darling? I bet if these damn people who are so in favor of war loved one another as we three do, they'd soon put an end to it all." Please, God, may Martha's words be mankind's prayer forever. She spoke for every mother throughout the ages and for the years to come.

Vince continued to be pulled from his original crew to fly on a lead plane as lead bombardier. He wrote to Martha: "It seems like they won't let me fly anything but lead..." I happen to believe that he had established himself as an "Ace Bombardier."

Vince's aunt, Sister Dorothy, wrote to him in early July 1944. She wrote: "What a striking comparison can be made in the world today. We in the good old U.S.A. are enjoying the blessings of peace, save for the absence of so many loved ones—and in so many countries even women and children are suffering the hazards of war. God grant that a lasting peace will soon be the heritage of the whole of humanity!" She continued: "No doubt you are seeing plenty of action. And, interesting no doubt. Well, the air force is doing a splendid piece of work, so I understand." Sister Dorothy was assigned to a home that provided care for mothers and babies, some of whom would be put up for adoption. She wrote that here "…we do not see anything like war scenes, but we manage to keep plenty busy. There are babies and babies and still more babies—each one a little bunch of happiness." She continued to seek God's blessing upon Vince, as well as the Blessed Mother's protection.

In the meantime, Vince's aunt, Sister Francis, wrote to him regarding her recent visit with Martha and the baby. She wrote: "How I wish this horrible war would end and that you could get home to them." She continued: "They tell me that you have seen some action in the past month. That means that you need extra prayers, and you are getting them." Both aunts reminded Vince that the feast day of his patron, Saint Vincent dePaul, was coming up on July 19. Sister Francis wrote that she has prayed to St. Vincent dePaul many times for Vince's safety.

Vince wrote that a good buddy of his had introduced him to poetry. He wrote to Martha: "I've been reading a book with the 101 best poems in it. Can you imagine that, me reading poetry? And believe it or not, I kind of like it. I never gave poetry much thought until lately, and it's good stuff. Corky more or less convinced me of it. He's quite a guy, hon. You sure would like him." When people are off fighting in a war, and they are put in dangerous situations as Vince was, they begin to reflect on many aspects of everyday life that we all tend to take for granted. They look around and begin to appreciate the little things, such as flowers and green grass. Poetry was just another thing for Vince to pause and look at, and he discovered yet another beautiful treasure that makes life worth living. Martha was pleased to read that Vince was enjoying poetry. Lieutenant Corky Corlis shared his book of 101 poems with Vince. Corky received this book from his mother when he was a teenager, and he carried it with him at all times.

On July 9, 1944, Vince was formally awarded his Distinguished Flying Cross medal for his direct hit on the oil production facility in Merseburg on May 12, 1944. He wrote to Martha: "I do have something important to tell you, or anyway I think it's important. I was awarded the D.F.C. (Distinguished Flying Cross) today. I'd like to write you how the award read, but I don't think I'm allowed to. It was for one of the raids I led awhile back…The D.F.C. is one award higher than the Air Medal." Vince was so excited and proud, but even more humble and modest. He added to this letter: "I'm afraid I can't tell you the exact number of missions I have, but I will say that I am a little more than 2/3 finished. It shouldn't be too long now, honey. Just keep your fingers crossed and hope and pray."

On July 11, 1944, Martha wrote to Vince about a friend of theirs who had been reported missing in action. They had just heard of two others in recent weeks. Altogether, five friends had been reported missing in action since Vince went overseas. Martha and Vince asked each other to write anything they heard about the missing men. Martha heard limited details from the wives, and Vince tried to pass on any reliable information he heard that he was allowed to write about. For example, shortly after reading of one fellow reported by Martha, Vince wrote to her that he had heard that the same guy was now safe. There was already enough stress with the war on and the separation of loved ones; now there was the added stress and anxiety of hearing about close friends missing in action. These were very anxious and tough times.

Upon hearing about the latest of the friends missing, Vince wrote: "Darling, I hope you haven't been worrying too much about me. If you have, I want you to stop. I promise you I'll be back to you, and very soon I hope."

Much later, they learned that one of the five friends who initially was reported as missing actually died when his plane went down. Earlier, before receiving the news of his death, his wife had written to Vince because she knew they had been stationed at the same airbase. She wrote: "I thought that you might be able to tell me some little something in the way of an encouragement. I'm just sure that he's safe because he told me he'd come back, and I know he will. I guess he'll be kinda curious to see what his new son looks like anyway." As late as December, 1944, she still had not heard anything definite regarding her husband. She wrote in a Christmas card to Martha and Vince: "I just know that he's alive somewhere and will walk in the front door one day soon. If you know anything, *good* or *bad*, please tell me, as eight months of this suspense is hard on one's nerves!"

This is one of the biggest tragedies of war. The loss of a loved one is bad enough, but then there is the lack of any word and not knowing for such long periods of time. There were so many brave young men who gave their lives in our nation's defense in World War II. How can we ever repay them, except to never forget them and to pray that they are in God's safe care? By the way, the young widow had a baby girl in September 1944.

On July 13, 1944, Martha wrote in one of her letters: "I miss you so much, Vince. Sometimes I just wonder how I'm still sane. I think it must be loving you and Little Vince so much. In fact, honey, I know it's that." On the exact same date, Vince wrote from an ocean away: "My love constantly grows for you, and I want you both so bad. I sometimes wonder if I can go on. I will though, because I know you are both back there waiting for me. Be good soldiers—it won't be too long." Their uncanny connection continued.

Knowing that Vince was missing the baby's early growth and development, Martha kept him informed of Little Vince's day-by-day progress. She reported his weight gain every other day or so. She reported when he discovered his hands, when he began to reach for her face and that he held her chin. She even reported that he laughed when she sang or talked to him. She wrote: "He loves for me to sing to him, and the three songs he likes best are 'Tangerine,' 'You'll Never Know' and 'Silver Wings in the Moonlight.' I sing those three all day long anyway, so I guess that's why he likes them best. He laughs when I sing to him." Since she was then writing twice a day, she had no trouble keeping Vince up to date. Vince wrote: "…I want to thank you for keeping me posted on Little Vince so much. You tell me every time he gains an ounce or grows an inch, and all the little things he does. That's what I like to hear."

Martha wrote to Vince about a friend who was about to give birth and her husband, who was about to be shipped out. Martha was hoping that he would not leave before the baby was born. Recalling her own situation made her all the more concerned for her friend. She wrote: "I know what it is to go through that without the only person there who really matters. Hon, at that time, no matter how much you love your mother and father, you still want your husband with you. I know I did, anyway. Even though I had a very hard time, I'd be willing to go through the same experience again if you were with me, but I don't think I'd like to do it over again with you away. I know that you were with me in spirit, and that you were loving me and praying for me this time, and that is why everything turned out OK. But while we're on the subject, hon, I don't see how any woman can stop at having one child just because of the pain she was caused. Every time I glance at Little Vince, I just think of what a small price is paid for so great a thing—a few pains. Everyone who knows all about my little troubles says to me, 'Martha, I bet you won't have any more, will you?' They are quite amazed when I still want my other four, and believe me, Vince, when I say I do." She continued: "I could rave on and on for hours about how wonderful I think children are...but it's 1:00 AM, so I'd better sign off. I'll be back tomorrow..."

What a beautiful and strong woman Martha was. And here I thought my father was the hero. My mother was every bit a hero as well, in my book.

Vince responded to Martha's letter about having more children as follows: "...I'm so proud of you. I couldn't help but cry when I read your letter today. Honey, I know I couldn't possibly realize the pain you went thru with Little Vince, but believe me I wanted to be there just as much as you wanted me to be. I know what you mean when you say the only person in the world who matters wasn't there, 'cause I wanted to be there so bad it hurt my heart to no end. I promise the next time I'll be there with you every second of the time. What makes me so proud of you is after going thru all that pain you don't want to stop at one child. Darling, I just wish I could share half of your pain. You are so modest— you say your 'little troubles,' when you had such big ones."

The next mission for the crew was on July 13, 1944. The target was Munich, Germany. Lieutenant Robertson was again their pilot. They endured flak on this trip but engaged no enemy fighters. The mission lasted 8 hours and 50 minutes. This attack was one of four carried out by the 92nd Bombardment Group from July 11 to July 16. This series of attacks, which struck at the industrial areas of Munich, involved 100 planes from the 92nd. Direct bombing hits were made on the Bayerische Motoren Werke, the Afga Dye Works, the main railroad station, and a large oil depot as well as other important facilities. The success of these raids prompted a commendation from Lieutenant General Carl Spaatz, Commanding General, United States Strategic Air Forces, who wrote that the damage caused by these attacks had undoubtedly been a severe blow to German war production. He went on to write that the bombing results would directly affect Germany's ability to continue the war. Lieutenant General Spaatz acknowledged that these missions required great endurance while operating under difficult conditions. Over the four days of attacks, the 92nd group lost four planes and their crews.

On July 17, 1944, Martha received four letters from Vince. She wrote: "I really hit the jackpot today, darling." Within those letters, she learned that Vince had received his promotion to first lieutenant, as well as being awarded the Distinguished Flying Cross. She wrote: "Golly, Vince, I'm so proud of you and love you so much. I know you're very happy about your promotion, and believe me, I am too." She wrote in a second letter that same day that she told little Vince about his daddy's good news: "When I told him about your promotion and the D.F.C., he laughed. He's got a swell disposition and makes friends with everyone. Just like you, Vince. You know, I am sure a lucky gal. I have the most wonderful husband and baby who ever lived. I'm very proud of you both and love you both very much."

Vince had written to Martha that Grubby was coming along nicely and that he was in the best of spirits. This was obviously a slip-up by Vince, for Martha did not know that Grubby had been injured. She wrote to Vince: "Hon, what is the matter with Hodges? You said that he is in good spirits and will be up and around soon. I didn't know anything was wrong with him. Please tell me all about it…" Upon reading this, Vince realized that Martha could not have known about it. He had not told her because he was not allowed to write about it, and besides, he didn't want her to worry. And Grubby did not tell his wife initially because she was expecting a baby any day. It was simply an oversight on Vince's part to even have written anything regarding Grubby in a letter to Martha. He would have to explain the situation to her at a much later time. Martha later received a letter from Grubby's wife, who wrote that he had been wounded, but even then his wife did not know the extent of his injuries. Shortly thereafter, Grubby returned to the United States, where he was greeted by his wife and his new baby boy.

On July 18, 1944, Vince's original crew was back in the sky with a newly assigned pilot, Lieutenant Jack Glasco. Lieutenant Robertson had completed his missions and was returning to the States very soon. Their target was the principal research and development center for Nazi experimental weapons, which included jet propulsion aircraft, flying bombs and rockets, located in Peenemunde, Germany. It was the deepest penetration into northeast Germany. The mission lasted 9 hours and 57 minutes. They approached the target by coming in over the Baltic Sea. They encountered flak but no enemy fighters. Thirty-four planes of the 92nd Bombardment Group participated in what has been called the most important mission of the month of July 1944. The attack was highly successful, with bomb hits all over the target area. Smoke could be seen rising 12,000 feet into the air. Commendations came from Lieutenant General Spaatz, Lieutenant General Jimmy Doolittle and Major General Williams. Lieutenant General Spaatz characterized the attack on Peenemunde as one of the finest examples of strategic precision bombings ever accomplished. Major General Williams said that attacks on the Nazi research and development center proved the air force's ability to destroy the designated target regardless of location or enemy opposition.

Vince may have been flying on this particular day with yet another crew, or he may have been on a plane that had to return to base due to engine problems. Again, details are sketchy.

On July 19, 1944, Vince wrote to Martha and the baby: "Darlings, I have a confession to make. For the past two days I haven't written, not because I didn't want to, though. You know how it is, now and then things turn up that keep you from doing the things you want to do."

Vince was pulled for a special assignment as the lead bombardier in a mission to bomb an aircraft/ball bearing facility in Ebelsbach, Germany on July 21, 1944. The mission was described as having excellent bombing results. While there was no flak at the target area, and no enemy fighters were encountered, apparently there was strong ground resistance, because 11 of the 12 American planes on the raid were hit by enemy fire. However, all returned safely.

Martha wrote to Vince in a letter dated July 23, 1944, that she was separated from the baby for awhile. She went to church to make her novena for Vince while the family took the baby to the park. When they met up at home, Martha took the baby and started to talk to him, essentially apologizing to him for leaving him for so long a time. She wrote: "Well, Vince, he did everything but jump up and talk to me. He grabbed hold of my nose and wouldn't even let go. His little eyes were as big as saucers and he was really almost talking. He would laugh out loud, and then his hands would fly. You see, my hair is getting pretty long again, so I've been wearing it up in front and down in back. Well there was a curl hanging down and he was trying to touch it. I finally let him get hold of it, and brother, he really pulled and held on to it. He is such a darling, and is so darn pleasant. He goes to anyone, and just talks and laughs with them. He looks so much like you that I almost cry when I look at him. You could never deny that he was your son, honey, because he is the image of you." Later, she wrote: "He looks and acts exactly like you." She also wrote: "You should see him laugh and talk to your picture. He sure does love his daddy." I can just see my father's chest swelling up with pride at Martha's words.

Vince responded to Martha by writing: "I know what you mean when you say you miss him when he is gone from you for a long time. I was just thinking how wonderful it is that babies know their mother instantly even though they are so young. God sure takes care of that, doesn't He." When I reflected on this quotation, I began thinking about the fact that my father lost his mother when he was only two years old. And now, here he had a baby boy he had not yet seen in over two months since his birth. I can only imagine the anguish my father went through during his separation from Martha and the baby. I love him so much more for what he had to endure. I love my parents so much more for the sacrifices they both made in the cause of freedom.

Perhaps the monotony at the base was starting to get to the aviators, or maybe it was the the pressure of combat, but one night the fellows had quite a night in the officers' club. Vince wrote: "The 326th threw a personnel party tonight, and what a brawl it turned out to be. It started out to be just a quiet social affair until somebody pulled out a couple quarts of Scotch. We were playing football there in the club and just about wrecked the place." As Vince anticipated, the next day they heard from the colonel. Vince wrote: "He didn't appreciate our way of having fun very much. Can't blame him, though. We acted like a bunch of nitwits. Our CO called a special meeting today, but I got off the post before I could get my can chewed out." Prior to leaving the post, though, Vince got up feeling pretty stiff. He wrote: "I could hardly move this morning when I woke up. My knee was all knocked up, my big toe felt like it was broken and my eye was mighty, mighty sore. In other words, I was a mess."

Martha responded by writing: "Hon, I thought I'd die laughing when I read about your football game in the club. I was just sitting here thinking of what fun we had in the club at Dalhart and trying to visualize what it would have looked like had you all played football. I can imagine how mad the 'Old Man' got, and I bet he did some 'bitching.' Say, you must have gotten quite beat up that night. I hope you feel alright now. You'll have to have football games more often, and then you won't get so stiff."

Upon receiving a bunch of letters from Martha at one time again, Vince wrote: "I don't know what it is, but your letters sure have a magic power of some kind over me. I feel so good when I get them." Martha expressed similar sentiments regarding Vince's letters.

Martha had not been to the movies in approximately two months. On July 24, 1944, she went for the first time since the baby was born. She and her sister Mary saw *Christmas Holiday* starring Deanna Durbin and Gene Kelly. For a refreshing change, there was no war theme. She thoroughly enjoyed it and encouraged Vince to see it if he had the opportunity. Coincidentally, Vince wrote to Martha about a week later and said that she had not mentioned that she had been to the movies lately. He understood that she had been very busy with the baby, but that it would do her good to get out once in a while. In this particular letter, he mentioned that he had just seen *Lassie Come Home*, which he really enjoyed. Ironically, Martha had been to her second movie within six days before ever receiving Vince's letter of encouragement. She and Angela went together and saw *Two Girls and a Sailor*, starring Van Johnson. She wrote to Vince and told him not to miss it. Within another few days, Vince saw *Cover Girl*, starring Rita Hayworth. He thought this movie was "...very, very good," and continued: "They should put more shows out like it."

Vince was sent back to the 305th Bombardment Group from July 26 to July 31, 1944. He was kept extremely busy over there. He flew four missions in four days between July 28 and July 31, 1944, catching only about twelve hours of sleep during those days.

On July 28, Vince was lead bombardier on a raid somewhere over Germany. From all indications, he was in the thick of air combat during this mission. Their squadron encountered intense gunfire while flying to the target. They encountered between 15 and 20 enemy fighters, four to six of them going right through their formation and then returning. The enemy fighters were in all sorts of colors and markings to confuse the Americans. One Nazi Me-109 was camouflaged to resemble an American P-51 Mustang support fighter. There was American fighter support on this mission, but not during the initial wave. Nevertheless, the Americans had good bombing results. In briefings prior to this mission, the aviators were instructed to bomb targets of opportunity, sometimes as alternate or backup targets. They were instructed to bomb any military installations, bridges, enemy troops, columns, convoys and concentration of troops or equipment, but not if "adjacent to built-up areas." They were again advised that they must bomb only targets that were positively identified, and that a visual sighting must be made.

The Germans were cunning in their air techniques. In May 1944, a B-17 joined a formation and flew over the target with the other bombers but never opened its bomb bay doors. It was observed to have an unidentifiable white vertical marking, and it apparently disappeared after the bomb run. In June 1944, another strange B-17 showed up during flight. Initially it trailed behind, then caught up and then flew ahead. It was speculated that the enemy repaired or mimicked a B-17 and flew it up to join the Americans, possibly to learn and study the techniques of the Army Air Corps.

On July 29, 1944, Vince was again a lead bombardier. He was back to Merseburg/Leuna, Germany, where undoubtedly the target was again the oil and fuel plant. It appears that the Americans lost eight B-17s on this one mission.

On July 30, 1944, the target was an airdrome in Munich, Germany. Part of the payload was a leaflet drop. Many American aircraft were damaged during the multiple raids on Munich that day, which included industrial targets. Of the 337 planes that incurred some damage, 71 incurred major damage.

On July 31, 1944, Vince was again a lead bombardier on another target in Munich. This mission was led by General H. M. Turner. As the aircraft headed into the bomb run, they discovered they could not bomb visually, so they turned around and came a second time using their PFF radar equipment.

Vince's mail had backed up over at the 92nd. When he went to retrieve it, he found 16 pieces of mail, half of which were birthday cards. He turned 22 on July 30, 1944. He was delighted to receive all those cards on his actual birthday. He commented in a letter to Martha on July 30: "Today seems no more like a birthday than Christmas does. Didn't even have a little drink to it. That'll all come when I get back. Roger?" He continued: "When I get home I'll let you shake the hand that shook a general's. I'm only kidding you, honey, but we did have a general flying with us on one of the raids we led. Pretty ritzy, huh?" Martha responded: "Honey, you're really doing alright for yourself, aren't you? Having a general ride with you sure is ritzy."

On July 31, Vince wrote that he had been up for 24 hours. He was very tired and wrote Martha only a short letter. In this letter, he wrote: "I don't have much news for you 'cause what I've done since yesterday is strictly secret, although it'll be all over the papers tomorrow. Even though we can't write about it." Even though he had accomplished so much in the previous four days, I am not sure exactly what he was referring to as far as possible news coverage is concerned.

As I further reflect on my father's comment that his recent activity would be "all over the papers tomorrow," I realize that he might not have been referring to any particular significant event; he might just have been somewhat frustrated because aviators could not write about mission events, but the press certainly reported on them as often as they could.

Vince wrote to Martha about a recording he had heard that he really liked, a song called "Lili Marlene." He explained that it had quite a story behind it. Apparently it was a German song sung by a Swedish girl. The words were reportedly written in 1915 by a German, Hans Leip, in the form of a poem. According to Vince, it was adopted by the Germans fighting in Africa as their theme song. However, the Allies also liked the song, and they also adopted it. Vince further explained that the British made a short movie about the background behind the song. He enjoyed the movie very much and hoped that Martha could one day see it. He doubted that the recording was available in the United States, but he asked Martha if she would look for it. Martha wrote back to Vince that she had found the recording. There were only two copies, one sung by a man and the other sung by "Hildegarde." Martha bought the one sung by the woman. She wrote: "I've been playing it ever since I got home, and I like it a lot. The tune is catchy, I think, and I like it more every time I play it. I'll take good care of it for you until you get home, darling." On the day before Martha wrote to inform him that she had found the recording, Vince included the lyrics to the song along with his letter.

15

Is the End in Sight?

On August 1, 1944, Vince returned to the 92nd Bombardment Group. He wrote that it seemed that all he had done in England was pack and unpack, and that it was getting a little monotonous. He was hoping that the next time he packed, it would be because he was on his way home. In a letter on that date, he instructed me as follows: "Vince, you be a good little boy for your Mommie, 'cause she deserves it. She is the best in the world, but I guess you have found that out by now."

Vince was happy to be back with the fellows with whom he had served so long. However, on August 3, 1944, he wrote to Martha that earlier in the day he had said good-bye to two of his close friends. One was Lieutenant Paul Robertson, who had been with Vince since the beginning of his original crew. The other was Lieutenant Forney; he and Vince had been together since June 1943. These two officers had completed their missions and left for the replacement center, which was where one went before heading back to the United States. Vince wrote that he was sure going to miss them and hoped and prayed that he could join them soon. Vince wrote: "That's what I hate about this war; you meet such good friends and then have to part from them." It must have been a bittersweet feeling for Vince. He continued in this letter that he and a buddy had been to the club that evening "…doing a little drinking, and I am a little high." He continued: "Don't know what we have been celebrating, but I just felt like getting drunk and I did." Before he ended the letter, he apologized to Martha twice for getting drunk. He wrote: "I hope you will forgive me for getting drunk, but I just had to. I've been so lonesome for you two here of late. The closer I get to finishing the lonesomer I get. If you both only knew how much I loved you, you could understand. My love for you is so great it burns my heart constantly."

It is really not hard to understand when you ponder what these men had endured. More importantly, Martha understood. She responded by writing: "Honey, you don't have to ask my forgiveness for getting a little 'high.' You have just as good a time as you can, darling. Just be very careful not to get 'stinking' when you have work to do. On your free time, you do just as you want to make yourself happy. Anyway, according to your letter, you did your celebrating on the third of August. That was Willie's birthday, hon." Since that was her dad's birthday, Martha figured in retrospect the celebrating certainly had a reason, even if Vince had not been sure why.

Vince received a letter from his sister, Angela, dated August 7, 1944, in which she really poured her heart out. She wrote of a friend who had just had her second baby within fifteen months. She wrote: "Darn the war—I could have had another too if it weren't for the old war." Even though she was the mother of twins, she meant every word of it! Her husband, Charles, had been gone overseas, and she hadn't seen him for almost two years. They eventually had a total of seven children.

Angela, who was raised by their Aunt Mary, continued to live with her while Charles was in the army. Angela wrote about Aunt Mary and how crazy the twins were about her: "When she gets home they make her wait on them hand and foot. I can't even take them to the bathroom! She spoils them so. Sometimes it makes my blood boil, and we have had some terrific fights. A couple of times I couldn't make up my mind whether to get a place of my own or not. I pour out all of my troubles to Martha; she's the only one I can talk to, and she has helped me so much. I only hope she doesn't mind me telling them to her. Please don't say anything to Charles, as he thinks everything has been perfect here since he went overseas, and I don't want him worrying about such things. You don't know how glad I'll be when this war is over, for more reasons than one." She asked Vince to try to visit Charles on his next pass, for he was stationed somewhere in England.

Angela continued her letter: "Another thing—have you written to Daddy? I know how you feel, I felt the same way too, but I guess I'm one of those soft-hearted persons who forgives and forgets. You can't imagine how much he's waiting and hoping to hear from you. I get a letter every week and in each one he's still hoping. One of these days he'll explain himself and pay us back what he owes, but I'm forgiving him before that. He does have a lot of good in him, but you haven't heard much of his good side, this I know for a fact. Remember, honey, he was perfect before Mother died; the shock of her death is what set him off. I can't write any more about it, but please drop him a line." Vince had been estranged from his father for years. For all intents and purposes, his father had abandoned Angela and Vince upon the death of their mother. I believe this hurt Vince deeply.

Later, Vince wrote to Martha and indicated that he did not realize some of the troubles Angela was having. He felt bad that he had not written to her more often. He also acknowledged that Angela had opened his eyes about his father, John, which prompted Vince to write to him. He felt bad that he hadn't previously realized some things pertaining to his father. Incidentally, John was back in the army as an enlisted man while Vince was over in England. John had been stationed at Camp Beauregard, Louisiana, but had recently moved to Fort Sam Houston, Texas. Interestingly, Martha later wrote to Vince: "You know, darling, Aunt Mary has her faults, as we all do, but honest, if it weren't for her, Angela would have had a tough time getting along with those two children."

Martha wrote to Vince on August 8, 1944, that the baby was "cranky" today. She was not sure whether he had a belly ache or whether he was cutting teeth, noting that he had been biting his little fist. Suz fixed the baby her old standby recipe, which consisted of a little warm water with a few drops of liquor and a little sugar. Martha wrote: "Whatever it was, he got over it and went to sleep until 15 minutes after his feeding time."

On August 8, 1944, Vince was on a tactical mission to bomb the German lines in the Caen area of France. Again he was a lead bombardier. The goal of this mission was to attack positions very close to the front lines of our Allied ground forces, and it called for absolute accuracy in bombing. A large concentration of German troops and materiel needed to be neutralized so that our troops could advance. Coordination with ground forces was essential. The bombing netted excellent results; tragically, however, 25 Canadians were killed and another 131 were wounded because American bombs accidentally fell on them when flak hit the lead aircraft in another squadron, causing their bombs to be released early. One B-17 was hit and went down. No chutes were observed.

Over the two-day period of August 7–8, more than 5,000 tons of bombs were dropped in support of the Canadian First Army offensive toward Falaise, France. While German troops retreated and many may have escaped on foot, very little in the way of motorized equipment was able to move after the American bombardment.

On August 10, 1944, Vince and a buddy were feeling kind of down. He wrote to Martha that to break the monotony "...we chased each other around with fire extinguishers, just like a bunch of kids. More fun though. Helped to pass the afternoon away. I swear, hon if I don't soon finish up, I'll go crazy around here. I don't know what it is, but something's got me." He wrote: "I can't go on much longer without you two." He informed Martha in this letter that his division was awarded a presidential citation for action back in January 1944, prior to his arrival in England. Nevertheless, Martha wrote: "Honey, I think it's wonderful about the group being awarded the Presidential Citation. I'm so very proud of you, darling, and love you so much." In response to Vince's comments about being down, she wrote: "Hon, I know just how you feel about being in the dumps. Somehow I too feel very low here of late. We'll just have to keep going, darling, and soon we will be together again. God grant that it will be very soon, darling."

On August 12, 1944, Vince was again assigned as lead bombardier, flying with Major Winget and Captain Gall. The target was a German fighter park at Chaumont, France, approximately 20 miles northeast of

Paris. This was a new landing site for enemy fighter planes, and Allied officials thought that it had assumed a very important role for the Germans. Vince led 36 planes in the bomb run, and the results were described as excellent. In all, 70 airplanes were involved in this attack, and the mission was accomplished without any problems. No flak or enemy fighters were encountered, and there was good American fighter support. In a letter dated August 13, 1944, Vince informed Martha that he had only two more missions to fly, and then he would be done.

On August 15, 1944, Martha had the sad duty to inform Vince that one of their five friends who had initially been reported as missing had actually been killed. Upon reading about this latest report of the death of their friend, Vince wrote back that the news was "shocking." He added: "It gripes me to no end when I think of all the good boys that have gone down over here. How I wish this darn thing would end."

In an effort to keep Vince informed about his little son, Martha wrote to Vince in mid-August: "Honest, hon, you should hear the baby laugh. Then when you get him real excited, he 'yells.'" She reported further that while the baby was in the backyard, propped up in his carriage, watching his diapers blowing in the breeze, he got hold of a lady's slip hanging on the clothesline and tore the lace. Martha wrote: "Can you imagine that, darling? Don't we have a destructive child, though?"

When Vince read that Martha's sister Rita was back home while Jack continued his training, he inquired as to where everyone slept at Suz and Willie's home. He had been wracking his brain trying to figure out where they all slept in their modest row house in Baltimore. At this time, there were Suz and Willie, Buster, Martha and the baby, Rita (who is now pregnant), Mary, Catherine, Butch and Joey. Martha simply responded: "Say, darling, we have plenty of sleeping quarters, so don't you worry about that! Do you know that before Rita came home, I had the whole front room bed for me, and Little Vince slept in his basket. Anyway, around our house, there has always been room for one more, and there always will be." Three days later, Martha purchased a crib for the baby. She wrote that the baby "laughed and yelled" when she put him in his new crib.

Martha and Vince continued to write about some additional movies that each saw and recommended to each other. Martha wrote that she saw *The Story of Dr. Wassell*, starring Gary Cooper. She thought it was wonderful but seemed to think that Vince had already seen it. Vince was able to catch *Christmas Holiday*, starring Deanna Durbin, which Martha had recommended earlier, and he enjoyed it. He also saw *Two Girls and a Sailor*, which he thought was wonderful and which was also recommended by Martha. In addition, Vince saw *Summer Storm*, starring George Sanders and Linda Darnell. Like others he had enjoyed, he recommended that Martha see this "wonderful" movie as well.

On August 17, 1944, Vince and a buddy went to town. He wrote: "When we started home is when the trouble started. I thought I knew a short cut, so we proceeded to cut thru some woods and fields. Well, after about an hour, I conceded that I was lost." After getting directions from some Englishmen, "...we finally found the road to the field, but it was about an hour later. I don't think I'll ever live it down. My legs feel like they are about to fall off from all the walking we did."

On Sunday, August 20, 1944, Vince and the fellows had been lying around in Alex's room all day. The reason they were there was because Alex was the only one with a heater in his room. Vince wrote: "I guess you're wondering why we want a heater in the middle of August. Well, to tell you the truth, I'm wondering myself. It'll really be good to get back to a country that has set weather. It's so unpredictable over here." Vince was having difficulty trying to write this particular letter due to "...six guys shooting the crap." He continued: "Every time more than three guys get together around here, every mission you've ever been on is the topic of conversation. Just like the mailman on his day off, taking a hike."

Vince wrote to Martha on August 21, 1944, and mentioned that he had been playing cards and chess with Alex at the officers' club. He wrote: "I get a kick out of playing chess with Alex. He taught me how to play and has yet to beat me. I'm not bragging or anything, but he gets so p_____ off, that I just sit there and laugh my head off at him." Vince went on to write about his squadron, the 326th: "It's funny about our sqd. Everybody is jealous of it. We are the only ones that ever throw a party, have the best bombing record in the group, almost the whole 8th Air Force. All the fellows get along good and promotions come thru pretty fast. The last five crews that came to this group all asked to be put in the 326th. Don't know how they found out about our sqd., but somewhere down the line we have a pretty good name." He continued: "I was supposed to go on pass today, but didn't find out until this afternoon. I told them where to stick it and would take my pass when I felt like. Us old crews get away with murder, but that's the way it should be."

The next day Vince wrote: "This life over here is sure starting to get me down. Same thing day in and day out. We have the run of the place and have sure been taking advantage of it. A lot of the single fellows are volunteering for another tour 'cause they've never had it so good."

On August 23, 1944, Major Glenn Miller and his orchestra played at Vince's air base. He mentioned that the drummer, Ray McKinley, stole the show. Vince wrote that Ray McKinley had a "top-notch orchestra of his own." Glenn Miller had just been promoted from captain to major during the past week. Major Miller was quite a hit with all the guys. Tragically, Glenn Miller presumably died when his plane went missing over the English Channel in December 1944. His body was never found.

Vince wrote that he was going over to division headquarters the next morning to take some kind of test. He was not sure what it was all about, but would let Martha know about it if he could. The next day he wrote: "I think that test I took today was a lot of hooie. They didn't get much from me. Half the stuff they asked us I had forgotten the day I graduated. Seems as though they want to get a mean average from lead combat bombardiers and navigators so they will have something to go by with new crews. Personally I don't think you can make lead teams by test. I believe it's the guys who are the luckiest." It sounds like my father was being a little bit cocky here, but at the same time modest.

Vince watched two reels of film on the invasion of New Britain by our ground forces and thought they were excellent. He wrote: "Those guys go through hell. We all bitch about conditions over here, and we have no right to. Why, we are living in heaven compared to those boys. I think I've done the last of my bitching for a long while."

On August 23, 1944, there was a write-up in each of Baltimore's then two daily newspapers regarding the accident that occurred on June 18, when Vince's crew lost its command pilot and the pilot had his foot blown off. The story received a fair amount of coverage and quoted the hometown native, Lieutenant Vince Gisriel. While everyone was very proud of Vince, including Martha, nevertheless, she was quite shaken up earlier that day. She wrote to Vince: "Well, Vince, I sure got a scare this morning. The phone rang, and it was for me. I was upstairs, so Mom asked if there was a message, and the man said 'No,' he wanted to talk to me. I came down, and it was a man from the *Sun* office. He said, 'Mrs. Gisriel, I have a report that Lieutenant Gisriel was in a plane crash in June, and I would like some details.' Vince, I almost died. I told him I didn't know anything about it, but he asked me a few questions, and I told him what I knew. I asked him what report he had, and he wouldn't tell me but said that it would be in the evening paper. Then, about 15 minutes later, a man from the *News Post* called. Now, I can't wait for the paper to come."

I can just imagine the initial shock my mother had when she heard the reporter's very first words: "Mrs. Gisriel, I have a report that Lieutenant Gisriel was in a plane crash...." and then "in June." Vince could not write to her about it. Martha had to hear it from an unknown reporter.

After reading the articles that appeared in the papers about Vince's crew and the dangerous situation that had occurred in the skies over Hamburg, Germany, Martha wrote to Vince: "Well darling, you're quite a hero so far as everyone who knows you is concerned." She continued: "Hon, my feelings are so mixed up, I don't know what to say. First of all, I think I'm grateful to God and His Blessed Mother for watching over you while in such danger. Then, I feel so sorry for Grubby. I knew that something had happened to him, but never dreamed it was anything so serious—but thank God that he is still alive. Then, I'm so happy and proud of you that I could jump up and down. Vince, I'm really glad that I didn't know all about it before. I probably would have gone crazy worrying.

Honey, were you hurt? Please tell me all you can, as I'm sure I know the worst of it now. I've been answering the phone all evening, hon."

Vince had become a real hometown hero. Many people knew about it within a few days. The nuns at the parish school knew about it and were proud of Vince. Doctor Brown brought it up to Martha right away when he saw her and the baby. A fellow at the telephone company called Martha and wanted to do an article on Vince for the company newsletter. Vince's father, who was stationed in Texas, sent Aunt Mary a clipping from a Dallas newspaper that ran the story. Apparently the Texas papers were full of the story because their "nearby hometown hero" was Grubby, from Sweetwater, Texas. What a true hero he was.

On August 26, 1944, Vince was off on another mission. The target was the Nordstern synthetic oil complex in Gelsenkirchen, Germany. This facility was described by the officer briefing for the mission as one of the three most important oil targets left in Germany, and this plant alone produced an estimated 10,000 tons of fuel per month. While no enemy fighters were encountered, the aircraft did draw intense gunfire from the ground, and the flak in the target area was intense and accurate. The lead airplane was hit by flak on the bomb run, making it difficult to keep the target in the bombsight optics. In spite of that, the bombing results were good. Colonel William Reid, their group commanding officer, was flying as command pilot in the lead plane, directing the entire mission. When his aircraft was hit with flak, he was injured. After receiving first aid, he returned to his duties and guided the formation safely home. Upon returning, it was discovered that Colonel Reid's plane had sustained damage to the hydraulic system, which meant they had no brakes. He ordered parachutes to be opened and trailed from the waist and the radio room, which caused the plane to swerve off the runway, but it stopped safely. Several planes had sustained battle damage. Vince's B-17 had flak damage and its number 4 (right wing) engine was shot out. The mission had excellent fighter support.

On the evening of August 28, 1944, Vince was sitting in his quarters listening to the radio. He had just picked up a program from Paris. He wrote: "The Parisians are going wild with joy. You could hear them, screaming and yelling and even crying. I guess I don't realize how it is to be subdued for four years." What a powerful moment for my father! In recent weeks, he had played a vital part in the liberation of France. How proud he must and should have felt as he listened to the joy that he had helped to achieve.

On August 29, 1944, Vince received an oak leaf cluster for his Distinguished Flying Cross and also one for his Air Medal, both for bombing enemy targets.

In her never-failing effort to keep Vince up to date with the baby, Martha wrote: "When I feed him his pabulum now, he just has to hold the spoon and then he blows (or something) when he gets a mouthful, and pabulum goes all over the place."

Back on August 21, 1944, Martha responded to the news that Vince only had two more missions to fly. She wrote: "Oh Vince, that's such wonderful news. I hope and pray that by the time you get this letter you will be all finished." In her second letter of the day, written later that evening, she informed Vince that on that afternoon she had made her novena for him, as usual. She had also lit three candles for him, as usual. However, on this particular day, she had lit a votive lamp in honor of the Blessed Mother for him. She added that the votive lamp would burn for nine days. She closed her letter, as usual, asking him to be careful and keep praying very hard, but "Harder than you've ever prayed before, hon."

Vince flew his last mission on August 30, 1944, exactly nine days after Martha lit the votive lamp. Vince led on his final mission. The target was the industrial center and docks around the port of Kiel, Germany. The officer conducting the preflight briefing characterized this target as of great importance to the German navy and submarine fleets. Thirty-six planes attacked the target. No enemy fighters were encountered, and the flak was moderate and inaccurate. A number of bomb-crew aviators described the American fighter support as the best they had ever seen. On Vince's last nine missions, he flew with seven different pilots.

Between July 1, 1944, and August 31, 1944, I have counted seven cards and 161 letters between Vince and Martha. Single-handedly, they kept the U.S. Postal Service afloat during the war years!

16

The Telegram

On or about September 1, 1944, Vince sent a telegram to Martha that simply read: "MISSIONS COMPLETED LOVE, VINCE GISIEIEL" As usual, someone botched the spelling of his last name. However, you can bet Martha knew who he was. Then on September 2, 1944, Vince wrote in a 12-page letter: "Just in case you haven't received the cable I sent, I have completed my missions. Isn't it wonderful, honey, I'm a 'man with a future'—Can hardly believe it's true. I finished up on the 30th. I guess you think I have forgotten how to write now that I'm through. I'm sorry about that, but believe me, this is the first chance I've had to write. A lot has happened since the 30th, and I hardly know where to begin."

He continued: "I'll begin from the time the engines stopped on that last one. What a feeling that was, hon. It's something unexplainable. You keep pinching yourself to make sure it isn't a dream. From the time we were briefed, I sweated. It seemed like the rest of my life depended on this one mission. Going over I was nervous and jumping, and even after bombs away, I knew the mission wasn't over. There was still that long trip home. Coming across the sea, all I could think of was hitting that runway and pulling to a stop. Finally the English coast was sighted; then I knew it wouldn't be long, but something could still happen. What a feeling it was when I saw the field—but nothing can compare to the sensational feeling that comes over you when you jump out of the plane. It's something that can't be explained."

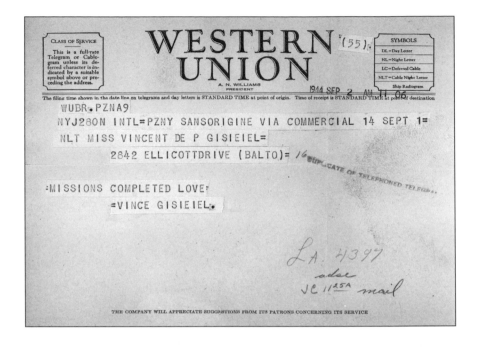

Vince had jumped out of that plane 34 previous times after dangerous missions. I am sure it was a relief each time, but he knew he would return to the skies again after each of the other missions. This one was different. He knew it was over for him. He had made it safely through all 35 missions, thanks to Almighty God, His Son, Jesus, the Holy Spirit and the Blessed Virgin Mary, in Whom Martha and Vince had constant hope and confidence. All their prayers were answered, and he knew it and he was ecstatic. Thanks to Martha for her prayerful vigilance.

A group of Vince's buddies were there to meet him as he came off his last mission. He was so happy to see them. They had a bottle of Scotch, and they insisted that Vince start it. Vince wrote: "I really didn't want it—I was so hungry. I didn't get to eat before going up. To be a sport I drank some. After all the congratulations and stuff we ran over to Danny's plane. He finished also. Well, he and I like to went crazy—hugging each other. The first bottle of Scotch was gone by now, so the boys pulled out another one, and Danny started that one." He continued: "Altogether

7 fellows finished up, so you can imagine how the club was after the mission. I was so tired and happy I couldn't drink, but stayed there and really had fun."

Vince continued his letter of September 2, telling Martha that early the next morning, he set out to visit his brother-in law, Charles. His sister, Angela, who was married to Charles, had hoped that Vince would have the opportunity to visit with her husband since they were both stationed in England, and Vince knew that this might be his only opportunity to see Charles before going back to the States. He took a chance and headed for a town near where he thought Charles's camp might be. With the assistance of the Red Cross Club there, he was able to find Charles in a short time and arranged to meet him later that night. They had only about four hours to spend together, but they had a great time catching up with each other. Vince found Charles to be looking "superb."

Afterwards, Charles drove Vince to Bristol, where they got lost searching for the train station but had a lot of fun looking. Once they found it, Vince caught a late train to London, where he met up with Danny and some other buddies. The next afternoon they headed back to the airfield. They arrived there four hours late because they could not catch an earlier train, and missed a party put on by the 326th Squadron, one that they had planned to make their own farewell party.

Upon arrival they learned that everyone had been looking for Vince and Danny because their orders to head for the 12th R.C.D. (replacement center) had arrived. Vince continued his long letter: "You could have knocked me over with a feather. They usually take about eight days. That's when my troubles started. Here I wasn't packed, nor cleared the field [processed out for reassignment], and I was going around like crazy. I had to get up early this morning and start clearing the field. I would never have made it today. Luckily we are leaving tomorrow morning. I'm still not completely packed. Now do you see why I haven't written? I've been on the go constantly, and will probably be from now on. If you don't hear from me every day from now on, you know it's because they've got me running." Vince wrote this letter while very tired. He informed Martha that he had only slept about 12 hours in the last three days.

On that same day, September 2, 1944, Martha wrote to Vince that she had received his cable regarding the completion of his missions. She wrote: "Well, darling, I'm so happy that I could cry, laugh and do almost anything. I received your cable this morning and Vince, I'm so thankful to God and His Blessed Mother for protecting you during the course of your missions. You don't know how relieved I feel, and everyone else does also." She continued: "I hope they won't keep you over there, darling. Oh, Vince, I'm so excited that I can hardly write…Gee, I hope you'll soon be home so you can see your little son. I was telling Little Vince about the cable I received, and he laughed. I'm sure he knows what it's all about, Vince, because he's been so excited today."

Vince arrived at the replacement center on or about September 3, 1944. He sent a letter to Martha dated September 4, 1944, and wrote: "Just a quickie to let you know I arrived safely at the 12th R.C.D.—my first step to getting home. Don't know how long I will be here—probably anywhere from 10 days to two weeks or maybe longer. It's quite a job sending a man home, you know. Will be kept very busy here, so in case you don't hear from me, don't worry. Roger!" He continued: "Everything has happened in such a hurry, I don't know what end is up. I still can't believe it's all true. That's all I have time for now. I love you both dearly. Won't be too long now, darlings. Just keep your chin up, and I'll be home before you know it. Then I can really show you my love for you." He ended: "May God and His Blessed Mother bless and protect you always…"

On that same date, Martha wrote to Vince: "Boy, the proverb of, 'Like Father, Like Son' sure is true about you two. As far as I'm concerned, you are both perfect, and everything I hoped and prayed for all my life. I thank God every day for having both of you." She continued: "…I love you much more than anything in this world. I love you so very much, my heart aches. I miss you so much, it's pathetic, and it gets worse and worse as the seconds pass by. Little Vince loves and misses you very much also. We both hope and pray that you will be home with us very, very soon. Please be very careful, darling, and keep praying very hard." She ended: "May God and His Blessed Mother bless you and protect you always…"

For the last several months, Martha and Vince had ended almost every letter this way.

On September 5, 1944, Vince wrote a V-mail to Martha from the replacement center: "I know how you hate to receive V-mail, but everything is such a secret here I hardly have anything to say. Don't have very much time to say it, either. I guess it's best you stop writing me, as I won't be here by the time your letters get here. Unless you hear different, you can stop writing." On September 13, 1944, Martha wrote: "Well darling, I received your short but very, very sweet V-mail today. It sure made me feel good when I read that I'd better stop writing because you would probably be home before you received my mail. I'm going to keep writing to you anyway, hon." Two days later, Martha wrote: "Well hon, I didn't write to you this afternoon because I thought I'd stop writing. But I just had to write. Somehow I feel so much closer when I write to you." Even though Martha continued to write, it appears that all of her mail postmarked on or after August 22, 1944, never reached Vince until weeks later. Some September 1944 letters apparently did not catch up with him until November.

It obviously was important to Martha to keep writing. On September 5, 1944, she wrote "Happy Anniversary" to Vince, acknowledging that they had been married fifteen months earlier. She was hoping and praying that "…we will be together to celebrate our 16-month anniversary." She wrote in this letter: "I received two wonderful letters from you this morning, darling, and they sure made me feel wonderful. Your letters are sure comforting, darling." She continued: "Listen honey, you know I don't mind you're not writing to me when you are so tired, or busy, either. You've been wonderful about writing to Little Vince and me so often. I know I couldn't have stood being separated from you so long without your cheerful letters. I know that you write whenever it is possible, so what more could I ask of you? You're just a darling, that's all. I love you so much."

Martha wrote to Vince that she had to walk the baby to sleep for about an hour one evening. She added: "That's gonna be your job, honey. Just kidding!" She also informed Vince that the baby "…is eating me out of house and home." He is closing in on 16 pounds.

Martha reflected on Vince's accomplishments in completing his missions and his being a lead bombardier when she wrote on September 6, 1944: "Say, darling, I'm sure proud of you, and so is Little Vince. You really must have done a good job, darling. I knew you would, though. You are the kind of a person who will do what you are supposed to, no matter how difficult it might be. I love you so much, hon. You're just superb, that's all." She ended this letter by expressing her love in yet another creative way by writing: "My love for you grows and grows as the seconds pass, and even now it is higher than heaven's highest cloud, and way down below the oceans." A few days later she wrote that "…there just aren't any words in the world, to tell you how very much I love you."

On September 7, 1944, Martha wrote that she and her sister Rita took the baby down to St. Edward's School to visit the nuns. She stated that "…they were very glad to see the baby. He really performed for them, laughing and carrying on. They were all holding him and they were really having fun. You know, most babies cry when they see those black habits, but not 'Our Little Punkin.' It makes them feel good when the babies don't cry, so they think Little Vince is swell." Later I attended first and second grade at St. Edward's School. Who knows—I may have been trying to figure out a way to obtain good grades by charming the nuns at a very young age.

On September 9, 1944, Vince sent Martha another V-mail from the replacement center stating: "Just a note to let you know I am OK and thinking of you often. There just isn't anything I can say to you as to what I am doing here. You will just have to sit tight and wait."

Martha had called Angela to inform her that Vince was coming home and that he had visited with her husband, Charles. Angela was very excited to hear both pieces of news. She wrote to Vince on September 11, 1944, to express her excitement and to express her appreciation for his visiting Charles. She could not wait to see Vince when he returns and to hear all about Charles. Angela had been out in the country helping to run Charles's family farm due to the serious illness of one of his relatives. She had been very busy there with all the chores and cooking for her in-laws. She acknowledged that her letter writing had suffered quite a bit lately because of all her added responsibilities, which included taking care of her twins. She wrote to Vince: "The twins have been so damn bad since we've been out here—I don't know what to do with them. I have to keep my eyes on them every second. Four times this afternoon I had to climb in the pigpen to get them out of there—also in the chicken houses." The twins were 2½ years old. They were quickly becoming farm boys.

Martha wrote to Vince on September 11, 1944: "Rita received a letter from Jack this morning, and he told her that he was getting his shots. Gosh, it looks as though he's getting ready to go overseas. I sure wish something would turn up to delay his going at least until after the baby is born. I feel sorry for anyone who has to go over there. I certainly wish this darn thing was over."

Martha also informed Vince that the International League Baltimore Orioles won the pennant by "one point." It was the first time they had won in 19 years, and 25,000 fans greeted them at Penn Station upon their return home. At first I thought my mother meant they won by one run, but I checked into it. She was referring to the fact that the Orioles ended their season with a record of 84 wins to 68 losses, while the Newark Bears had a record of 85–69. Mathematically, the Orioles would have had a won-loss percentage of .552, while the Bears had a .551 percentage. Thus, the Orioles actually won the pennant by .001, or one tenth of one percent!

The Orioles went on to defeat the Louisville Colonels in the Junior World Series. Interestingly, the last game of the Junior Series at Baltimore's Municipal Stadium drew over 20,000 more fans than the last game of the 1944 Major League World Series held in St. Louis. That year the Major League World Series was known as the "Streetcar Series" or the "St. Louis Showdown" because it was between the St. Louis Cardinals and the St. Louis Browns. The fact that the Baltimore game drew a larger crowd is said to have contributed to Baltimore eventually obtaining a Major League franchise. Ironically, it was the St. Louis Browns who would move to Baltimore ten years later to become the current Major League Baltimore Orioles. In all fairness, Baltimore's Municipal Stadium had a larger seating capacity than St. Louis's Sportman's Park. After the fire that destroyed the previous Oriole Park, the International League Orioles moved to the bigger Municipal Stadium.

Martha further wrote that Little Vince was "...so glad that you are finished over there. He is anxiously awaiting your return, darling. He loves you so much, just like his mother!"

On September 12, 1944, Martha wrote to Vince to acknowledge that she read that he had arrived safely at the replacement center, and she was glad for that news. She wrote further: "Well darling, our little son weighs almost 16¼ lbs. now, and is a little over 26½ in. tall. Now, can you imagine what a brute he is? He's so cute, I could eat him up. Every day he gets more like you, and that makes me very happy."

Vince sent Martha what appears to be his last letter from overseas on September 13, 1944. He wrote: "Another quickie to let you know everything is still alright. I guess you've been worrying 'cause you haven't heard from me. Well don't, hear, honey? I'm sorry for not writing very often, but I expected to leave here a couple of days ago. Just say a little prayer and I'll be home before you know it. I can hardly wait to get home. It's been a long time now, and I am missing you more every second." He continued: "I'm hoping some mail reaches me soon. It's been two weeks now since I've had a letter from you. They are holding all our mail up someplace, but I don't know where."

On the evening of September 14, 1944, Martha received a telephone call from one of Vince's buddies, who had just flown to New York from England a few days earlier and had seen Vince before his departure. Vince had asked the fellow to call Martha when he arrived in Baltimore, primarily to let her know that her husband was fine but still waiting to leave for home. At this point, Martha figured that Vince could not be too far behind his friend in the process of returning to the United States. She wrote: "I hope you fly, because you'll be home so much sooner. If you were to walk in the door right this minute, it wouldn't be too soon for me."

Since she had received very few letters from Vince while he had been at the replacement center, Martha had become quite anxious about his return home. She wrote on September 15, 1944: "I didn't get any mail from you, darling, so maybe you're on your way. Gosh, darling, I sure hope you are." Then, on September 20, 1944, she wrote: "Well, honey, no mail again today, so I guess you know how I feel. Gosh, honey, I'm just on edge waiting for you to call me or walk in." By September 23, 1944, there was still no recent mail from Vince. Martha wrote: "Well, honey, no mail again today. I'm hoping that you are almost home now, darling. Gosh, hon, I just can't wait, and neither can Little Vince. I tell him that you will be home soon, and he does everything but talk to me. He's getting awfully big, Vince. I hope and pray that you will be home to see him very soon." She continued: "Well, hon, I went downtown again today, and I finally got two dresses and a pair of shoes. One of the dresses is a blue wool, and the other is a black crepe. I was especially interested in getting a nice black dress for when you come home. Well, I didn't get exactly what I wanted, but I do like the one I got. In fact, I like everything I bought and hope you will too."

Martha was really beginning to get anxious, for on September 24, 1944, she wrote to Vince: "Gosh, honey, I thought sure you would be home by today. I've been a total wreck ever since I received the cable, just waiting for you to come home. I'll try to be patient, though." Martha wrote Vince yet another letter, on the evening of September 25, 1944. However, Vince must have arrived home on September 26, 1944, because Martha's letters stopped as of September 25, and she didn't write again until October 29, 1944. Martha and Vince had not seen each other since mid-February, 1944. They had been separated for over seven months.

Between September 1 and 25, 1944, I have counted one card, one telegram, two V-mails and 40 letters between Martha and Vince.

Needless to say, there was great joy and happiness in Baltimore when Vince finally arrived home. Words could not describe the relief my mother had upon his arrival. I can only imagine the joy in my father's heart when he returned home to Martha and at the moment he met me for the first time in person. So many people were genuinely delighted to see Vince back home safe and sound. I cannot find the appropriate words to express my appreciation to Our Almighty Father for how He protected my dad. My father made it back from England with hardly a scratch. I am convinced that it was Martha's and Vince's faith, prayers and devotion to Our Almighty Father that brought him back safely. Reading about their strong faith has rekindled my own faith in God. Reading and writing about my parents has been a real blessing for me. It is something I will always treasure.

On October 1, 1944, Sister Dorothy sent a note to Vince stating: "Just want to join with the folks in giving you a glad 'welcome back' to the good old U.S.A.—and to rejoice with you in the happy reunion of which good old Baltimore is the scene. I know you are grateful to God and His Blessed Mother that you have been preserved safe thru the many dangers and hardships that have been yours during the past months. God grant that you may enjoy every moment with your precious little wife, darling son and cherished loved ones! You deserve it. Be assured of my continued love and prayers."

From all indications, Martha and Vince were together from September 26, 1944, until October 28, 1944. After what would have been a long and well-deserved rest and stay at home, it appears that they finally had the opportunity to go on a honeymoon of sorts. Vince was sent to Miami, Florida, from approximately October 22 until October 28, 1944, in preparation for his next assignment. He was able to take Martha with him. They stayed at the Sovereign Hotel. Both suffered a sunburn while in sunny Florida.

17

The Best Bombardier
in the Whole Wide World

Prior to their departure from Florida, Martha and Vince said good-bye to each other on October 28, 1944, while standing on her train bound for Baltimore. Vince then went to another station and boarded a train bound for Fort Worth, Texas. The next day, from his train he wrote: "I don't have to tell you how much I miss you. Saying good-bye to you last night was like cutting my heart out. When I stepped off your train I was afraid to look back again. I know I couldn't have stood seeing you leave." He continued: "Darling, until we are together again, don't worry too much. When you get to thinking about things just pick up Little Giz and he'll tell you how much he and I love you. It won't be long before all three of us are together again." He ended: "I love you both beyond all possible thoughts and words, and miss you the same." "Giz" was a nickname for all the Gisriel boys for at least the last three generations, since Gisriel is pronounced "Giz-ree-ool" by most of us. Even my two daughters, Beth and Emily, were called "Little Giz" and "Baby Giz" in their younger years and are even to this day by friends of their older brothers.

Likewise, Martha wrote on October 29, 1944, from her train: "...I sure miss you, Vince. Gosh, I've been a sad-looking sack ever since I left you. Hon, I sure am a sissy. After you left me last night, I came to my seat and was sitting here, just crying my eyes out..." She continued: "I'm very anxious to see 'Punky.' I'll tell him what you told me to, and I'll kiss him a whole lot every day for you. Vince, I've made up my mind that no matter where you go, Little Giz and I are going with you. Hon, I just can't stand being away from you. I only hope and pray that you will be sent to a decent place. There I go, griping again. Vince, don't think I'm not thankful that you're in Texas, in preference to being in combat. I thank God every day for sending you back to me and Punky, and shall, every day of my life. I promise not to gripe any more, darling." Apparently, "Punky" was one of my new nicknames.

Vince was on his way to Midland, Texas, where he would attend instructor school. Somewhere in Georgia, the railroad switched the cars on his train and he found out there was no dining car. He did not eat from the time he left Florida the previous evening until 3:00 o'clock the next afternoon, when he had a box lunch. When his train arrived in Montgomery, Alabama, there was an hour and a half layover. He wrote: "…you can imagine where I headed for. That's right, the closest café. Had a delicious sirloin steak with French fries, slaw, peach pie à la mode, milk and coffee. I'm telling you I was starved. It cost me, but it was well worth it." In Montgomery, they switched trains yet again. This time, he was on a "Streamliner."

The next morning, Vince woke up in New Orleans, where he had several hours of layover. He joined some other officers traveling with him and ate breakfast and lunch in New Orleans. He wrote to Martha on October 30, 1944, noting that he would arrive in Fort Worth sometime the next day. He wrote: "…I'll be glad to get off of this buggy." He continued: "One consolation I have today is I know your trip is over. I guess everybody was glad to see you, especially Little Giz. How's the little guy? Missed you like all heck, huh? Can't blame him for that; look what he was missing—You." Further, he stated: "Here it's only been two days since we parted, but golly, it seems like weeks. Let's pray that we three can be together again very soon." He signed this letter "Daddy Giz."

By October 30, 1944, Martha was home, having arrived in Baltimore at 6:20 AM. She wrote to Vince: "I made it very plain, when I came home, that if you went someplace decent after Midland, Punky and I were going with you. Much to my surprise, there weren't any remarks made. Mom said that if that would make us happy, then it's the thing to do. She also said that she thought Little Vince would make a good traveler, because he is such a toughy."

On October 31, 1944, Vince sent a cable to Martha telling her that he had arrived in Fort Worth safely. Later that evening, he wrote that he had just pulled into Midland, Texas. He and three others were staying over in Midland at the Hotel Scharbauer. They were due in camp the next day. He wrote: "Had my first bath in four days, and I feel like a new man. Really needed it." He wrote to Martha that when the train passed through Sweetwater, Texas, he got off and inquired about Grubby. He spoke with a man who knew Grubby well, and he learned that Grubby was home with his wife and baby boy. He also learned that Grubby did not have his artificial foot yet. Vince hoped to see him while he was stationed in Texas. He signed this letter "Papa Giz."

Keep in mind that Martha and Vince had been together from prior to October 1, 1944 to October 28, 1944. Yet, from the 29th of October until the 31st, I have counted one card, one telegram and 6 letters between them.

On November 1, 1944, Vince arrived at the Central Instructor School (CIS) of the Army Air Force at Midland, Texas. On that day, he wrote to Martha: "Good evening, darlings, here I am at the base, and all I can say is, give me a discharge. This isn't such good news, but it's a fact. We'll probably be here from 9 to 12 weeks and there's nothing much I can do about it. The instructor school is 9 weeks and I probably won't start for 3 more weeks. I'm working on a leave, but it looks hopeless, and I mean hopeless." Reading this prompted Martha to write two days later: "Vince, darling, that sure (t's) me off, to hear that you are just sitting around down there. Can you understand this army? I can't, but then maybe it's me. They rushed you through Miami, for what? To let you sit around in 'God's Country' for three weeks."

Vince continued his November 1 letter: "The post is much better than I expected; in fact it's nice. Very clean and pretty big. The town of Midland isn't bad either, but the housing condition is awful. There just isn't a house to be found. One guy that brought his wife out had to leave her in a town 104 miles away. How about that!" He signed this letter "Big Giz."

Martha wrote to Vince on November 1, 1944: "I've sure been down in the dumps ever since you left me at that train Saturday night. As always, though, your letter perked me up." She continued: "Well, darling, Jack left this morning. Poor Reets was crying, so I did too. Honest, I guess I'm not very patriotic, but I just can't understand why people who love one another have to be separated. But honey, I'm sure going to go with you after you leave Midland." Martha ended her letter: "...I love you with every ounce of life in me. I could never explain how very much I love you really, darling, because my love for you increases as the seconds pass by. I miss you very, very much, and hope and pray that we will be together very, very soon. Little Vince loves and misses you very much also." She signed this letter "Mrs. Giz and Little Giz." She even signed a few letters as "Mama Giz" or "Mommie Giz."

On November 3, 1944, Vince had the opportunity to call Martha long distance. She wrote on that date: "Well, darling, I didn't get any mail from you today, so I guess you know how blue I was. But Vince, you're sure an angel, 'cause you always do something to pick me up when I'm awful low. Yeah, hon, it was that wonderful phone call. Vince, I'm so glad you called me. I've just been on pins and needles since I left you, so it was wonderful to hear your voice." Vince wrote on November 3 as well: "It was wonderful hearing your voice again, and it was just what I needed to boost my morale." Martha wrote later in the month that their long-distance calls cost $19.68 for the billing period. The call from Midland on November 3 was $8.05 plus tax. Martha and Vince thought they only spoke for about a minute, but apparently they did not. That was a lot of money in 1944; however, it was important for them to be "in touch."

Martha continued in her November 3 letter: "Honey, I think I know how you feel down there, 'cause I feel the same way. I try to keep busy so the time will go faster until I can be with you, but it just won't work. I'm busy all right, but I just stop doing things and sit and think of you, and that ain't good. Little Giz sure helps my morale a lot, but then he is so dear and sweet to me, and I love him so much, just like he's you, that I miss you even more. (I wouldn't dare read this over, because I know I can't put down on paper what I'm trying to tell you.) Anyway, Vince, it all boils down to this. I can't stand being away from you, and I couldn't stand being away from Little Giz either, so I'm going to hit the road as soon as you'll let me. Now don't get me wrong, hon. I understand very well that we can't be together while you are down in Midland. I really want to be there though, honey. But even if you go clear to California, we're going, too."

Partly because there wasn't much else to do, on the evening of November 3, 1944, Vince and some buddies went to a local high school football game, where Midland was playing San Angelo, Texas. In his letter he reported that it was a "walk away" for San Angelo. When they left the game "…the score was 50 to 7 and they were still going strong." He enjoyed the game even though it was one sided. He wrote: "They really go in for high school football down here. Even broadcasted it over the radio."

Vince had asked Martha what she wanted for Christmas. Her response was: "…I know what I want for Christmas. I want you, so I'm coming down to see you. I'll tell you more about that later, but I'll see you before you leave Midland." Vince responded to Martha's inquiry as to what he wanted for Christmas by asking for a radio if she could even find one—it was difficult with the war on. He also mentioned that he could always use some Jockey shorts and tee shirts. He further mentioned cigarettes, particularly his brand, Pall Mall. However, he wrote: "What I really want for Christmas, and not all that, is you and Little Giz, lock, stock, and barrel. I might not have you, but I'll be with you spiritually, as I always am."

On November 4, 1944, Vince wrote that he had started the Novena of the Seven Sorrows to the Blessed Mother. On November 5, 1944, Martha wrote that she had started another Novena to the Sacred Heart for Vince. They continued to be very connected, even so many miles apart. In this letter, she further wrote: "Joey just kissed me good-night and told me to 'write to Vince and say I love him.'" Joey was going on two and a half years of age.

I would be remiss if I did not write about my Uncle Joe Owens. Joe is Martha's youngest brother, who was born in June 1942, shortly after Martha and Vince met. Martha was 20 years old when her mom and dad had their eighth child, Joseph. During the many months when Martha and Vince were separated, particularly when he was in England and prior to the birth of their first child, Martha spent a great amount of time with her baby brother. Joe was a great source of joy and happiness during a time when she was lonely for Vince. As Joe grew into a toddler, she simply enjoyed his presence and companionship, as though he were her own. Not only was Joe a pure pleasure for Martha, but it is obvious from her many letters that he brought real sunshine and happiness into the Owens household during a bleak time in our nation's history. It is also obvious that there was much joy and happiness in the Owens family, period. They were a close-knit, good Catholic family who loved God and each other as much as any family could. Suz and Willie did a great job in raising their children. I had the privilege of growing up close to my grandparents, aunts and uncles. Believe me, it was a happy experience. Joe and I were basically raised as cousins even though he was technically my uncle. However, as I reflect back, he was really like a brother to me, and I love him as such.

On November 4, 1944, Vince wrote to Martha that he was to begin taking a couple of classes a day on Monday, November 6. This was earlier than he thought, and he hoped that he would complete the course sooner than he thought. Perhaps Martha's sentiments regarding how the army seemed to waste so much time were felt somewhere up the chain of command. However, on November 6, 1944, Vince wrote to Martha: "Grab hold of something, honey because this is funny. Tomorrow I am off for San Angelo. Yep, I'm being transferred again. It beats me what the deal is. Rumors say they have opened up a CIS there to take care of the overflow here. Sounds logical anyway. Will have to let you know more about it when I get there. All of Class 45-2 is going there. We were supposed to have left at 3 o'clock this afternoon. We found out at 2, so you can imagine—we didn't make it. Leaving around noon tomorrow." Vince continued: "I guess you wonder why I think it's funny; well, really honey, it is. You'd have to know Midland AAF to appreciate it. Their heads are so far up their _____ (and locked) it's pitiful. They go around in a trance all the time. I'm kind of glad I'm leaving, even though I am unpacked and settled. The town of San Angelo is about 80 miles S.E. of here. It is much bigger, and they say housing conditions are much better. I feel sorry for the fellows that got their wives settled in Midland or Odessa. Most of them had to pay a month's salary in advance. The guy I was telling you about that had his wife in Fort Stockton just got his wife and kid settled this morning; now he's off again."

Vince continued his November 6, 1944 letter: "Well, I got 1 hour and 5 minutes flying time in today. Flew with 3 Negro cadets. Oh, yeah, I forgot to tell you they have Negro cadet bombardiers. In fact a class of them graduated Saturday. They're pretty sharp, too. I wasn't instructing them or anything. Just went along for the ride."

He further continued: "Met a guy today that was in the same hospital with Grubby in England. He said when the subject of bombardiers was brought up all Grubby would talk about was his bombardier."

In response to Martha's letter dated November 3, 1944, Vince ended this letter writing: "I just read your letter over for the third time, and the more I read it the better I like it. Especially the part where you can't live without me or Little Giz and you are going to hit the road. That's music to my ears, 'cause, darling I want you so much to come. I also realize it won't be right away but it will be, and very soon I hope. I'm sorry to disappoint you—that is, about your seeing me before I leave Midland. Guess you'd better make that San Angelo, now, huh?"

Within a few days, Martha responded: "Vince, it's good you told me to get a grip on myself when you told me that you had been transferred. Golly, Vince, I'm still confused about it. You be sure to let me know what the deal is and how long you will be there and when you start, etc. Also if you know whether or not you get a choice, when you finish up. Honest, Vince, it's enough to give you gray hair wondering what this army is going to do next. However, I'm glad that you are being transferred to a nicer field, or town, anyway. And listen, honey, I'll see you in San Angelo, before you leave. (if I have anything to do with it!)." She added:

"Was glad you ran into someone who knew Grubby. I know that Grubby thinks very highly of you, Vince, because when Ann Mogg went to see him at Mitchell Field, all he did was talk about how brave you were and how much he thought of you."

In her letter of November 6, 1944, Martha went on to acknowledge that she and Vince were in agreement about her joining him when his current course was complete. She wrote: "I think we both feel the same way, honey, 'cause sometimes it's all I can do to keep from crying. Then, sometimes, there just isn't any way to keep from crying, so I do. I feel better for a while, but then that empty feeling comes back."

On November 6, 1944, the eve of the 1944 presidential election, Martha wrote about it. Apparently, she and Vince had a friendly disagreement as to who should be the next president. She wrote: "Say, honey, if I could only be with you, I wouldn't even argue about who the best man is." She continued: "I'm really a Democrat, but I don't think it's democratic for one man to be in office so long. I just hope that the 'right man' goes in." Franklin D. Roosevelt was about to be elected president for his fourth consecutive term. The 22nd Amendment to the U.S. Constitution, which limits the president to serving no more than two four-year terms, was proposed in March 1947 and ratified in February 1951. Martha was ahead of her time!

Martha wrote to Vince on November 7, 1944, predicting the outcome of the election: "By the way, darling, I think your man is going to win!" She also informed Vince that she finally saw the movie *Going My Way*, with Bing Crosby. She wrote: "Golly, it was good. I thoroughly enjoyed it." Perhaps it inspired her closing in this particular letter, when she wrote: "Vince, there has never been a song or story written that would express my feelings for you."

Vince arrived at the San Angelo Army Air Field on November 7, 1944, to attend instructor school at Concho Field there. He wrote to Martha on November 9, 1944: "I have a little dope for you on this CIS, or what is going to happen to us after the course. The director of training talked to us today, and he gave us the big picture. We are divided into three categories while we are here. One, those who want to stay in the training command and instruct cadets; Two, those who want to go back overseas; and Three, those who want neither one nor two will be sent to the air forces. They are the three categories, and you get your choice of one, or I should say, you apply for one; whether or not you get it remains to be seen. There are two classes graduating the same time, one at Midland and one here. Both have 200 officers in them. Out of the 400 officers, 125 will remain in the Training Command to instruct cadets. No one is asking for #2 category except the crazy men, and I'm not one of them. So that leaves the rest to go to air forces."

Vince continued: "Now here's my trouble. I don't know whether to ask for One or Three, and I want your advice on it. If I get in One, I'll be instructing cadets either in Texas or New Mexico, but my chance of going back overseas is very small. Now if I get in Three, I might get closer to home, but in the air forces you don't know what will happen to you." He was referring to the four divisions of the air force; namely the first, which was in the northern and eastern states; the second, in the central and southeast states; the third, in the Gulf Coast region; and the fourth, on the West Coast.

Vince continued his detailed letter: "I myself would rather be in the air forces, but I'm a little scared that after 6 to 12 months they might put me on a crew again. Chances are 10 to 1 they won't, but you can never tell. Darling, what do you think I ought to do, or should I just let things ride and let them decide. *Please send your advice.* Remember tho, that what ever I ask for, I still might not get it." He wrote further: "Oh, yeah—if you get One, you have to go back to Midland for three more weeks of training unless you are to instruct at San Angelo, and then you take the three weeks here. That's the big picture. I hope you can make heads and tails out of it. I'm afraid to go back and read this—it'll confuse me too much." He continued: "Went in town tonight to look the place over. Found S. Angelo to be a pretty good town."

Vince painstakingly laid out the various scenarios to Martha as best he could, pointing out the benefits and the pitfalls of each. He was hoping for some guidance, but he probably realized that the ultimate decision would have to be his to make. I am sure that uppermost in his mind was what was best for his family. Later Martha wrote: "Well, honey, I'm just as confused as you are as to what you should apply for. Golly, Vince, I don't know what to say. I don't think I could stand having you go overseas again, honey. So please try to get something that will keep you over here."

On November 8, 1944, Martha wrote: "Well, darling, I see your 'boss' won. That's an awfully long time for one man to be in office, but they say that everything happens for the best, sooooo!"

Vince wrote to Martha and Little Vince on November 10, 1944: "I love you both so much it's hard to put it into writing. For you, Punky, my son, it's a love no father on earth can equal, and you, Tanny, my wife, it's a love no husband on earth can equal. Husbands and fathers have loved, but theirs is only a drop in the bucket compared to mine. Mine is something out of this world." He asked Martha in this letter: "Do you have any idea about when you and Giz should start hitting the road? Let me know what you think about it, darling. Until tomorrow I love you both with a burning Love that will last forever." "Tanny" was just one of the many nicknames my father had for my mother. I keep thinking it may have been short for "Tangerine," one of my father's favorite songs of that era. However, I have not yet been able to confirm it.

On November 11, 1944, Martha wrote to Vince acknowledging the fact that he had been in the service now exactly two years to the day. She wrote: "Gosh, it seems so much longer than that." When you consider what they had endured to this point, I can understand why my mother would feel that way. Perhaps it was coincidental that Vince would have left for active duty on Armistice Day, November 11, which we now call Veterans Day.

On November 12, 1944, Vince wrote that he might finish the course at San Angelo by December 16, 1944. He could not figure out how they could finish the course in that short time frame. However, he did state that they would be going to class from 8:00 AM until 6:00 PM, six days per week. He also wrote that he hit the jackpot again by receiving four letters the previous day and two cards, three photos and seven letters on that day, apparently all from Martha. Some of it was mail just catching up with him because of his frequent moving about. On that same day, Martha wrote and informed Vince of yet another friend who had been reported as missing in action.

They continued to exchange information and recommendations regarding motion pictures that they saw. Vince saw *Mrs. Parkington*, starring Greer Garson and Walter Pidgeon, and suggested it to Martha. Martha saw *Greenwich Village*, with Don Ameche and Carmen Miranda, and wrote that it was a pretty good movie. Later, Vince saw *And Now Tomorrow* and thought it was "swell." He wrote to Martha: "I think you'd like it very much. Don't miss it if you can help it." Even later, Martha wrote that she saw *Kansas City Kitty*, starring Joan Davis. She really enjoyed this movie "…because it was light, and no war."

Vince finally started classes on November 13, 1944. He had five hours of navigation and one hour of physical training. He wrote: "The P.T. is what hurt. I went out there and knocked myself out. I'm really in p____ poor shape. Was blowing like a horse after 10 minutes. You know, it's been nine months since I've had any athletics to speak of. Sure glad we only have three hours a week. Maybe by the time I get out of here I'll be in good shape." Vince explained to Martha that he had to finish 90 hours of navigation in the course. The next day he wrote: "Talk about somebody being stiff—boy, I could hardly move when I got up this morning—you know, from those athletics yesterday. I believe every bone and muscle in my body must have been affected. I'll probably feel better after a couple days of P.T."

Martha had advised Vince that they had $500 saved up. He wrote: "Honey, I think that's swell that we have $500 in the bank…Won't be long before we'll have a nice big down payment on that house of ours."

On November 14, 1944, Martha wrote that while she wants to be with Vince very much, she thought that perhaps she should not join him with the baby until he is "sort of permanently settled." She was thinking that probably will occur sometime after he completed his current course at San Angelo. She wrote: "If I had anything to do with it, Vince, we'd be with you already." She continued: "Vince, I can't understand it, but I'm nearly crazy being away from you. I understand it really, it's 'cause I love you so very much. When you were overseas, I knew that I couldn't be with you, but now I just can't bear being away from you."

In her letter to Vince dated November 15, 1944, Martha mentioned Thanksgiving. She wrote: "I guess you know that Baltimore is celebrating Thanksgiving Day on Nov. 23, while Texas still observes the old date, Nov. 27. (That's something you can give your 'boss' credit for, hon. He changed the date!)" Vince would later explain that while most of Texas celebrated Thanksgiving later in the month, in the service it was also changed to the 23rd. He wrote: "I'm in the army, remember (as if you could forget) and when the 'boss' says it's to be the 23rd, it's the 23rd."

Separation was starting to affect Vince again. On November 16, 1944, he wrote: "I love you both so much it hurts. Doesn't hurt because I love you, but because we aren't together like we should be. I need you both so much, but yet I know we can't be together for a while. It just gripes the heck out of me. Why do people that love each other as much as we do have to be separated? I guess that is something that can't be answered. Must be fate."

By November 17, 1944, Vince was still focusing on which category to request for future assignment. He had thought about it and discussed his options with an instructor. He explained to Martha that while he would probably have to remain out west, the training command would probably keep him out of combat the longest. He also pointed out that the hours of work were more predictable; his instructors were currently working eight hours a day, with Saturdays and Sundays off. He wrote: "I'm almost hoping I'll stay here. It shouldn't be too hard to find a place to live, and I think you'd like it here." Vince's instructor offered to sign him up as requesting an instructor job, and Vince said yes.

Martha wrote to Vince on November 17, 1944: "Say, hon, did you know that the Army-Navy game was shifted to Baltimore? Anyway, there has been quite a feud about it. The Sec. of the Treasury went to Washington to see if he could have the game in Philadelphia and 'your boss' said no! Then Sen. Tydings (Maryland) went and asked if it could be played here, and 'your boss' said yes! How about that?" Martha never referred to the president by his name; she always referred to him as "your boss" when writing to Vince. Apparently Martha was not very fond of President Roosevelt. I always wondered whether it was because she felt that he was responsible for our entrance into World War II. Some of the women in the Owens house referred to him as "Roseball." In retrospect, I do not believe the United States had any other choice but to enter World War II. Researching for this story has convinced me of this even more so. Hitler had to be stopped, and America was needed to stop him. Otherwise, I believe he intended to conquer the world. His atrocities against the Jewish people and others were beyond unconscionable. It had to end.

Incidentally, Martha and Vince used a word quite often in their correspondence that I have not found in the dictionary. The word is *joed*. They used it when they wrote about being tired or worn out from long activity. For example, Martha wrote following a walk on a brisk November day with the baby in his carriage: "...when I came home, I was really joed." Another example is when she wrote to Vince about returning to physical training: "Boy, I bet that P.T. does joe you."

On November 18, 1944, Vince wrote to Martha: "The colonel gave us a little talk again today. Mostly about what we are doing wrong. He did say that those with the best grades and most initiative would be instructors in the training command—that is, if they wanted it. Also that some would go as instructors to the air force, some to radar and maybe some to combat. Those going to radar, he said, would probably leave within 10 days. So I might be on the move again. About those going to combat, I think it's just those that mess up someway or another, so don't you worry about it." He continued: "I thought last week's school schedule was tough, but the one coming up this week is even worse. Every other day we go until seven o'clock. Nice of them, don't you think? These guys living in town with their wives are really p_____ and moaning. And I can't blame them either."

On that same day, November 18, 1944, Martha wrote to Vince about the baby: "...Vince, if you could hear him yelling Da-da-da all day, you'd just squeeze him so hard. I almost died until he said it, and now he says it all the time. Sometimes when I'm feeling very blue and he says it, I could just cry my heart out, but instead I kiss him, once for you and once for me. Vince, I'll be so glad when you finish that course so Little Giz and I can come with you. I love and miss you so very much."

Vince wrote on November 19, 1944: "We start flying tomorrow, and then every other day after that. Our flying here consists of setting up the autopilot, a couple navigation missions, and dropping about 30 bombs. I don't think we drop any bombs, but our instructor will drop them.... he'll make different mistakes intentionally and we have to correct him. All it is, is practice in instructing cadets."

Vince flew his first mission while at San Angelo's Concho Field on November 20, 1944. He wrote: "It was just a practice flight, so it didn't mean much. It sure felt funny synchronizing in an AT-11 after flying in a B-17 all this time. I guess I'll get use to it again, tho." In his letter of November 20, Vince elaborated more on his 90 hours of required navigation training. He realized that Martha was somewhat confused, for she understood that he was training to be a bombardier instructor and not a navigation instructor. He explained why he was receiving so much navigation training. He wrote: "The bombardier course has been extended to 24 weeks, just twice as much as when I went thru." He pointed out that he had very limited navigation training. He continued: "Now the cadets get about 9 weeks of it. So if I'm going to instruct cadets, I'll have to know something about it. I know most of it, but had to learn the hard way—in combat. To be a bombardier—that is, a lead bombardier—you have to also be a navigator. Finally the training command found that out. Twenty-four weeks is sure a long time to be training a guy for bombardier tho, don't you think?"

Martha had written to Vince and mentioned that there had been a "feud" in the family, but it did not involve her. Upon reading about it, Vince wrote to Martha: "Boy, I'm glad we don't have any trouble that way. And if we did, you know what I'd do. You don't. Neither do I. Boy! I got out of that one fast. I'm just kidding you, honey. You can get along with anybody, and that's because you're so sweet and wonderful. And I love you dearly for it."

On November 21, 1944, Martha was back to the movies again. She and her mom and sister Rita went and saw *Gypsy Wildcat* starring Maria Montez and Jon Hall. She wrote: "Boy, was it good? I liked it a lot." On that same evening, Vince saw *My Friend Wolf*, which he enjoyed. Two days later, Martha, Rita and their mom saw *The Merry Monahans,* starring Peggy Ryan, Donald O'Connor and Jack Oakie. She wrote "Boy, was it good? If you get the opportunity, be sure to see it. I sure enjoyed it. Rita and I laughed so loud that Mom said we embarrassed her."

Vince wrote to Martha on November 22, 1944, and informed her that his clothes from Midland had finally arrived at San Angelo some two weeks after his departure. He must have left in a hurry without a whole lot in hand, and apparently, he had been short on clothes. He wrote: "Each night I've been washing a pair of socks out. I can cut that out now."

In this letter, he told Martha that he did actually drop his first bombs on that date. Apparently, that part of the training was unexpected for him. He was learning with a new aircraft. He admitted that he had a poor score, but acknowledged that it didn't really mean anything, so he wasn't worried about it. When Martha read that Vince was not happy with his bombing score, she wrote: "So you're dropping bombs again, huh, hon? If I were you, I wouldn't worry….Everybody knows that you're the best bombardier in the whole wide world."

Two days later, he wrote: "We flew a bombing mission today, but instead of us dropping the bombs, our instructor did and we acted as instructors. More fun! It was our chance to get back at him. We just chewed his _____ out, and plenty. Only kidding…" Vince reminded Martha of his awful score the other day, and continued: "…well, his was even worse. He'll never live it down, either. We're going to see to it."

On Thanksgiving Day, November 23, 1944, Martha wrote: "I went to the 9 o'clock Mass and Communion for you. It wasn't a Holy Day, but I have so much to be thankful for that I went to church." She wrote that they had a very nice dinner, adding: "No turkey, but chicken and all that goes with it." It is yet another reminder that the war is still raging.

Vince wrote on Thanksgiving Day: "I have so much to be thankful for. Having such a fine family, and God sparing me from the fate of combat.

I am really thankful for it too." Vince added: "What a dinner we had this afternoon. Only good one I've had since I got here. It consisted of turkey (all white meat), mashed potatoes, corn, asparagus, cranberries, two kinds of pickles, tomatoes, stuffed celery, hot rolls, pumpkin pie and ice cream. How's that sound? Only cost 75 cents too. Pretty good, huh?" As earlier written, Martha had said to Vince that she would live in a soap box if she could be with him. In this letter, Vince wrote: "I bought a soap box today, and am going to hold you to what you said. It's a little small, and I want to see you get into it. Don't forget now, that's a bargain." A few days later, Martha responded: "Honey, I think it's wonderful that you bought a soap box for us to live in. Giz, don't you think I wouldn't do it, and I can assure you that I'll keep my end of that bargain."

A few days earlier Martha had asked Vince if he thought being assigned to radar would make him sterile. Vince responded in his Thanksgiving Day letter: "About radar making you sterile, I really don't know for sure. That's what some people say, anyway." He ended this letter by writing: "I love you both very much and miss you like all heck. As the seconds go by, I can feel my love for you in my heart grow bigger and bigger. The love light in my heart shines with a glow of beauty for you both." He then did something that I have not found previously. On the outside of the envelope of this letter sent airmail, he wrote: "Fly to Mommy Little Letter, I can't." In his very next letter, he ended by writing: "I love you both so much now my little heart pitter-patters all day from it. And I will keep on loving you until eternity and then beyond that." After two years in the service, with over six months of combat, Vince had not lost his romantic touch a bit.

On November 26, 1944, I was six months old. My father sent me a letter addressed to Master Vincent de Paul Gisriel, Jr.:

> My Dearest Little Giz,
> "Happy Birthday," Son! Sorry I can't be there in person. You're too little to understand now, but they tell me there's a war on, and I have to be here and you there. It won't be long tho and you, Mommie, and I will be together again. Mommie

tells me you are growing into a big boy, and can do just about
everything but walk and talk. It won't be long before you'll be
doing both of them. I hope you wait until I'm around before
you do either, but things like that can't wait, they just happen.
Take real good care of Mommie for me and tell her I love her.
Again "Happy Birthday." I love you, dearly.
Your devoted "Daddy"

How can I be more blessed. My father was a good man who loved
my mother and me with all his being. He loved his country and he was
doing his best to protect and defend it. More than anything, he loved
God, Our Father, His Son Jesus, the Holy Spirit and the Blessed Mother,
and he passed that love on to me. How could anyone ask for more in a
father? Thank you Heavenly Father, the Creator of love and all men and
women! He enclosed a set of aviator wings with the letter.

Upon reading the letter from my father to me, Martha wrote: "Vince,
I think the letter you wrote to Little Vince is beautiful. I cried when I
read it, and Little Vince laughed. I think the wings are wonderful. I know
that he will treasure the letter and his wings all his life. I've showed it to
a million people, I believe. Only a few read the letter, though. I felt as
though I wanted everyone to see it, and they all thought it was swell."
Now, in this book, Martha's wish has come to fruition, for many more
can read my father's loving words to his son.

Martha wrote to Vince on November 26, 1944: "Well, darling, Our
Little Son is six months old today. Can you imagine it, honey? One half
a year old? Golly, it seems like just yesterday that he was born, and then,
too, it seems ages. I just can't imagine us without having Little Vince. It
seems as though he's been here all the time. I kissed him and wished him
a Happy Birthday for you, early this morning. Vince, he's so wonderful.
I just can't wait until we three are together." What more can I say about
a mother who loved me and wanted me so much and was always there?
I am doubly blessed. Again, thank you Almighty Father!

In this letter, she informed Vince of the death of two more friends
and a third missing in action. She wrote: "Golly, if this war would only

end." While saddened to hear the news regarding the death of two friends, Vince seemed to think the fellow reported as missing may be safe, having worked as an intelligence officer following his combat tour of duty.

On November 26, 1944, Vince also wrote to Martha: "I thought the last two weeks of school were rough, but after seeing this coming week's schedule, it's even worse. Every other morning we have to be down the flight line at 7:30 and go until 7 PM." He also wrote about seeing the movie *Princess and the Pirate,* starring Bob Hope. He wrote: "I thought it was very good—go see it if you have the chance." He continued: "Before the show started, the post orchestra played for about a half hour. They played two of my favorites, 'Silver Wings in the Moonlight' and 'I'll Walk Alone.' They were very good."

Vince continued this letter even further: "Darlings, I'm so doggone homesick for you two tonight, I don't know what to do. I've just been sitting here thinking, when you and Little Giz come out to where ever I am stationed, we can get an apartment or maybe a house even. We've never really lived alone, and it'll be lots of fun, I bet. It'll be just like civilian life maybe. I'll come home and you'll be getting dinner ready, and maybe I can help you with it, that is if you'll let me. Then after dinner I can help you with the dishes or put Little Giz to bed or something useful. After that we could sit and listen to the radio, or read, or do a little loving, and we have lots of that to catch up on."

Martha responded: "Darling, don't be too homesick, 'cause we're going to be with you real soon. Hon, won't it be wonderful to have a place of our own? And you know doggone well that I'll let you help me do anything. I think about it so much that I'm eating my heart out. About those evenings, after the dishes are done, and Little Giz is asleep, I'm strictly in favor of catching up on our loving. Oh, Vince, won't it be wonderful? No matter how busy it keeps me, it will still be heaven, being with you and Little Giz."

On November 27, 1944, Martha wrote to Vince regarding two of his close friends. One was already overseas, and the other was headed there. She wrote that she is sorry about it and added: "Why, oh why can't this old war end? I hope and pray that it will end, very, very soon." She also reported on yet another motion picture: *Since You Went Away*. She wrote: "Gosh, it was good, but so terribly sad. I cried and cried."

On that same day, Vince wrote to Martha: "The colonel gave us another little chat again today. It seems a couple of the fellows are screwing up and he's getting p____ off. It was more of a threat than anything. If it keeps up he's going to have us marching to class and have a curfew. Isn't that the height of chicken crap! All the fellows who are living off the post with their wives are supposed to move back on the post. You can imagine the number that are doing it. That's right. None!"

As he had done in his earlier training, prior to going overseas and into combat, Vince kept Martha posted on his progress in school. He wrote to her: "...my average ground school grade in all the tests we've had so far comes to 90.5%."

Vince mentioned to Martha how tired he had been, and posed the question: "Must be getting old, huh?" She responded: "No, darling, I don't think old age is creeping up on you. I think it's the darn long days—you have to be on the go down there." Vince wrote on November 30, 1944: "Today in P.T. we went over the obstacle course for the first time, and was it rough. It's the roughest one I've ever seen. I was puffing like a horse when I got thru, and I don't mean maybe."

Between November 1, 1944 and November 30, 1944, I have counted 62 letters between Martha and Vince.

On December 1, 1944, Vince wrote to Martha: "Talk about being cold this morning. You know I had to be down the flight line at 7:30 AM, and I froze my little *can* off. We were supposed to fly at 11,000 feet and drop qualification bombs, but the clouds were down to about 2,000 feet. So we just went up to about 1,000 feet and did some low altitude bombing. I'm not sure, but I don't think we drop any more bombs. The rest of our flying will be navigation missions, I think." Vince informed Martha that after receiving an 88 percent score on a bombsight test, he is now carrying an average of 90.25 percent. He also informed her that he finally wrote to the sister of the officer who was killed in their plane back in June. He wrote to Martha: "It took me a heck of a long time to do it, but I'm sure glad I got it off my chest." Vince ended this letter by writing: "I love you both so much it hurts my heart. It's the kind of hurt that you want to be in your heart. I call it my 'love hurt.'"

Martha responded: "Say, Giz, I'm sure proud of you. You're getting some swell marks down there, hon, and I'm glad you're working so hard. I mean, trying so hard." She added that she was so glad that he had written to the sister of the officer who was killed in action. She wrote: "I know what a tough job it was, but aren't you glad now that you wrote to her?"

18

The Best and "Merryest" Christmas

On December 2, 1944, Vince wrote to Martha and the baby: "Darlings, grab hold of something again, because this takes the cake. I'm now writing from a train on the way to Langley Field. It was as much a surprise to me as I imagine it is to you. Today at 2 PM I was told to report to the Officer's Personnel Section, and they told me to be ready to leave by 9:30 PM. Well, you could have knocked me over with a feather. You can imagine the running around I've been doing, clearing the field. I don't know how I ever made it, but I did. No one seems to know what we are going for, or if they do, they won't tell us. I'll let you know as soon as I get there what the setup is. I got caught with my drawers down. Had my check for $262 but no money, and I couldn't pay my mess bill. I was p____ off as it was, so I goes prancing into the colonel's office and starts raising heck. You know me—I'm usually quiet about things like that, but I was really mad today. Really took the colonel by surprise, too. It wound up where he made the Officers' Club cash my check, by order." Vince informed Martha that he expected to arrive at Langley Field, Virginia, on December 5 and that he would try to call her that evening to let her know what it was all about. He asked her to stay home to await his call if she could.

On December 5, 1944, Martha received Vince's letter written from the train. She wrote: "I received a letter from you this morning, but, I didn't grab hold of anything in time, so it knocked me over. I noticed it was postmarked Dallas, Texas. Gosh, honey, I'm glad and sorry, and just feel real confused. I'm so glad that you're so close to home, Vince. But then if you're going to take radar, I'll be a total wreck, wondering if they'll send you back overseas." She continued: "Vince, do you think you'll be able to get home on a weekend pass, or for Christmas? Golly, hon, I sure hope you can." She wrote further: "Say, hon, you sure were caught with your pants down. I can imagine what a wreck you must have been trying to get ready to leave, clearing the field, and with no money. I'm glad you gave that colonel heck, honey, but honest, I can't imagine you getting mad. You know, that's something I've never seen, and hope I never do." She also added: "I kept Little Giz up until 7:30 PM hoping you would call. I was going to let him jabber to you, but he got sleepy, so I thought I'd better put him in the sack....He laughed when I told him that you were going to call us, but he laughs all the time anyway." Before Martha could even finish this letter, Vince apparently called from Langley to announce his arrival and to inform her that he was coming home. She never mailed the letter. Vince may have seen it upon his return home on December 6, 1944. However, the unfinished letter was eventually put in the same envelope with Vince's letter dated December 2, 1944. It may have remained there for over 60 years, until I read it.

All correspondence between Martha and Vince ceased between December 6, 1944 and December 14, 1944, for Vince was home on leave.

On December 15, 1944, correspondence started back up again when Martha wrote to Vince: "Honey, you have only been gone 12 hours and fifteen minutes, but it seems like 20 years." On December 16, 1944, Vince wrote to Martha: "It's only been a day now since I last saw you and already it seems like weeks." Vince explained that he was awaiting a class assignment. He informed Martha that the guest house on the post had burned to the ground just prior to his arrival back at Langley. The wife of a tech sergeant had been killed in the fire from smoke inhalation. This was the same guest house in which Vince's Aunt Helen was to stay upon her arrival at Langley over the Christmas holidays. You see, not only was Vince stationed there, but Aunt Helen's younger daughter, Nonie, who had enlisted in the Air WAC, was also stationed there. Aunt Helen had two good reasons to visit Langley Field.

Later in the day, Vince learned that he was to start classes on December 18, 1944. The course was scheduled to last twelve weeks. While Vince had not yet seen his cousin Nonie in person, he had reached her by telephone. Vince wrote a second letter to Martha on December 16, 1944. In it, he wrote: "Was talking to Nonie on the phone and she had some very good news. At her office they got a TWX stating that no man back from combat would be sent over unless he so desires. Sounds good, huh. I also met a couple guys going thru in this course who said the same thing. You know what I'm going to start bucking for—a job as permanent instructor here. That wouldn't be too hard to take. What say?"

Martha responded on December 19, 1944: "Honey, I really feel swell since I heard that rumor about you not going back overseas again. Golly, I hope that's true. I'll pray very hard that you will be a permanent instructor down there. I'll say it wouldn't be hard to take." She also mentioned that her brother, Buster, had begun to put up the model train garden for Christmas. She wrote: "…boy, Little Vince was all eyes. Then, when they had the train going around, he really got excited. He almost jumped right out of his little teeter-baby chair. Gosh, I bet he'll be excited on Christmas." Martha also acknowledged Vince's phone call to her earlier that evening. She wrote: "Vince, I sure thank you for calling me. It was so wonderful to hear your voice." She ended by stating that she would be waiting for his telephone call in two nights. On December 19, Vince also wrote: "It was really swell to hear your voice again. I miss you so doggone much it did me wonders to talk to you."

In his letter of December 19, Vince elaborated on the school setup at Langley Field. He explained to Martha that one week they went to class in the morning, and the next week they attended class in the afternoon. He was scheduled to begin flying after Christmas. Then he would fly every other day. He added: "I hate to think about flying. They say it is really cold up there." Vince ended his very next letter with one of his classic closings: "My heart just keeps pounding out a love call to you both and it gets louder and louder each second. My love has gone way past infinite and then some."

Vince wrote that he had the opportunity to meet with Nonie. They went to the PX and had something to eat. Vince wrote that they "sat there for a long time just talking about this and that." They had not seen each other in months and had a lot of catching up to do. Remember, they were raised like brother and sister. Later that day, they went to town and had dinner. Vince had "Chicken in the Rough" and thought it was delicious.

Vince continued: "It was funny—Nonie has to have a pass to be able to be with me (isn't that awful?), and we were just waiting for some M.P. to stop us, but doggone it, they wouldn't. Now, if she didn't have a pass they would have swarmed all over us." She needed a pass to be with an officer because she was an enlisted Air WAC.

Vince arrived home on December 23, 1944, just in time for Christmas. I can only imagine the joy that Martha and he felt and shared because they were together and because he was home for their baby's first Christmas. When you consider the year they had endured, it would have meant even more.

Another Christmas blessing and gift to the entire family was the arrival of Rita and Jack's baby girl, Dianne, on December 24, 1944. Jack, who was stationed at Chatham Field, near Savannah, Georgia, decided that he wanted to go home to visit Rita and the baby. Since his crew was preparing to ship out, he knew he could not obtain a pass to travel home, but he decided to leave for home anyway. On Christmas Eve, he headed off the post, only to be stopped by a military policeman. Jack showed the MP an old pass, and quickly the MP pointed out that the pass was no longer valid. However, Jack explained his need to get home and promised the guy he would be back as soon as possible and before his unit shipped out. The MP must have had the Christmas spirit, because he let Jack go off post.

Jack rushed into town, purchased a roundtrip train ticket, and headed for Baltimore. Upon his arrival, he proceeded directly to the hospital to visit with Rita and to meet his newborn daughter, Dianne. After his initial visit with Rita and the baby, he visited his parents' home and that of Rita's family. Apparently, Willie was very worried for Jack—that he would not be able to return to his post on time. Martha's sister Mary recently recalled that the former first sergeant was beside himself that his son-in-law might be in trouble.

Jack then went to the hospital for a second visit and to say good-bye to his young family. By evening, he was back at the train station. This was where the excitement began. Because it was Christmas Day, the trains were packed and probably running late as well. Even though he had his return ticket, he could not catch a train back to Georgia. He pondered his options and then noticeed an express, nonstop Silver Meteor from New York bound for Florida coming down the track. Even though it did not stop, it slowed down enough to grab the mail satchel, and this enabled Jack to hop on. In those days much of the U.S. mail went by train, and the postal service actually sorted letters in mail cars so that it could be distributed along the nation's railways to the various cities and towns. Mail was dropped along the railway lines as well. However, this particular express train was not scheduled to slow down again before it reached Florida. This southbound train took a more rural route, avoiding cities and towns, to facilitate a quicker trip.

After Jack's athletic feat of boarding the train, he took a seat. The conductor came along, noticed him, and asked, "Where did you come from?" Jack explained his situation and how he just had to get back to Georgia. After all, he had paid for a round trip and he had his return ticket in hand. Like the MP, the conductor must have had the Christmas spirit. Not only did he let Jack stay on the train, he even told him to try to get some sleep, and he would wake him when they were approaching the Savannah area. The conductor had the engineer slow the train down near Savannah so that Jack could jump from the moving train. The conductor even told Jack how to jump and roll to avoid injury. At the appointed moment, Jack jumped and sat in a cow pasture until dawn, when he could see his way back to the post. He made it safely back in time and he was able to see the treasures of his life, all within a short period of time. This story reminds me of the old saying, "Where there's a will, there's a way." It could not have happened to a nicer guy, for my Uncle Jack is one of the finest men whom I have ever known. He is one of a kind and quite a gem of an individual.

Life in the military went on, for Vince was back at Langley on December 26, 1944. It got harder and harder for him to leave his family following each visit home. He wrote upon his return to the field: "Good afternoon you two precious, lovable persons. I'm back again loving you like all heck, and after being away from you less than one day, I miss you like all get out."

Vince went on to describe his trip back to Langley on Christmas Day. He wrote: "I'll start from the beginning and let you know how I made out on the trip down. We got to Wash. about 8:40 and stood in a line until 12:30 midnight before we got a bus to Newport News. You can imagine how late that made me and how I was sweating. Hit Newport News about six and it was seven before I got down to the flight line. I was marked absent, but no one seems to care whether we were there or not. I report to our echelon leader and he checked me off and told me to get my stuff and stand by with the crew I was flying with. Luckily, between 6 and 7, it started to rain and the ships hadn't taken off yet. The way it turned out, flying was called off completely. Thank goodness. I was sweating blood coming down here, but now that everything had turned out I'm OK."

On the following day, Vince wrote: "Darlings, I wanted to tell you this last night but I had to rush so I didn't have time. I had such a wonderful time while I was home. It was the best and Merryest Christmas I ever spent. I had everything I wanted, namely, you and Giz. What more could a guy ask for? I thank God that he let me get home for the holidays."

Martha wrote to Vince on December 26, 1944: "Well, honey, as soon as you left last night, I got real blue. I missed you so much last night and today. I always do miss you like heck, but for some unknown reason, it has been awful since you went back last night." She added: "I was so lonesome for you when I went to bed, so you know what I did? I slept on your side of the bed."

When Vince got back to his barracks, he called Nonie and was surprised to learn that Aunt Helen was still at Langley. He arranged to meet them both that evening to take Aunt Helen to the train station for her return trip to Baltimore. Aunt Helen said that she had a wonderful time. Vince believed that she did indeed, because "…she was sure sorry to leave." They were joined on the trip to the train station by Nonie's friend "Sparks." "Sparkie," as he was also affectionately called, turned out to be an important person in Nonie's life, because they were later married while both were in the service. Vince stood for them at their wedding, and he was the only other person there other than the priest. They were married in the rectory. Sparkie would go on to make a career out of the military, eventually retiring from the air force with 26 years of service to our country. He attained the rank of master sergeant.

Martha wrote to Vince on December 27, 1944. She wrote that while she did not get a letter from him that day, nevertheless, she sure felt wonderful. She wrote: "Yep, that telephone call did it again. Vince, it was heaven to hear your voice." In this letter, she informed Vince about the baby's seventh month checkup. She reported that everything was fine, and the baby could begin to eat the yoke of an egg. She wrote: "If only we can get eggs," yet another sign that the war continued.

Likewise, Vince wrote on December 27: "Good evening, darlings, I'm back again loving you more than ever and missing you like all heck. I'm very happy right now tho, and of course it's because I just talked to you over the phone. It was pretty quick, but wonderful to hear your voice. Those three minutes sure went fast. Seems like I just said hello when I was saying good-bye." Fortunately, when Vince was stationed at Langley, he was able to phone home often, sometimes every other evening. Vince continued this letter: "Didn't have to get up too early today—5:15 to be exact. Tomorrow is the one I dread. I have a 4:15 briefing to make and will probably get up about 3:15 AM. Isn't that a disgusting hour?"

Vince continued his December 27 letter: "I've almost finished *30 Seconds Over Tokyo*, and boy, is it good. It's really a wonderful description of it." The book was probably a Christmas gift. He was also enjoying the radio that Martha gave him. He wrote: "The radio is sure getting its use.

At first I could only get one station on it, but after I put an extension on the aerial and ran it out the window I can get just about everything on it, even Baltimore stations."

The next day, Vince wrote that he did get up at 3:15 AM. He was all set to fly that morning, but the pilot did not show up and they could not get another one. He had to wait down at the flight line until 10:15 AM. When no one showed up to fly the plane, he went back to bed.

Vince was able to go home for the New Year's holiday as well. Between December 1, 1944, and December 31, 1944, I have counted one telegram and 28 letters between Martha and Vince. While letter production has slowed down, they have obviously spent a lot more time together on weekend passes and other leave. Nothing beats being together!

19

So Close, and Yet So Far

On January 1, 1945, Vince left Baltimore to return to Langley Field, Virginia. He traveled all night, departing from Baltimore at 7:24 PM and arriving back at his barracks at 5:50 AM. He was able to sleep for an hour and a half before he had to take a navigation proficiency test. Only a twenty-two-year-old man in love can accomplish such things.

Apparently, when Vince left home, Martha was upset and angry, but not really with him, as she would write. She was hurt and annoyed for other reasons. In her letter dated January 1, she apologized for the way she acted when they parted. She wrote to Vince that she "...wanted to let you know how sorry I am for acting the way I did." She continued: "I was awfully hurt when you left, and still am. Honey, I'm going to tell you why I was mad, because if I hold it much longer, I'll explode." She explained that when he was home on leave, he received a lot of company, apparently friends stopping by who had not seen him for quite some time. She also addressed the fact that Aunt Helen put unreasonable demands on his time, wanting him to visit her when he was back in Baltimore. Martha felt that she and Vince had so little time as it was, and that their limited time could be better spent together, and alone. Martha further wrote: "I thought my heart would break when you left this evening, and I still do. Don't let this letter upset you, Vince, because I'll probably be sorry I mailed it after I do. If you get this letter before you call me, please don't mention it. Just tear it up when you read it, and we won't talk about it, any more. Well, darling, the more I write the worse I feel, so I guess I'd better sign off for now. I have already cried my eyes out, but I know I won't feel better until I hear that you aren't mad with me."

On January 2, 1945, Vince wrote a postscript that read: "I'm hoping you aren't still mad with me. I can't for the life of me think what I did. If I hurt you in any way, darling, please forgive me." Martha and Vince spoke with each other by telephone on January 3, 1945. Vince wrote that evening that he "…had to write and tell you how happy I am. Of course you know why—I just finished talking to you and you weren't mad with me. I've been trying to rack my brain ever since I left you to see what I had done to make you mad. I think I know what it is, but then maybe I'm wrong." He continued: "What hurt me most was the fact you wouldn't tell what was the matter. I was very selfish about the whole thing. All I could think of coming down on the train was the chance I had taken to come home and then you wouldn't let me in on it. Now that I know you feel better, I'm so happy. It just breaks my heart when I do something that hurts you, I love you so much." He added: "I said that I'd tear up the letter you wrote, but honey, if I did that, then maybe I'd never find out why you were mad. And I just have to know. I won't be satisfied until I have talked to you face to face and we have narrowed everything down. For the time being let's lay the whole issue aside until I get home again." Apparently, Vince had not yet received Martha's January 1 letter.

In her letter of January 1, Martha also mentioned the lack of privacy at the family home when Vince was home on leave. Apparently this was beginning to become an issue for them, particularly for Vince. In his letter dated January 3, Vince addressed it when he wrote: "…I'm sure if we were together more often, and had a place of our own, things would be altogether different. Don't get me wrong about you being home with Suz and Willie. Never could I show my appreciation for all they have done for us. I don't know what we would have done without them. They've been wonderful, and I love them so much for it. One couldn't ask for better in-laws."

The war lingered on and nerves appeared to be frayed, but Martha and Vince continued to pray for each other. Martha attended her novena frequently, and both went to Mass, Communion and Confession as often as they could. Their faith in Almighty God helped them to persevere. In a letter from a buddy, Vince learned that two of his friends had been reported as prisoners of war. This kind of news was never easy for Vince and Martha.

Vince was able to get a pass for what appears to be a long weekend. Upon his return to Langley Field, he wrote to Martha on January 8, 1945: "It's only been a day since I last felt your tender lips, but to me it seems like ages. I love you so doggone much it hurts to be away from you a long time, and one day is a very long time to me." Martha wrote that very day: "Honey, you've only been gone one day, but it seems like years. Gosh, hon, but I miss you."

Vince had traveled back by train and added: "The trip wasn't too bad this time. Only had to stand from Richmond to Williamsburg." He continued: "By 5:00 AM, I was in the sack snoring away. Got up in time to make PT, but after all the trouble we didn't have any. They took roll tho and the adjutant talked to us for awhile. He didn't have much news about a leave." Vince had already informed Martha that his course might be delayed for another two weeks. He was going to attempt to obtain a leave to come home during the delay. This prompted Martha to write: "Say, Vince, I sure hope the colonel gives you all a leave. Gee, that's terrible to make you sit down there doing nothing."

Continuing his January 8 letter, Vince wrote: "Forty-five more men will start school Monday. Don't know who yet, but should in a couple days. I'm one of 300 in a pool; 150 of them will be sent back to their original stations. The others will wait until classes start. Each Monday a new class of 45 will start. About the others, everyone seems to think they will get leaves if the colonel will ever get back. You see he went (so they tell us) to St. Louis with the screening test, etc. and has been weathered in."

Vince added: "Hon, one of the boys in the barracks came down with the mumps yesterday, and I thought you'd better watch out for Giz. Nothing like taking precautions, you know. Maybe it would be best to call Doc Brown and see what he has to say."

183

In her letter to Vince dated January 9, 1945, Martha told Vince that on this night, Little Vince would not go to sleep and kept screaming because of his teething, Joe was sick to his stomach and Rita's newborn, Dianne, was crying because it was time for her to eat. They had a regular nursery in full operation at the Owens family house.

Martha wrote that she and her sister Catherine saw the movie *30 Seconds Over Tokyo*, starring Van Johnson. She wrote: "Boy, honey, was that good? I cried and cried, and do you know what I think? I think Van Johnson looks something like you, or at least he did last night. It was terribly sad, though."

On January 9, 1945, Vince wrote: "Just heard some good news over the radio. Luzon has been raided. What do you think about it? Pretty good, huh?"

It appears that Vince's class had been delayed, and he was on leave from approximately January 10, 1945, through January 26, 1945.

On January 27, after his return to Langley, Vince had already written a letter to Martha within 12 hours of having kissed her and the baby good-bye. He wrote: "I don't have very much news for you, but I just couldn't go without writing you." He had also talked with her over the telephone within those 12 hours. He mentioned that the trip down was uneventful, that he had very good connections and had good seats. Martha wrote within 13 hours: "It seems so lonely here since you left. Golly, I wish we could be together. I hope you try to get a place down there."

Vince had passed his screening test, which meant that he would stay at Langley and not be shipped back to his original station at Midland, Texas. Upon hearing this, Martha wrote: "I sure hope you do real good down there so they'll make you permanent. I know you will do your best, though."

On January 28, 1945, Vince wrote: "Good afternoon, darlings. Here I am back again loving you another day's worth and missing you like all heck. Now it's been a day and a half since I've seen you two, and I'm just about going bugs. Honeys, am I homesick! I knew that leave would spoil me, but I didn't think it would be this bad." Vince learned that he would start school on January 29, 1945, and that it was scheduled to last 10 weeks. He asked Martha to be on the lookout for a car. He wrote: "If you find a good bargain, Willie can look at it and decide whether or not to get it." Vince also indicated that he intended to search for an apartment for Martha, the baby and himself. Apparently, apartments were hard to find, and the ones that were available tended to be out of town; thus the need for a car.

Martha responded: "Hon, I've been checking the papers every day for a car, but so far no go. I saw a '32 Ford, for $195.00. How do you like that? You know, hon, we're not going to be able to get a cheap car—or I mean, we shouldn't, because it might not hold up for that trip back and forth each week." Martha continued: "Vince, I'd just love it if we could only get an apartment down there. You know, hon, after you begin to fly, you just won't be able to make that trip, and lose your sleep, and expect to keep going. I realize, though, that you don't have very much time to look for a place. So I told Mom today that I was going back with you one weekend and try to find a place. Would you like that, darling?"

Martha wrote that she and her mom had gone to the movies and had seen Abbott & Costello in *Lost in a Harem*. She wrote: "I just laughed, Vince, 'cause it sure was funny. I liked it a lot." A few days later, she and her sister Mary went to see *Three in a Family*. She wrote: "...Vince, it was darling. If you haven't seen it, try to. It's sure good. I liked it a lot."

On January 29, 1945, Vince wrote that he started classes that day. He stated: "Just a repetition of what we had a couple weeks ago. The first whole week is nothing but navigation." In that letter, he added: "We're getting a break on the mess bill beginning the first of Feb. All meals will cost but a quarter. You know, they use to be 50 cents, and that really adds up." He also wrote: "Hon, about this coming weekend, I think I'll be home, but I'm not really sure yet. I won't be able to leave until 7:15 PM Saturday, getting me in Baltimore early Sunday morning, and then I'll have to leave early Sunday evening. Even if it's for only a couple hours, I'm going to get home if I can." Vince spent about 20 plus hours traveling on a shortened weekend just to see Martha and the baby for part of a Sunday. Some might think this is crazy; I know it was love!

The next day, Vince wrote: "The school here is beginning to get more interesting, but also tougher. I think I'm going to like it a lot, tho." In this letter he mentioned Martha coming down to Langley. On January 31, 1945, Vince wrote that he got his paycheck that day: "…but it was too late to cash it, so at the present I'm still broke. That's life, tho, isn't it."

On February 1, 1945, Martha spoke with Vince by telephone. Following their conversation, she wrote: "Say, hon, I bet you were tired today after flying five hours. Golly, that was long, wasn't it? That's the first time you've been up for a couple of months, isn't it? No wonder you were too tired to look for a place to live." Vince also wrote following their phone call. He apologized for not looking for an apartment, acknowledging that he had had the afternoon off to do so. He wrote, however: "I was so doggone tired when I got down today, and then after taking a hot shower, I was really tired. And hungry too. I ate at 4:00 AM and then didn't eat again until 5:30 PM." He continued: "Oh! I knew there was something I didn't tell you. You know I said that all meals were going to be 25 cents from now on, beginning today. Well do you know why? The field has been put on rations, and that's all they can charge. The quality of the food isn't the same, but so far it hasn't been bad. Now it's all cafeteria style, no civilian help. I guess that's why it's so cheap." He added further: "Oh, yeah—there's something else I forgot to tell you. I was home today, but I was upstairs about 12,000 feet and couldn't very well drop down to see you. Yep, I flew right smack over Baltimore; I couldn't exactly see our house, but could see the area. I sure felt like bailing out and seeing you, but thought I'd better not."

The next day, February 2, 1945, Martha went to the movies with Angela. They saw *Something for the Boys*. Martha wrote: "And boy, was it good? I sure liked it…" She continued: "Oh, yeah, we got in a fight with some snippy girls behind us. Not a fight, but just said something. No wonder, hon, they told the whole story, because two of them had already seen it." Later, Martha and Angela went to see *Meet Me in St. Louis*. Martha wrote: "…it was really good." Vince wrote about a movie he saw, *Roughly Speaking*, starring Rosalind Russell and Jack Carson. He wrote: "The show was really good. I enjoyed it immensely. If you get a chance to see it, don't miss it."

On February 2, 1945, Vince wrote to Martha that he had found an apartment. He wrote: "...I'm not bragging in the least. It's a dump. I'll tell you all the details when I see you tomorrow (I hope). I guess I never should have taken it, but I was desperate. I had to pay a week's rent ($10) to hold it, but that's to be expected. The way I figured, it would take a couple weeks for you to get organized and get down here, and in the meantime I could hunt up another place. You know—just keep the other place in reserve just in case. There's a class finishing up this week, and maybe there'll be some vacancies in Hampton." Vince went home for a very short weekend. He described it as a "few hours," but nevertheless "wonderful"

Martha and Vince had been married twenty months as of February 5, 1945. Martha wrote to Vince on that date: "Honey, I received your card and it was wonderful. Vince, I didn't think you were going to remember it. But you did, darling, and it sure made me feel very happy. I hope you found my card in your bag. Anyway, I hope you had a very nice anniversary day. Just think, hon, 20 months today. That's a pretty long time, isn't it, hon? But it seems just like yesterday."

In Vince's letter dated February 5, 1945, he wrote to Martha: "Darling, they've done it again. Our class has been split up and half of us have been moved up...now I only have eight weeks to go instead of nine." He continued: "The classes are really getting interesting, but hard. I sat in class all day today with my mouth open. The little knowledge I have of electricity is helping me a little. I think after the war all this will come in pretty handy for me. I think I'm going to like the course very much."

By February 7, 1945, Vince had started an aggressive search for a nice apartment. He put his name on one list at an apartment complex operated by the military that already had 140 names ahead of him. He went to another community, and they would not even take an application because they were so backed up with people wanting to rent. He had Nonie and Sparks on the lookout for him, as well as an Air WAC who worked on a daily bulletin that sometimes ran ads for apartments. In addition, he went to town and walked "…all over the place." He wrote: "I'm not giving up easy. Every chance I have I'm rushing into town. Say a few prayers so I get a nice place." Martha had written the day before: "Hon, I'm so glad you're going to try to get an apartment tomorrow. I'll be so tickled and happy when we three can be together."

On February 8, 1945, Vince wrote that he had stopped in Nonie's office. He wrote: "She's got everyone working on an apartment for us." On that day, Vince had training on the supersonic trainer. He explained that it was a trainer that simulated flying conditions. The next day he was scheduled for night flying. He interrupted writing the letter to telephone Martha. He continued the letter after the phone call, and wrote: "Just finished talking to you, darling, and you sounded wonderful. I don't know what I do when you're not with me. Sometimes I don't know how I can go on. What keeps me going is knowing I have you and Giz waiting for me."

Martha wrote a letter to Vince dated February 9, 1945. In it she teased him about his letter of February 6th. She wrote: "By the way, hon, are you in love or something, because your letter was dated 'Sept. 6th'?" She continued in this letter: "Hon, our Little Son is so darling. I swear, he's really at his cutest age. I'm so glad we're going to move with you so you can enjoy him too. You know, you really don't see the cute things when you come home, like on the weekend. But when we three are together, we'll really be happy. You know, Little Vince doesn't see you often, but he sure must think of you constantly. He calls Daddy all day long. Oh, yeah, Vince, I have to tell you this. Every morning, I let Little Vince look out the window. Well, this morning he was watching the trash truck. Well, this real short man came around from behind the truck with two big tubs on his shoulder, and Little Vince yelled Dad-dad, dad! I thought I'd die."

Due to Vince's scheduled weekend flying during the second week of February, he was not able to get home for the first time in several weeks.

Vince called Martha twice on February 10, 1945. He informed her that he had found a nice apartment. She wrote on this date: "Vince, I'm so happy and excited about the apartment. Boy, we're really going to have fun, aren't we? I'm just dying to get down there. It sure sounds swell." She continued: "Gee, honey, I'm sure sorry you couldn't get home this weekend. I miss you so much. However, I'd rather you wouldn't come up and have only an hour at home, and then have to rush back and fly." Martha added: "Oh, yeah, hon, I'll try my very darndest to get down there by next weekend, but you know, hon, I have an awful lot to do. I'll be so glad when we get settled, won't you? Boy, I'm really eating my heart out, Giz." She continued further: "You should hear Mom and the family, hon. You'd think they were moving too. They're all real excited, and, of course, are helping me to get ready." Martha wrote that she intended to obtain a small ice chest or icebox for the apartment. By the way, I still call a refrigerator an *icebox* even to this day. We really did have an icebox in my parents' first home back in Baltimore. I can still remember the iceman delivering a block of ice to the house in the late 1940s.

Jack was about to be shipped overseas, so Rita went to the closest town to be with him prior to his departure. On February 11, 1945, they returned home together at 8:00 PM. Jack would be home for just a very brief period. He was due back at his post the next morning at 6:00 o'clock. Martha wrote on this date: "I think it's wonderful that Jack got home. I sure wish he didn't have to go over. Both for Jack and Rita, too. I know how she feels. And I know that she'll feel worse and worse as each day goes by." Martha ended this letter by asking Vince to remember Jack in his prayers. Vince responded that he surely would.

Martha went to the movies again with Angela and saw *Hollywood Canteen*. Martha wrote: "…boy, it was swell. I laughed and laughed and thought Angela would die laughing at me." Later, Martha, Angela and Suz went to see *To Have and Have Not*, starring Lauren Bacall. She wrote: "Boy, wasn't that good? That Lauren Bacall is really 'all-reel,' isn't she? I really enjoyed it."

On February 11, 1945, Vince wrote to Martha: "I guess you're just as excited about the apartment as I am. I can hardly wait until you and Giz get down here and we get settled." Vince was planning to buy some used furniture from a woman. He asked Martha to tell him what she thought about it. He explained to Martha how everything came together. He wrote: "I was really lucky to hit this apartment. I just happened to ask a man sitting on the steps if he knew where a certain street was. Then I asked him if he knew anyone who had a vacant apartment. I got to talking to him, and he mentioned his daughter who was living upstairs and said she was planning on selling her furniture. So that was it. I looked at the furniture and apartment and thought it wouldn't be a bad deal. The man's wife thought it over and decided to rent me the apartment." Later that evening, Vince was scheduled for night flying.

Jack left for his post at 4 o'clock on the morning of February 12, 1945. Martha wrote that day: "We all wanted him to call us, but he didn't. I don't think Jack is much on saying good-bye."

Martha was planning to go to Virginia on Saturday, February 17, 1945. Vince was anticipating her arrival. He was even planning to acquire his ration card to purchase groceries. He wrote on February 12, 1945: "I can see where that's going to be fun, especially when it comes to the meats. I sold them, but I know nothing about them. I'll do my best." As a young man, he had worked in a local grocery store in Baltimore. He continued: "I'm so excited about you coming down I don't know what to do. I'll be in a fog until Saturday, I know." Vince wrote their apartment address in this letter. They would be living at 3611 Myrtle Blvd., between East and LaSalle Avenues in Hampton, Virginia. He acknowledged that he would have to coordinate with her as to where and when to meet on Saturday. Willie and Suz were planning to drive and bring Martha and the baby from Baltimore to Hampton. Vince would need to know what route Willie would travel in on as well.

In this letter, Vince wrote: "You know I flew last night and then had a class at 8:00 this morning and right now I'm really joed. When I hit that sack tonight I'm really going to sleep." There is that word again, "joed"!

Vince wrote to Martha on February 13, 1945, and mentioned a few things they would need for the apartment—such as a toaster and an alarm clock—in case there was a spare one at home. He was planning a menu for the weekend and arranging for accommodations for Suz and Willie and little Joe, who was also traveling with them. He was planning on hot dogs for Saturday and a roast for Sunday. He wrote: "Tomorrow I have off from 9:00 AM to 1:00 PM, so I'm going to do my shopping then. I don't know where to begin, but I think I'll manage (I hope)." He continued: "I just know I'm missing something, but I'm so much in a whirlwind you'll have to forgive me. I'm so excited about it all. I just can't wait for you two to get here."

By February 15, 1945, Martha's travel plans had changed somewhat, in that she had decided not to bring the baby for the weekend because he had been cranky and feeling bad. He was not sleeping his regular schedule. He was waking up throughout the night, and Martha had not been getting her regular sleep either. She told Vince that she hadn't been to bed before 1:30 AM all week. Martha had so much to do to get ready for her departure for Virginia, but the baby had demanded so much more of her time. She admitted that she was tired and added: "I don't know whether I'm pregnant or just so excited, but I'm so nervous. My whole insides are real shaky." She anticipated that when things got settled, she might "...just sleep and sleep and sleep."

By February 16, 1945, Martha had decided to cancel plans to move to Virginia on the upcoming weekend. She had considered possibly going to Virginia alone, at least for the weekend. However, the baby was still not himself, and she did not want to leave him back home when he was feeling bad. Baby Dianne was also sick, and she had cried a good part of the previous night. Martha wrote that between Dianne and Little Vince "...Rita and I were up all night." Martha also explained this to Vince during a telephone conversation on that date. Naturally, Vince was disappointed, but he understood that the baby's health was more important than moving that weekend. He later wrote: "First of all we must think of Giz's health, and there's no sense in taking any chances. I imagine you are just about knocked out yourself. Please take it easy, will you, darling." Eventually, my cousin Dianne was called by a nickname, "Dee."

As the following week arrived, Martha's travel plans were on hold again. By February 19, 1945, decisions were made day to day. It all depended on how well the baby was feeling. By February 21, 1945, he was feeling worse. His sleep pattern continued to be out of sorts. He had developed a fever. Doctor Brown had him on two medications, one of which was ear drops. Doctor Brown had also cautioned Martha regarding an outbreak of scarlet fever going around, but he was pretty sure the baby's problem was teething.

Vince wrote to Martha on February 21, 1945. He explained that he hadn't written as much because he thought she would be joining him. Martha understood perfectly. They also spoke by telephone. He was amazed to learn how much she had already sent by train in advance of her move, and at such little cost. He had not yet received it, but would arrange for its pickup or delivery from the railroad depot. He informed Martha that he could not come home that weekend because he had to fly again.

Ever since December 1944, shortly after Vince arrived at Langley, I noticed that his mail was addressed to "Shell Bank, Langley Field, Virginia." I could find no reference to "Shell Bank" until his letter dated February 21, 1945. Often when Vince wrote he used stationery bought at the PX with a military logo preprinted on the letterhead. On that date, he used stationery that depicted Langley Field with two planes flying over the field and "U.S. Army Air Force" underneath. Apparently, Shell Bank was a remote section of Langley Field separated from the main field. On this letterhead, he had denoted in his handwriting where Shell Bank was and what part was called Langley Field. He further added a circle under Shell Bank and wrote: "The Mud Hole." I have since learned that Shell Bank may have been so named because it was apparently a built-up area of Langley Field made from dredged materials including shells from the bottom of an inlet of the nearby Little Back River.

On February 22, 1945, Martha wrote to Vince. She reported that the baby was feeling much better. She mentioned that there was another feud in the family, during which she was in tears. She wrote: "I wasn't in it at all, but it just got me down. I guess it's war nerves, huh?"

Martha did go to Virginia the weekend of February 24, 1945. She traveled alone—without the baby. Little Vince was well enough so that she could leave him home under Suz's care. After her weekend visit,

Vince wrote on February 26, 1945, and mentioned that it had only been 19 hours since he had put her on a bus to go back to Baltimore. When he left her, she was standing in the aisle of the bus, and he was eager to hear how her trip home turned out. They spoke by phone on that date, and Vince learned that Martha had to stand most of the way. He was sorry to hear that, but relieved that she arrived home safely.

On that same date, and less than 24 hours following her departure from Langley, Martha wrote: "I was so lonesome all the way home, but when I got here, there was a letter waiting for me, and that sure made me feel good. Then, too, seeing Little Vince helped me a lot. As soon as I came in, he put his arms out to me and gave me a kiss." She continued: "My trip was a little rough, but Vince, it was well worth it. I had such a wonderful time. I'll be so glad when Little Giz and I come down for good. It won't be long, honey. Everyone at home was very glad to hear that I like the apartment so much. I'm still talking about it, and also the post. I slept most of the day, but I'm still fogged out. I think if I get a good night's rest tonight, I'll be super."

On the next day, Martha informed Vince that Jack had left Manchester, New Hampshire, but Rita was not sure where he was at that time. On February 28, 1945, Vince's aunt, Sister Francis, sent Vince notification that she had enrolled him and his brother-in-law, Charles, in a Solemn Novena to Our Lady of the Miraculous Medal. The novena ran from February 19 through February 27, 1945. As a member of "Mary's Kneeling Army," she had prayed that the Blessed Mother would watch over them and protect them. Coincidentally, she was currently assigned at St. Paul's Church, in Portsmouth, Virginia, not far from where Vince was stationed.

Between January 1, 1945, and February 28, 1945, I have counted two cards and 51 letters between Martha and Vince.

20

Hampton, Virginia

On or about March 1, 1945, Martha and the baby finally joined Vince in Hampton. All correspondence ceased between them from March 1, 1945, until July 2, 1945. Thus, Martha, Vince and the baby enjoyed four months together living alone as a family in their own apartment.

Rita dropped a note to Vince with a message from a friend of his. In the note, she informed him that Jack was in Iceland as of March 3, 1945. It happened to be his birthday. He and his crew were waiting for the weather to break before going further overseas. She wrote: "Please pray for him, Vince."

Within the first two weeks of Martha's arrival in Hampton, her brother Buster visited the family. He traveled by steamship on the *City of Norfolk*. After his return home, he wrote to Martha and the "lieutenant," to let them know that he arrived home safely, because he knew his sister would probably worry. Buster knew his sister all too well. He had quite a trip home due to rough water. He noted that the vessel had a narrow beam and rolled quite a bit. Later, they ran into dense fog. He wrote that the fog was such that "…you couldn't see as far as you could spit." The captain cut the boat to one-quarter speed and blew the whistle every two minutes. Nevertheless, Buster enjoyed the trip very much and struck up a friendship with the second assistant engineer of the crew. You see, Buster, in spite of his polio and inability to walk without crutches all of his adult life, loved the water and boats. As a matter of fact, he later taught boating courses sponsored by the United States Power Squadron. In his letter, he wrote that he missed Little Vince. Buster is my godfather, and growing up, I was very attached to him, and I love him very much. Sadly, he died in 2006.

Buster said in his letter that he might come back for a visit again, and if he did, he would bring his own bread. Apparently, Martha and Vince must have run out of bread when he was there. Knowing Buster, he probably needled my father to no end about it.

On March 22, 1945, Suz wrote a letter to Martha, Vince and Little Vince. She apparently felt that Little Vince had not adjusted to the relocation very well and that it was affecting his sleeping at night. Thus, she was also concerned that Martha and Vince were not getting enough sleep. She was not convinced that the baby continued to have teething problems. She wrote that she and the family back home missed the baby very much. Suz had a theory that the problem with Little Vince was that he was lonely and homesick. Obviously, she preferred that Martha and Little Vince were back home. Suz was like a mother hen, and she always said that she liked her chicks to be close to home. God bless her! She had no qualms about expressing her feelings. In her letter, she wrote: "Guess I'll be put down as an A.1 Mother-in-law. But I've never told you wrong so far." She was quick to add: "Tell Vince he's still my honey." Suz ended her letter by telling Martha and Vince that her phone bill was $23.00. She then wrote: "Think we better buy the company."

Before long, Martha and Vince learned that they were expecting their second child. Martha had an inkling back in February that she might be pregnant. On April 9, 1945, Suz wrote again, telling them how much she and Willie missed the baby. She wasted no time in writing: "First I'd better tell you this, because Dr. Brown told Willie and I both he wanted us to make it clear to you both. He says he wants you to promise him you'll come up here to stay at the beginning of your seventh month. He says from there on he wants to check regular on your condition so he can be sure you won't have the trouble you did before. So be sure and remember."

Suz was in her glory. The family was already rearranging the house in their minds to accommodate Martha and the baby upon their return home. Suz wrote: "It may be a *little* crowded, but hell, we can make out, and Dr. Brown said it's the best place on earth for you." Suz was encouraging Martha and Vince to plan to stay with them even after the war, until they could buy a place of their own. Suz relayed that Willie thought that Martha and Vince should buy some shares in a local savings and loan company so that when the war was over they would be able to buy the house they wanted and would have their down payment. In the meantime, Willie had already paid for Martha's next delivery stay at the hospital.

On or about April 13, 1945, Martha and Vince received a brief letter from a friend, Jeanne, which brought extremely good news. Their friend wrote: "This is the letter I've waited a whole year to write. Yesterday I received a cable from Philip saying: 'Darling—am well & unharmed—be home soon—missed you terribly—all my love—letter follows.' Needless to say I'm happy and grateful." Philip was one of the friends they had earlier heard was missing in action.

Martha and Vince were together when Germany initially surrendered on May 7, 1945. Therefore, there is no written correspondence between them regarding this major event. However, they undoubtedly were extremely happy to hear that news and probably enjoyed a collective sigh of relief.

Vince received a letter from the vice president and general manager of the the Chesapeake and Potomac Telephone Company of Baltimore City, dated June 11, 1945. Vince had been away from the phone company since being called to active duty in November 1942. The company vice president wrote: "While you are away we like to feel that you are thinking about your friends and your associations with the Telephone Company just as we are thinking about you and looking forward to having you with us again." The letter went on to explain a revised employee suggestion plan that offered the payment of awards for all suggestions accepted. They still considered Vince an employee eligible to participate in the incentive program. What a great source of comfort for a guy serving his country and away so long, to know that he had a job with a good future waiting for him upon his return.

Suz wrote to Martha on or about June 17, 1945, acknowledging receipt of the word that Martha, Vince and the baby would be returning to Baltimore via the steamship. They were scheduled to arrive on June 30, 1945. Suz told them that she and Willie would be there to pick them up at the dock at 6:30 in the morning.

21

Patience or Endurance? (Or Both?)

Martha returned home on the advice of her doctor, as well as the encouragement of her parents. On July 1, 1945, Vince returned to Langley alone. It is evident from her letters to Vince that she missed him very much. On a number of occasions throughout July 1945, she wrote that she wished that she had not returned home so soon. She also missed their apartment. They gave it up upon her return to Baltimore, and Vince moved back on post. On July 2, 1945, in her first letter to Vince since her return, she wrote: "Honest, Giz, I'm so lonesome up here. I miss you something terrible, and I think Little Vince does, too. He was really in a rare humor today. To begin with, he woke up at about 7:45 AM, and you know he should have slept much later. Well, he wouldn't eat any breakfast, so I gave him a drink of milk and then took him up to bathe him. Well, he really performed. He wouldn't get in the bathtub. I was so darn mad. I had to hold him up with one hand while he climbed up the side of the tub and wash him with the other. He screamed the whole time, and by the time I was finished, I was really p____ off."

Vince was also missing Martha and the baby very much. He also wrote on July 2, 1945: "Here's hoping you two aren't missing me as much as I am *you all*....Just think, not even a day has gone by, but to me it seems like years." He added: "I still can't get over how good Giz was yesterday. I think it's remarkable. Sure sorry to hear he was bad today. You really don't think he misses me, do you? If he don't, he'd better had."

Martha ended her letter of July 2 by writing: "…I love you with all my heart and soul, plus every ounce of life I have in me and my big belly. Little Vince loves you very, very much also and so does whoozit. We miss you very, very much, Giz, but you are in our minds and hearts every second." "Whoozit" was their new unborn baby.

While they spoke over the telephone earlier on July 2, a violent thunderstorm was in progress in Baltimore. It scared Martha and she told Vince about it. Later that night, it apparently hit Vince's area. He teased Martha by writing: "That storm you were telling me about, it's just about to hit here. Funny thing—I'm not scared and I don't see why you were. Oh! Yes I do. I wasn't there to hold your hand. Or I should say pull down the shades to keep the lightning out. Huh!"

Vince had just returned to Langley a few days earlier when the Fourth of July holiday arrived. It prompted Martha to write: "I was sort of disappointed that you didn't get home, but I got to thinking about where you were last year, and I sort of consoled myself. Even though we couldn't be together, at least I know where you are and about what you're doing." Martha again wrote that she regretted returning home so soon. She continued her letter of July 4: "It seems as though I lived down there a real long time, and I really don't live up here." Vince wrote on July 4, 1945: "My life seems so empty these days.…I knew it would be bad when you left, but it is worse than I could ever describe." He also missed the baby, writing: "Gosh, I do miss him."

Martha told Vince that the family went to the park on the Fourth. Little Vince did not care for the swings, but he liked the sandbox, and as Martha wrote: "The payoff was the sliding board. Boy, did he love it. We'd put him about halfway up and then would hold him while he came down. He would laugh and scream and really had fun…"

With the many successes of our armed forces and their allies, the American people were optimistic that the end of the war might be imminent. Martha reflected that optimism when she wrote to Vince in her letter of July 4: "Have you heard anything about your office or that school closing down? Or about 'that discharge'? That's what I'm really interested in."

On July 5, 1945, Martha informed Vince of another friend who was killed. He had finished his tour of duty overseas, returned home, and while he was on leave, his wife had a baby girl. After his leave, he returned to Florida, where he was assigned to a B-29, and had just recently been killed. Each new report of tragedy took a heavier toll.

Vince had been playing softball on a team at Langley. They had been playing pretty well, and their team was tied for second place. On July 6, the team won 13 to 7. Vince went 2 for 4, with a double and a triple.

Vince was able to go home the weekend following the Fourth. However, he hitchhiked part or all of the way home. Martha wrote on July 8, 1945: "Vince, please promise me that you won't hitchhike home any more."

Movies continued to be the favorite pastime for the whole family. Martha, Buster and their mom and dad went to see *Diamond Horseshoe*, starring Betty Grable and Dick Haymes. Martha wrote: "Gosh, it was good. I really enjoyed it." A few days later she and Rita saw *Patrick the Great*, starring Donald O'Connor. Martha thought this was a "swell picture." She wrote: "...I made believe you were with me, 'cause I figured you'd be in your movie around the same time I was." Vince had told her earlier that evening over the phone that he had planned to go to the movies, and he did. Vince wrote to Martha about the one that he saw, *A Bell for Adano*, starring Gene Tierney. He thought it was "pretty good." Two days earlier, he had seen *Pillow to Post*, starring Ida Lupino. He thought it was "...very good. Something different for a change."

Vince wrote on July 9, 1945, about having to wait for a long time to get a bus back to Langley. He was thinking more and more about purchasing a used car to use to travel back and forth from his post to home. He wanted Martha to think about it. He also informed Martha that Sparks had left for overseas but was expected to return soon. He also added: "I think you looked so wonderful with your hair like you had it fixed yesterday. I hope you leave it that way."

On July 12, 1945, Martha wrote to Vince and asked him to keep an eye out for soap flakes in which to wash the baby's clothes. They were having difficulty finding them back home—yet another example of how war disrupted everyday life.

Martha enjoyed reading the funnies in the newspaper, but apparently one of her favorites, "Chief Wahoo," was not carried in the Baltimore daily newspapers, so Vince tore them out of the local Virginia newspaper and sent them to her. She appreciated it, for she was really into the story as it slowly unraveled day after day, like a soap opera. She apparently became interested in this comic strip while residing in Hampton.

Vince was able to go home the following weekend, as well as the next several. Martha was considering going down one weekend by steamboat, but she was unable to get reservations for her requested date of travel. By now she was six months' pregnant. Vince wrote: "I hate to see you have to come down here on that train. I know what a helluva trip it is, and especially on the weekend. Honey, believe me, I want you to come down very much, but also I don't want you to knock yourself out doing it. Remember, you're pretty far gone to be knocked around on one of those trains." Martha was frustrated because of her inability to schedule her trip to Langley on the weekend of her choice. She wrote: "Gosh, I'll sure be glad when you're out of this man's army."

By mid-July 1945, Martha was having difficulty with Little Vince going to sleep. She wrote on July 16, 1945: "As long as you sit up there and let him play he's fine, but just lay him in that crib and you'd think he was being murdered." It sounds to me like at this point in my young life I had learned to enjoy attention. Thank goodness, this behavior apparently stopped by the end of July. With my mother expecting and my failing to sleep on a regular basis for a while, it was disturbing her needed rest. On July 18, 1945, Martha informed Vince that little "Whozit," short for "Whoozit," was really kicking lately, and kicking hard at that. She wrote: "Honest, sometimes he kicks so hard, I get scared."

Being back at Langley without Martha and the baby was tough for Vince. He wrote on July 18, 1945: "I love you both, oh, so much that I wonder how I can go on with you two so far away. I've just been living from weekend to weekend." Movies continued to help Vince get through the week from one weekend to the next. Vince had the opportunity to see *Christmas in Connecticut*, starring Barbara Stanwyck. He wrote to Martha: "...honey, don't miss it. It is really good—in fact it's the best picture I've seen in a long time. I split my sides open laughing." The next evening, he saw *Junior Miss*. He thought it was good, with some very funny parts in it, "…but not as good as the other one." Later, Martha wrote that she went to the movies with Catherine and Suz and saw *Keep Your Powder Dry*, starring Lana Turner and Laraine Day. She wrote: "Boy, I sure liked it."

As I have mentioned, my parents wrote about some of the smallest details and events going on in their lives, and both continued to enjoy it. For example, my mother wrote about putting the wash out on the clothesline only to have it rain and then continue to rain for two days, during which the clothes would remain on the line. I thought about it and realized that they had no dryers then. Once the clean clothes were dripping wet again, there was no sense bringing them back into the house, for there was no place to hang them to dry. My journey back in time to the early and mid 1940s has brought back memories, but it has also reminded me of how tough everyday life was at that time—that is, when you compare it to the conveniences of our modern world. And yet, it was a simpler life, and people may have been just a little bit happier, when you take World War II out of the picture. I do not know for sure, but I suspect that has been an age-old question that will remain for every generation to ponder about the prior one.

On July 20, 1945, Vince was trying to write a letter to Martha, but he could not concentrate because there was a program on the radio capturing his attention. It was *People Are Funny*. He finished the letter after the show was over. He was really enjoying the broadcast. In this letter, he reported that his softball team had won its game that evening by a score of 5 to 1. Vince batted 2 for 3 in this win. However, he injured his finger from a foul tip, and he wrote: "…it's every color in the rainbow. Pretty swollen too. Doesn't hurt much though." The next day, he headed home for the weekend.

During the following week, Dr. Brown came over the house to check on Dee because she had been sick. While he was there, Martha asked him if it would be all right for her to travel to Langley. She wrote on July 23, 1945: "…he told me he thought I'd better not travel. I didn't mention bringing Little Vince to him. Anyway, if I can get someone to keep Little

Vince, I'm still coming, but if I can't, I guess I'd better not try to come down." Vince had reserved a room at the Langley Hotel just in case Martha did come. The cost of a room started at $2.75 per night. As it turned out, Martha cancelled her trip, and Vince went home for the weekend.

On July 26, 1945, Vince wrote to Martha: "What do you think of Churchill losing? For myself I was surprised. I think it's for the best tho. And how about the peace terms to Japan? I can't decide whether I like them or not. Seems to me that a lot of the war criminals would get away. I think I would like to see them accept them tho, but then again those Japs are tricky people."

Little Vince was fourteen months old on July 26, 1945. Martha wrote to Vince to inform him that their little one was walking all over the place. On that day, he had spotted Joey's little toy telephone on the steps. Little Vince walked over to it, knelt down on one knee, picked up the receiver and dialed, and said "Hi-Dad!" Martha continued: "We all just roared. If only I had had a movie camera. Anyway, Joey spied him and went over to get it. There the two of them were, yelling and each pulling the phone. That kid sure knows how to take up for himself." This was the first written record of an argument in which I was involved, unless you count the day that I climbed the side of the bathtub while my mother tried to bathe me.

Martha ended her last letter of July 1945 by writing on the 31st: "I love and miss you so much, it hurts my heart."

August 1945, found the baby talking more and more and mimicking the adults. Willie swatted at a fly on his arm, and Little Vince did the same to his arm. Rita was still waiting for Jack to return, and Angela was waiting for Charles.

Vince wrote on August 1, 1945, that it was Air Force Day, and Langley Field was open to civilians for an air show. Vince gave a good account of the program. He wrote that the show started off with a helicopter demonstration, showing "...its ability to just practically hang in air." The next feature "...was a P-59 jet-propulsion buzzing the field and doing aerobatics. Man, how that thing can go." Vince continued: "The third thing on the program and what I thought was the best, was a demonstration of a C-47 and glider." He described how the C-47 took off with the glider, then flew around awhile and let the glider loose. The glider landed within 50 feet of a pickup station. The C-47 circled around and came down the field about 5 to 10 feet off the ground and picked up the glider from the pickup station, Apparently, when the glider cut loose the next time it did two loops. Vince added: "Without any engines I still don't see how he did it. He then landed, swung around in front of the reviewing stand and stopped on a dime."

Vince added that the show continued with B-17s and B-24s simulating a bomb run on Langley Field, and "…then a bunch of P-40s hopped on them." Vince wrote that the Navy had a bunch of their F-8-Fs doing lots of aerobatics. He thought they were good, too. He wrote: "All in all I thought the show was very good." The military personnel did have a time trying to keep the civilians out of their hangar, which was off-limits to them. Vince closed this letter by telling Martha that he was able to get some soap chips for the babies' wash.

Martha wrote to Vince on August 2, 1945. She informed him that her mom and dad and a number of the family members had gone crabbing down by the Annapolis bridge. They had caught 51 crabs and one soft crab. Those were the good old days. Martha wrote that they had a "swell time," but they were all sunburned and came home looking like "lobsters." Vince was home on leave for the first weekend of August 1945, but he was back to Langley soon afterwards.

By August 6, 1945, Charles was finally home. By my calculation, he had been overseas just about 35 months. Martha wrote to Vince on that date regarding what Angela had to endure: "I'm so glad for her. I just don't know how she kept going all that time. I think I would have lost my mind if you had been over there for even half that time." Martha ended this letter by writing: "I just can't wait for you to get out of that old army. Little Vince loves and misses you very much, also. He wants you to get out of that army too."

Vince wrote to Martha on August 6, 1945. While writing this letter and telling Martha what a short but wonderful weekend he had while home with her and the baby, he heard a bulletin over the radio. He wrote:

205

"Just heard some kind of announcement on the radio about an atomic bomb they are dropping on Japan. Didn't quite get what they were talking about, but am sure interested in it. I just heard Gabriel Heatter and if what he said is true it's just unbelievable. The communiqué has come from Guam, on the city they dropped the bombs [on], but I bet every family in the country has its ears glued to radio. Hon, what is civilization coming to?" He went immediately into his ending: "Sweeties, I can just about keep my eyes open, so I think it's best I sign off for tonight. I love you both with all my heart and soul and all my life, and miss you beyond words. Good-night, my loves." Then he ended with his signature close: "May God and His Blessed Mother bless & protect you always, for Your devoted Daddy & Hubby, Vince." For he knew the world was safe in God's Loving Hands, and he could rest comfortably.

The next evening, Vince wrote: "Well that atomic bomb is sure something. I'd love to know the real damage it did. I'm hoping a communiqué comes out on it at 11 o'clock. Those bombs could really bring this war to an end, I think." Vince also reported that his team had won their softball game 20 to 1, beating the team with whom they were tied for second place. Thus, now they "…have undisputed possession of second place."

Martha wrote to Vince on August 7, 1945. The last word from Jack was that he was in Naples, Italy, waiting for a boat to come back to the States. Martha reported that she had her eye on a new washing machine. She also commented on the tragic death of Major Richard Bong, a highly decorated air force pilot who had shot down forty Japanese planes in the Pacific, and who was killed after escaping from a P-80A Shooting Star jet during a mishap in flight over California on August 6, 1945. She wrote: "Wasn't that terrible? After all the time he was overseas, and in such great danger…." His death was a great loss to the air force and to the entire nation. He was one of our true aviator heroes.

In her letter of August 8, 1945, Martha commented about the events of August 6. She wrote: "How about those atomic bombs, honey? Honest, I don't know what civilization is coming to. They seem so darn inhuman, but then, we really aren't fighting with humans, when we fight the Japs.

I'm glad someone over here thought of the thing. You know Germany was only two years behind us on it. I'm sure that the Germans or Japs would have used it on us if they had had the opportunity. The only thing, it seems so eerie, 'cause people that go in that vicinity within the next 70 years they will die, on account of the radium. But I'm telling you, I bet you all those poor fellows who were prisoners of the Japs are darn glad to see them get it. Then, too, I think they are being given a fair chance. We only used one bomb, and now we are giving them a chance to give up." She continued: "Oh, yeah, how about Russia declaring war on Japan? That's good, too, isn't it? But I think that bomb sort of scared them, don't you? Hon, do you think you'll get a discharge now? Gosh, things look pretty good, so you surely should get out of that old army soon."

When Japan refused to surrender following the first atomic bomb, a second one was dropped on August 9, 1945.

Getting back to the other matters of the day, Martha informed Vince that she had put a deposit down on the washing machine she had her eye on, and, I might add, her heart set on as well. Martha also reported that Jack had written to Rita that he was leaving Italy on August 3, 1945. Martha wrote: "Boy, is she excited! She has every reason to be, don't you think?"

Martha added, regarding Little Vince: "Boy, you ought to see him walk. He runs around here like a bat out of hell, and boy, does he get dirty! I've been giving him two baths a day."

During the summer of 1945, Martha and Vince lent Buster some money to start a food concession business. While I am not sure how long Buster had that particular business, throughout his life he worked hard and became a very successful businessman, who was very generous and always thought of other people. What a great investment that proved to be for my parents, not necessarily from a financial standpoint, but more so an investment in the growth of another human being, and a brother at that. My father saw the value in helping an individual build self-confidence.

Even though Martha and Vince longed to be together, they continued to make the best of their situation. It helped them when Vince could come home on the weekends. When they were apart, a good day for both of them was when they each received a letter from the other and spoke by telephone that evening. From their letters, you can readily see that even after all the time that Vince had been away, receiving that letter, followed by a phone call, was something that they both truly treasured. Even old news was welcomed. For example, if Vince came home on a weekend, he might tell Martha something he had already written about before he left the post on Friday. She would then receive the letter on Monday after he returned to the post. She would write: "I received a letter from you this morning, and even though you had already told me what I read, it sure helped my morale."

On August 9, 1945, Martha wrote to Vince: "Giz, darling, do you really think the war will be over in two weeks? Gosh, I sure hope it is. I just can't wait till you get out of that army." Vince wrote on August 9, 1945: "Over the phone I said the war would be over in two weeks, and after listening to the news I think more so now than ever. I might be optimistic, but that's my privilege. If you want the exact date it's going to be, *21 August 45*. It's no use you getting all hepped up tho, it's hard to say how long it would be before the discharges start rolling in. I didn't mean to be nasty when you mentioned discharge over the phone, but you know how hepped up you get. Honey, I don't think anyone wants to get out any worse than I do." It is obvious that Martha could hardly contain her excitement. She wrote on August 10, 1945: "Well, darling, what do you think of the news? It sure looks good, doesn't it? I'm just waiting for you to get that discharge now. We had the radio on all day, and boy, I was really getting all worked up."

Martha continued her August 10 letter by telling Vince that Angela and Charles had stopped by the house with the twins. That evening Angela and Charles were going to the movies. It would be only the second time that they had been to the movies together since they had met. Their lives had really been put on hold due to the war. Martha wrote that Angela "…looks as though she's in heaven and Charles really looks good."

Martha wrote that she had been to some more movies. Suz, Willie, Rita and Martha saw *Son of Lassie*. She wrote: "Gosh, it was sure good. I liked it a lot." Later, Rita and Martha saw *Escape in the Desert*. She wrote: "It was pretty good. It was about four escaped German PWs. I got awful mad, but it was exciting. Another thing, the Nazis got it in the end." She also saw *Out of This World*, starring Eddie Bracken. She wrote: "Gosh, was it funny? I sure enjoyed it."

On August 13, 1945, Martha wrote to Vince to inform him that they had received a letter from Grubby's wife. By now, the pilot and the copilot of their original crew were both civilians. Also, one of their crew members was a new father and another was about to become one. She wrote: "Seems as though the whole crew are eager, huh?" She continued in this letter, writing: "Gosh, I certainly wish the official report would come through, don't you? This waiting is terrible. You know, there's a $5,000 reward for the person who caused that flash to be sent out last night." While the world waited anxiously for official word of Japan's unconditional surrender, apparently someone had broken the story prematurely.

Vince was able to go home for the weekend prior to Japan's surrender. He wrote on August 13, 1945, that his trip back to Langley was pretty good except for a flat tire. He was traveling with a buddy who had a car. He wrote: "Gosh, coming down in a car is so much better than those darn buses." Anticipating an announcement soon regarding Japan's surrender, Vince wrote: "Darling, about next week, I don't know what to tell you. Lord knows what they'll do when this thing pops. It's my opinion that everyone will be restricted until something comes out definitely about discharges, etc. So if I don't make it, you'll know it's because I think it's best to hang around here. Just bear with me." Apparently Rita had heard from Jack, which prompted Vince to write: "It's a shame he's on such an awful boat, but at least she knows he's on his way home." Vince also informed Martha that his softball team had beaten the previously undefeated first-place team, but it remained in second place.

Vince was off by a week on his prediction. Japan surrendered on August 14, 1945. Martha wrote to him on that day: "Well, darling, here it is. The war is over. Honest, I just can't tell you how I feel. I didn't scream or anything, but I'm just deeply grateful that it's all over. I guess you heard that 7:00 PM broadcast. We all had our ears glued to the radio, but it was just impossible to hear anything. You've never heard so much noise in your life. Whistles, horns, church bells and everything. But here's the payoff. Little Vince was so tired, so I put him in bed at 10 min. before seven. Then, when 7:00 PM rolled around, and all the noise, I thought sure Little Vince would scream. Well, I'll have you know that he didn't even wake up. I went up twice to see if he was all right, and he was." Like father, like son, for the world was safe in God's Loving Hands, and he could rest comfortably.

Martha continued her August 14 letter: "Rita and I went to the Novena at 8:00 PM. We thought they would have extra services, but they aren't having them until the official V-J (Victory over Japan) Day is announced. Church was just packed." She wrote that Angela and Charles came to town to celebrate, along with their relatives. However, "...not a single place was open." She added: "Well, honey, I tried to call you tonight, but the operator told me it would be about impossible to get thru tonight. They were really rushed. So I just cancelled it." And finally: "Well, hon, I could keep writing for hours, but it would be all jumbled up, because I'm listening to all kinds of celebration and everything else. I'll be back again tomorrow, and until then, I love you with all my heart and soul, plus another day's worth, plus plenty." She ended with her signature closing: "Please be very careful, darling, and keep praying, very hard. May God and His Blessed Mother Bless you and Protect you, always, for Your devoted wife & Son...."

Martha wrote to Vince on August 16, 1945 and mentioned that she had spoken to him by telephone. Apparently, Vince seemed to think that he would receive his discharge rather soon. She wrote: "I only hope and pray that you've got the right idea about getting out right away." She continued: "I only wish we had been together so we could have celebrated. I haven't done any celebrating at all, but you just wait until you get home. Vince, isn't it just wonderful? Golly, I just can't believe it. It seems like there's always been a war, to me. I can't realize how it will be, that's all." She continued: "Honey, I sure hope you get a discharge, real soon. Please let me know as soon as you hear anything. I really want you to come up this weekend, but if you think something might break, then I'd rather you stay there. Don't forget, you be sure to let me know as soon as you find out anything. Honest, I've been so excited since you called me, just thinking about your being a civilian. I just can't wait."

The next day, Martha wrote: "Well, darling, tomorrow is Sat., the day that I just wait all week for, usually, 'cause you come home. I sure hope you come up this weekend. I want to see you so much. If you don't, though, I'll understand and try to be patient. Gosh, I just can't wait for you to get a discharge. Won't it be heaven, Vince? There I go, getting myself all worked up again."

Martha and Rita went and saw another movie. This time they saw *Gentle Annie*, starring James Craig and Donna Reed. Martha wrote: "I enjoyed it a lot, 'cause it was different."

Martha wrote to Vince on August 18, 1945: "I sure am sorry you couldn't come up this weekend. I miss you so darn much. But then, if not seeing you this weekend may mean that you'll be home for good in a very short while, then I'm perfectly contented. But, gosh, I sure miss you." Martha added a P.S. to this letter that read: "Honey, you're almost 'Mr. Giz' now. Hope it's real, real soon. Right this minute wouldn't be too soon for me."

On August 19, 1945, Martha wrote that Suz, Willie, Joey, Rita and she went to V-J services at church. She wrote: "…the archbishop set today aside to give thanks." Martha also informed Vince that even though Buster could not get any hot dogs for his concession stand, he still had his best day ever. Martha wrote: "He took in $69.95. That was really good, wasn't it?"

Things were beginning to happen at Langley. Vince explained to Martha what was developing. He wrote on August 20, 1945: "They took the first 300 men alphabetically and made up a roster. Each man was contacted to find out his home address and how he wanted to travel to the separation center. From the home address they pick the separation center—of course mine would be Fort Meade [Maryland]. After they know how many go to Fort Meade, they wire all the names there, saying here are so many men we have available for discharge. When Meade has the vacancies they wire back saying send them such and such at a time.

Just like I said over the phone, that can be anywhere from tomorrow till two months, but actually I think it will be within a week or two. Of course it would take a couple of days to clear this field and stuff. Once you get to a separation center tho, it shouldn't take any time." He continues: "From the eleven officers in our office, five of them are on the list and six of our enlisted men are also on it. If we all go I guess the place will have to fold up."

On August 20, 1945, Martha wrote to Vince and told him that Buster, who can only walk with crutches, had to report for a pre-induction physical exam at 6:30 AM on August 29, 1945. Martha wrote: "How about that? Honest, he just tells everybody and makes such a joke of it. I think he'd really love to go, but I don't think they'd ever take him, do you? Anyway, if he fails to appear, he gets another notice and then will have to go right to Ft. Meade. Wouldn't that be a panic? You should hear Willie. Giving him orders, and then telling him to salute his superiors, then Buster carries the orders out."

Vince reported the score of his final softball game to Martha on August 21, 1945. His team lost 7 to 2. They ended the season with an overall record of 20 wins and 7 losses. Vince told Martha that he had run into a former schoolmate, Bob Schwalenberg, from St. Elizabeth's School in East Baltimore, who had been signed by the Pittsburgh Pirates. Bob had a car and offered to take Vince home on weekends. Vince wrote: "The whole trouble is I don't think I'll be coming home on the weekend any more, 'cause the next time I get home will be for good. Being alerted like this and going home would be too much of a risk, don't you think?"

Martha wrote to Vince on August 22, 1945: "Hon, we had another feud around here this evening. To begin with, it was real hot today, and neither of the babies slept very much. Little Vince only slept about 25 min. Anyway, I was just worn out when we had dinner, which was about 20 min. to seven. Well, you know how cranky Little Vince is about bedtime? Well, I got up from dinner to put him to bed when Rita did too. Then we both came downstairs and had just gotten seated..." when certain family members started making noise. She continued: "I said something about the noise right when the babies go to bed, and so did Rita..." at which time even more family members chimed in "…saying about how much noise we used to make when Joey was a baby." An argument developed. Martha wrote: "Well, anyway, it just got on my nerves, and I got up from the table and started to bawl (darn me)." Martha continued: "Honest, I guess maybe it's me, in this condition, but things sure get on my nerves an awful lot. Just little things, too. I sure hope I get over it."

On August 23, 1945, Jack called Rita from New York about 9:30 PM. He had arrived in the United States on that day aboard the *Peter Minuit*. Martha wrote: "You know, it was funny, but right before dinner, I dropped a fork. Well that means a man is coming. Then, after the baby was in bed, I was reading the papers, and the list of men coming into New York. Well I didn't see his name, but I said to Rita, I bet you $1.00 Jack came in on the *Peter Minuit* today, and I'll be darned if he didn't. He expects to come to Ft. Meade tomorrow." Martha continued: "Rita was so excited. They talked for about 40 minutes." Jack had previously mailed an envelope home to Rita, but she was not to open it, apparently, until he arrived home. On the telephone, she asked him what it was and he responded that it was money. Then, he asked her how much she thought it was. She guessed $300. He said that he had won that much in two nights. The suspense built as to how much it might be.

Martha continued her letter of August 23: "Jack said they had a swell trip over, except it was so long. They had pinup contests on the boat, and Rita came out second. Jack said the only reason the other girl won was 'cause she didn't have very many clothes on." The ship had engine-room problems that prevented it from traveling faster than 5 knots. It took them almost three weeks to cross the Atlantic Ocean. That long trip back was enough to keep Jack in the States, for if he had arrived home earlier, he believed that he would have been shipped to Japan. On his trip going overseas, his crew was delayed for approximately 48 days due to bad weather; thus he was in a combat zone far less time than he otherwise would have been. The prayers of so many loved ones and friends for Jack were heard by Our Father in Heaven as well.

Martha further continued her letter of August 23: "You know what I woke up to see this morning? Little Vince sitting in bed with a Kleenex box torn to shreds, and Kleenex just all over his crib. You know his box of toys, on that little table next to the crib? Well, I think I put them on there, and he can just about reach the top of the box, so I guess he got hold of the Kleenex. Anyway, I jumped out of bed and gathered all the Kleenex up. I started to give him the devil, so he just kisses me." My mother often wrote that I was just like my father. I guess I used my charm on her just like he did.

By August 24, 1945, Jack had arrived at Fort Meade. Martha wrote on that date that he would not be home this evening though. She wrote: "Gosh, if I was Rita, I'd be just about nuts now."

Apparently, Martha and Vince had been talking about his pending civilian life and his returning to work at the telephone company. He must have brought up the matter of income. Martha wrote in her August 24 letter: "And don't you worry about our getting along on $40.00 a week. Don't you remember me? I could live in a soap box with you and the Little Giz's." Martha added: "Boy, hon, 'Imogene' has been setting me nuts lately. You never felt anything move around like that in your life. I really hate to go out because it's embarrassing." "Imogene" was the latest name for "Whozit."

Vince wrote to Martha on August 24, 1945: "Well, honeys, I finally have some news for you. Right about 5 o'clock this afternoon the separation centers started to wire back to Langley. As of then Fort Meade hadn't wired, but by now they should have. The fellows that have to go to California are leaving tomorrow. Those going to Fort Dix are leaving next Saturday. It goes on like that. Now when Fort Meade boys leave I don't know, but it should be sometime next week. We'll probably start processing tomorrow or Sunday, and that should take a couple days. Now don't you think that's good news? I'll keep you posted about anything new."

Vince and a buddy went into Hampton for dinner on August 24, 1945. He wrote: "We're so darn sick of stew (and that's what the mess halls had again) that we thought we'd get a good meal." After dinner, they went to a movie and "...saw of all things a shoot-'em-up cowboy picture...Walked out of it in the middle. Boy did it stink." Later that night, Vince got talked into a bridge game and won $1.72. He wrote: "The way we play is ¹/₁₀ of a cent a point so no one can lose or win too much money. It just keeps the game interesting."

Martha wrote to Vince on August 25, 1945. It was the second weekend in a row that he had not come home. She pointed out that it was another Saturday and wrote: "…I guess I'm just spoiled. But hon, honest, I feel like a chicken with his head cut off. I miss you so doggone much, and just can't wait until you get home." She informed Vince that Jack was still at Fort Meade. There were so many men at Fort Meade that it was causing a backup in processing. While Jack would get a 30-day leave, he was scheduled to report to Greensboro, North Carolina, on September 27. He was not eligible for a discharge just yet. When Martha heard about the backlog at Fort Meade, she began to wonder whether Vince would also be delayed.

On August 25, 1945, Vince wrote: "It was so wonderful to talk to you tonight. Just what I needed to help me through this sweating period. I'm sorry I can't be with you tonight, but I think it's best I stay here and sweat it out. It can't be too long now, I keep telling myself." To help pass the time, Vince went to another movie. This time he saw *The Valley of Decision*, starring Greer Garson, Gregory Peck, Lionel Barrymore and a host of others. Vince thought it was a wonderful picture.

Martha wrote to Vince on August 26, 1945 informing him that Jack had arrived home. She said that he really looked "swell." Martha wrote: "Dee was a darling when he arrived. She didn't cry or anything. She patty-caked and really showed off for him." She continued: "They made me open the envelope, and guess what it was? $800.00! How about that? Boy, that's really a nice little envelope full, isn't it?"

Vince had a very easy day on August 26, 1945. In his letter of that date, he acknowledged that he had been lazy. His day consisted mostly of reading the papers and napping for about three and a half hours. However, he did go to church in the morning and watched a ballgame prior to eating dinner. The waiting for his discharge must have been excruciating. Later that night, he went to the movies again. This time he saw *You Came Along*, starring Robert Cummings. He wrote to Martha: "It was really good I thought. The ending was very sad—you'd cry your eyes out." Martha wrote to Vince on August 27, 1945, to report on yet another movie she saw with her mom and dad, *Arsenic and Old Lace,* starring Cary Grant. She thought the movie was funny. She wrote: "Gosh, I sure laughed, but there were a few spooky scenes in it."

Martha continued in this letter dated August 27: "Well, darling, I just talked to you and it was wonderful to hear your voice. Honey, I can imagine how terrible it must be, just waiting, but please don't get discouraged. Just remember that I'm as anxious for you to get out as you are. Every day I tell myself that that teletype will go thru today. Gosh, but I hope it's soon." Obviously, it went through real soon thereafter, because this was the last letter that Martha wrote to Vince.

In reading Vince's letter dated August 27, 1945, it is apparent that the waiting was starting to get to him. He wrote: "I've been so disgusted these past few days just sitting around hoping that something will come in from Meade. It's really putting me in a rut that I can't get out of." He continued: "Talking to you really helped me to no end. I feel so much better now after hearing your wonderful voice. You sure are a morale builder, darling."

Vince's last letter to Martha was dated August 28, 1945. In it, he wrote that he had "wonderful news." He wrote: "I called the man today and asked him if anything had come in from Meade. He said yes for fellows going by T.P.A., and only one by rail. T.P.A. is by car. Then he asked me my name and said yep, you're the one going by rail. So, darlings, I'm in. I think I was pretty lucky to be the only one going by rail. The orders won't come out until tomorrow—that's why I didn't call you. I want to make sure I'm on them before calling you. The way they will read is: Leave Langley Field on or about 2 Sept 45 reporting to Meade not later than 3 Sept 1945. Now that 'on or about 2 Sept' will depend upon how long it will take me to clear the field. It'll take at least three days if not longer. What I'm going to try and do is leave here sometime Saturday, come home, then report to Meade Monday morning. I don't know whether it'll work tho. Won't hurt to try." In a few days, Vince was home for good!

Vince was reverted to inactive status effective September 22, 1945. He remained inactive until April 29, 1955, when he was fully discharged from the United States Air Force. He received an honorable discharge. The words seem so ordinary until you ponder the significance of their meaning. He, like millions of others, served our nation with honor and dignity, and we must always remember the sacrifices that our servicemen and women have made and continue to make on our behalf, in particular those who have been prisoners of war, wounded or killed defending our great country. May God bless them and all Americans today and always!

Between July 1, 1945 and August 28, 1945, I have counted one card and 74 letters between Martha and Vince. Even to the end, they never let up.

22

In Conclusion

As mentioned, Martha once wrote: "Boy, we're going to have a lot to tell our grandchildren, aren't we?" Sadly, Martha never had that opportunity, for she passed away in May of 1977 at the age of 55 due to bacterial endocarditis. Only seven of her fifteen grandchildren were born prior to her death, and the oldest was only seven years old at the time. However, "GrandMarth," as she was called, has been able to share so much of herself and Vince with her grandchildren through their letters, which she treasured and saved, and which we have discovered. For many years, the letters sat in cardboard boxes in their basement. Eventually they were put in my sister Mary's attic. Most were generally undisturbed and probably never reopened since first read by Martha or Vince during the war. Vince died in October of 2003, at the age of 81, from respiratory failure due to pneumonia.

The majority of Martha's letters traveled with my father from post to post, including overseas and back. He treasured them as well.

In spite of the difficulties Martha had in the delivery of her first baby, she wrote to Vince expressing her desire to have at least four more children. Even earlier, as shown, she had drawn in a letter to Vince a depiction of him and her as stick people with five children, three boys and two girls. While she accurately predicted the number of babies they would later have, the genders were reversed, for they had three daughters and two sons. Rita was born shortly after Vince's return home in 1945. Mary was born in 1947, Mike in 1953 and Tracy in 1962.

As I read my parents' letters, I reflected on the love between them. It is very rewarding and comforting to know that my siblings and I were conceived and born as a result of a deep love between them. It is so apparent that they wanted children in their lives and that they looked forward to the day when they had a large family. I thank God for the loving parents that He gave to us.

Everyone who knew Martha knows how much she loved children. In spite of their young ages, my oldest sons do remember her, even though Vince III was only 7 and Greg was only 5 when GrandMarth died. My son Kevin, who was 4 at the time, just barely remembers her, while Jeff, then 2½ years of age, does not remember her; yet in their early years she touched their lives in a positive way.

My father was like other veterans of World War II. They did not talk about the fighting very much. They would answer questions but tended not to elaborate. They knew they had a job to do, and they did it well. They were proud of their accomplishments but were not very happy about the fact that they had to kill others to achieve victory. I believe that they realized that the young men who were their so-called "enemies" were very much like themselves, but these "enemies" happened to live in countries whose leaders were fanatics. I am sure that it hurt our young servicemen to have to kill other men in combat, but they had no other choice. It was a matter of kill or be killed. They fought to protect all of their loved ones back home, knowing that if they did not stop the aggression right then and there, someday it could spread to within our borders.

Knowing my father as I did, I believe that he often thought about the people on the ground who were killed by the bombs he dropped. I am sure he thought about the soldiers who died and the civilians who were working in the factories. Likewise, I am sure he thought about the innocent women and children who may have been killed by a bomb that strayed from the target. I am sure this weighed heavily on my father and many a man in his position. However, from everything I have read,

I am very confident that the Americans did everything they could to avoid the loss of life to civilians. As I have written, they often returned to England with a full bomb load when they were not certain they could hit a strategic target. They were adamant about not dropping bombs unless they were certain they had the target identified. They would not drop bombs indiscriminately just because they were over enemy territory. Their missions were against Hitler's war machine, not the civilian population, and the Americans took that very seriously. These aviators were men of honor and integrity, and that honor and integrity helped to win the war and to secure the peace.

My father knew the difference between right and wrong and how to go about his life without the guilt that could easily have overcome him. My parents were very successful at raising their children and in their family life. After the war, Vince returned to work for the telephone company, where he steadily advanced to management positions and eventually retired with over forty years of service. He was highly respected at the telephone company.

On one occasion, I applied for a position at the phone company, but I did not tell my dad that I was applying. I told the personnel manager that I did not want my father to know because I wanted to obtain the job on my own, and that I did not want to be hired because I was Vince Gisriel's son. The personnel manager then told me that he could think of no better reason to hire me than the fact that I was Vince Gisriel's son. As it turned out, I was not hired, because I was not really suited for the opening that was available. The men who interviewed me for the job convinced me of that. However, I left there that day feeling very proud of my dad.

Martha and Vince were very active in their parish life, each serving the church in their own special ways. Vince was very active in the community as well.

I spoke at my father's funeral about his generosity over the years, particularly towards Suz and Willie. Not realizing it previously, after I read my parents' letters, it became abundantly clear that Vince was forever indebted to them for all they had done for Martha and him, especially when he was away in the military service.

Some in my family have asked why I wrote certain words such as "ba__s" or "p_____ off", or even "_____." It is because that is the way my parents wrote them in their letters to one another.

During the writing of this story, I hesitated to accurately quote my parents on their feelings towards the Germans and the Japanese, as I have done so candidly. I considered simply leaving out sensitive parts of their verbatim quotes. However, this is what my parents felt and wrote at the time, and darn it, they made a lot of sacrifices, and my father put his life on the line every day that he served in the military and every time he went up in a plane, especially on 35 missions over enemy territory. If anyone deserved the right to their opinions, it was my mother and father and the millions like them who endured the war and all the suffering that went with it. Men gave their lives so that others could live and be free. Our servicemen and women and their families put their whole lives on hold because of the aggression of others. While these were private thoughts, they were, nevertheless, written thoughts, and they were written under the protection of the First Amendment of the United States Constitution, which my father swore to uphold and defend, something he did quite well. By all means, let their words go forth and be heard by all who wish to read, to listen, to remember, to study and to understand, so that perhaps some history will never again repeat itself. May God bless the German and Japanese people, especially the millions who had nothing to do with World War II, and may we remain at peace with them forever.

In all the years I knew my parents, I never remember them uttering an unkind word about the German or Japanese people. At times, they taught forgiveness and love by their silent example.

Can you imagine the fear that goes through a young airman's mind before takeoff, having seen so many other planes go down and knowing full well that this mission could very well be his last? I believe my father was scared, but I believe that he was equally brave, as was the crew that served with him, and they persevered. That scenario was multiplied over and over by millions of others, and that perseverance won the war. My mother helped by her own perseverance. She never stopped praying, and she never stopped writing, and her letters helped bring my father back home.

My father came back to the United States safe and sound. All ten men in his original crew came back alive. I am convinced that my father made it back safely because of my parents' prayers and faith in our Almighty Father, His Son Jesus, the Holy Spirit and the Blessed Mother. I also believe that the prayers of so many of my parents' family members and friends were heard by God, and that those same prayers helped to bring an end to the war. Again, I am forever grateful to God for protecting my father.

Reading my parents' many letters has shown me how much faith they had, and how they trusted in God to help them through that incredible time. Working on this story has renewed my own faith. Incidentally, my mother remained faithful to her novenas until her death.

In case you were not keeping score, I read 1,154 letters written by my parents to each other between November 12, 1942 and August 28, 1945. I am told that there may be another dozen or more that I have not read spread among various family members. However, I feel that I have captured the essence of their thoughts at the time, as well as their love for one another. In addition, I also read 2 V-mails, 3 postcards, 10 telegrams and 24 cards between them during this same period, as well as numerous other cards and letters from friends and relatives written to my parents.

As I reflect back over the many months that I have read about my mom and dad, I continue to be amazed by their sheer endurance. My father endured almost three years of military life, which included six months of some of the most dangerous work a man can do. During most of that time, he was away from the love of his life, Martha.

I guess you would have to be a father to appreciate how hard it is to be away from your baby for as long as he was, not to mention what he missed in those early months. Then there is the endurance of my mother. The story I have written tells it all. I honestly do not know what is worse—being in combat or sitting home worrying and wondering whether your spouse will make it safely home. I can only imagine the weeks and months that she waited for him to return.

During the many hours spent in reading my parents' hundreds of letters, there were many times when I laughed. There were other times when I was deeply moved or saddened by what I read, and it brought a tear to my eye. There was one particular paragraph in chapter 14 when I openly wept. It was when I wrote about my dad losing his mother when he was only two years of age, and then he had a baby boy whom he had not seen in over two months following his birth. It was then that I realized how much I missed both of my parents and how I wished that I could speak with them again and discuss these events in their lives. I will have to put that on hold for a while.

In conclusion, this is what I believe. There is a God and He is a loving Father Who cares deeply about each of us, and while some in life are hurt and suffering, He cares very much about them and He will not forget them. He is a mighty Protector, and if we just ask, He will hear us and He will answer in His own way and in His time. I am also convinced that the love in a family is one of God's greatest gifts to all mankind.

Working on this story has given me a greater appreciation for what our men and women in the military service do for us every day. My prayer is that every serviceman and woman, returning from battle or serving our country, knows that they are loved and appreciated by a humble nation and that we are forever indebted to them.

Finally, we have such a great country, and we must all work to do our part to keep it that way.

In 1968 Vince and Martha celebrated their 25th wedding anniversary.

Vince Jr.'s wedding day, October 12, 1968. From left, Vince Sr., Bonnie, Vince Jr., and Martha.

The Gisriel kids in 1965: standing, Mike and Vince Jr.; sitting, Rita, Tracy (on Rita's lap), and Mary.

The Gisriel kids (and Vince Sr.) in 2001: back row, Tracy, Vince Sr., and Vince Jr.; front row, Mike, Mary, and Rita.

Ordering Information

To order additional copies of this book, send check or money order made payable to:

Marvin Press, LLC
P.O. Box 1944
Salisbury, MD 21802-1944

Send $19.95, plus $3.00 postage and handling, for each book. Maryland residents, add 6% sales tax to the price of the book ($1.20).

To pay by credit card, visit
www.heartsawaybombsaway.com

To order by telephone, call
410-251-1360